PERGAMON INTERNATIONAL LIBRARY
of Science, Technology, Engineering and Social Studies

The 1000-volume original paperback library in aid of education, industrial training and the enjoyment of leisure

Publisher: Robert Maxwell, M.C.

THE LIMITS OF POWER
The Politics of Local Planning Policy

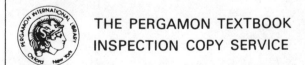

THE PERGAMON TEXTBOOK
INSPECTION COPY SERVICE

An inspection copy of any book published in the Pergamon International Library will gladly be sent to academic staff without obligation for their consideration for course adoption or recommendation. Copies may be retained for a period of 60 days from receipt and returned if not suitable. When a particular title is adopted or recommended for adoption for class use and the recommendation results in a sale of 12 or more copies, the inspection copy may be retained with our compliments. The Publishers will be pleased to receive suggestions for revised editions and new titles to be published in this important International Library.

THE LIMITS OF POWER
The Politics of Local Planning Policy

by

ANDREW BLOWERS

The Open University, U.K.

PERGAMON PRESS

OXFORD · NEW YORK · TORONTO · SYDNEY · PARIS · FRANKFURT

U.K.	Pergamon Press Ltd., Headington Hill Hall, Oxford OX3 0BW, England
U.S.A.	Pergamon Press Inc., Maxwell House, Fairview Park, Elmsford, New York 10534, U.S.A.
CANADA	Pergamon of Canada, Suite 104, 150 Consumers Road, Willowdale, Ontario M2J 1P9, Canada.
AUSTRALIA	Pergamon Press (Aust.) Pty Ltd., P.O. Box 544, Potts Point, N.S.W. 2011, Australia
FRANCE	Pergamon Press SARL, 24 rue des Ecoles, 75240 Paris, Cedex 05, France
FEDERAL REPUBLIC OF GERMANY	Pergamon Press GmbH, 6242 Kronberg/Taunus, Pferdstrasse 1, Federal Republic of Germany

First edition 1980

British Library Cataloguing in Publication Data

Blowers, Andrew
The limits of power — (Urban and regional planning series; 21). — (Pergamon international library).
1. Local government — England — Bedfordshire — Political aspects
2. Local government — Great Britain — Political aspects — Case studies
I. Title II. Series
352 96 094256   JS3325.B/ 79—40767

ISBN 0 08 023016 4

Printed in Great Britain by A. Wheaton & Co., Ltd., Exeter

For Gill

Contents

List of Tables

List of Figures

Preface

Academics who spend part of their lives in politics are a fairly common breed in national government and they are not uncommon in local government. Some have realised or discovered that their political interests and knowledge can inform their academic research. I do not suggest that individual academics take up a political career merely to further their academic one since the motivation and dedication required of public life is unlikely to tempt many from the quieter reaches of academia. I do not think that academic politicians are directed more by the imperatives of their research than by the exigencies of pursuing their ideological purposes. But it would be foolish to eschew the serendipity afforded by the combination of academic and political interests.

I was for four years, 1973–7, Chairman of the Environmental Services Committee of Bedfordshire County Council. In this role I was attempting to develop policies inspired by partisan attitudes but conditioned by the need to achieve consensus and compatibility with policies being pursued, often for different reasons, by other organisations. The conflict between party and a wider public interest was particularly acute since my own party did not have overall control at the time. The happy coincidence of an intellectual and political interest in planning eventually led to my conceiving a book based on the knowledge and experience I had gained of the planning process from the inside.

I have not attempted to write a book exposing the rapacity of developers or the myopia of officials. I am, in any case, comforted by the belief that British local government is not on the whole riddled with corruption nor in the pockets of rampant capitalism. It is run by men of good-will who have a deeply embedded sense of loyalty to their profession or party, and who subscribe, though in different ways, to some vague notion of the public interest. On the other hand, my book is not intended as a bland defence of the *status quo*; indeed, I hope it raises issues that deserve the closest attention if the mistakes of the past are to be avoided and if the current malaise of planning is to be overcome. This is a critique not an exposé.

My main intention has been to illuminate the political realities of policy-making in planning. I have used various sources, some of them conventional, others inaccessible to the ordinary researcher. The academic literature on the subject has been plundered to help frame the overall picture and to relate what I have to say to the work of others who have trodden this field. Much of my primary source material – agendas, reports, minutes, or press cuttings – is publicly available but unhappily little used, partly, I suspect, because it is intrinsically boring to those not directly concerned with the decisions it relates to. Unless one is involved, it is very difficult to piece together coherently the many fragments of detailed and often impenetrable literature that pours from the presses of our government bureaucracies. Other sources are not open to the public. Among these are correspondence files and other internal memoranda which may be vital but often remain hidden, if not confidential. The inaccessibility of the political process is protected by the carapace of secrecy which is one of its inherent features. Much of my source material is not to be found in the written word, but is the essence of the interactions at committees, or between decision-makers. I attempted to record viewpoints and comments expressed verbally by keeping a diary of the events of the period I describe and this proved to be a valuable resource when I came to the difficult task of trying to connect up the various stages in policy-making. I believe my method based upon the valuable and unique insight it gave to the process does reveal much of what lies hidden, and goes some way towards explaining the how and why of certain decisons.

The concepts with which social science has to deal are necessarily evaluative, and I have made no attempt to disguise that fact by assuming a kind of bogus neutrality. Clearly I hold certain views of the planning process and I was ideologically committed to the prosecution of particular policy initiatives. I have tried to provide an academic account of my views through an interpretation of the events and interactions which compose the political process of planning. My perspective is presented through an analysis of the institutional and structural background. The planning process is shaped by certain procedures, rules, and political and bureaucratic institutions. As a leading politician in a local authority I enjoyed greater insight into local politics, and greater access to the experience of politics at a local level than would have been possible from the outside. My interest lies in the institutional and structural determinants of the process, not simply in recording from the inside the motivations of particular individuals.

The relationship between theoretical perspectives and experience is a major problem of discussion in the philosophy of the social sciences, and has implications for the character of empirical research. This is not the place to discuss this issue in detail, but I do not take the view that the social scientist simply confronts a body of data or a sequence of events and then proceeds to infer relevant theories from them. He necessarily approaches his material with hypotheses in mind, and the material becomes meaningful in terms of these hypotheses. The material he is concerned with does not exist independently of his conception of it, nor of his assessment of its significance, nor yet of its significance within society generally. Of course, there are certain basic descriptions (of events leading up to a decision, for instance) which can only be challenged on grounds of their completeness or empirical accuracy. But explanation involves more than empirical observation as if the material were somehow independent of the social scientist's outlook. There are clearly problems in assessing what counts as explanation and the adequate relationships between hypotheses and the evidence used to test them. What I have attempted to do is to take certain problems and issues that seem to me to be interesting and to provide evidence for my interpretation of them. In doing so I hope I have revealed the local political experience of these issues in a way which offers some explanation for them. For example, I have tried to demonstrate the relationship between conflict over planning policy and uncertainty. I have suggested why planning policy tends to reflect the existing pattern of power in society. The generalisations which I have made may well strike echoes in the work of other researchers and in fields other than planning. Certainly I have found in my discussions with a range of people that my explanations coincide with their own presumptions. In pursuing these issues I hope I have made some contribution to the explanation of the character of planning and politics at the local level.

The case-studies which form the major part of the text are used to test generalisations. There is, of course, a sense in which such generalisations emerge as particular cases are pursued. It is an iterative process and, for this reason, I have posed issues in the opening chapter and have stated more formally my propositions in the final chapter. I am far more concerned to demonstrate the interrelationships of events, actors, and institutions within one situation than to provide examples which can be used for comparative analysis. Such an approach, I consider, is more likely to lead to better theoretical understanding of politics, government, or planning than a series of supposedly comparable analyses from different authorities. The choice of case-studies needs some explanation. From all the possibilities I eventually selected four. These struck me as the most interesting I came across during my four years as chairman, and they provide sufficient variety to demonstrate the various forms of planning currently practised. The topics considered are minerals, transportation, land development, and structure planning. The planning methods discussed include development control, strategic planning, and transportation planning.

Although the book focuses on planning in a non-metropolitan or 'shire' county, it also considers the other administrative layers in the planning process, the district councils, the regional bodies, and the role of central government, notably the Department of the Environment. In the latter case, the appeals and inquiry procedure and the quasi-judicial function of the Secretary of State are considered in relation to specific cases. I have tried, from the perspective afforded me in county government, to examine the connections between all levels of government and its relations with the private sector, interest groups, and the general public. By concentrating on one authority and a few examples, I hope to realise my aim of providing a deeper understanding of the process as a whole.

The structure of the book revolves around three broad concepts — planning, politics, and power — which are introduced in the first chapter and developed in relation to the literature in Chapter 2. From these concepts certain themes are developed which are illustrated in the empirical chapters which form the bulk of the book. Certain themes are prominent at certain points. Thus the theme of conflict and uncertainty underlies the chapter on transportation (Chapter 5); the theme of incrementalism versus comprehensive planning is central to the chapter on land development (Chapter 6); the theme of consensus and continuity is developed in the chapter on structure planning (Chapter 7). In each chapter several themes are present and the focus on the interaction between leading policy-makers, and the concentration and dispersal of power is fundamental to each example. The final chapter attempts to pull the themes together and reformulate them in a series of statements which stand as the conclusion of the book. The book ends with a consideration of the planning process and the possible changes that might be brought about in the future.

The book is not addressed to any particular audience. Having spent the most fruitful years of my academic career in a faculty where interdisciplinary teaching and research are the norm rather than the exception, I have been exposed to the work of colleagues in various social science disciplines. My initial interest in planning and geography has been broadened to include politics and administration. Although the book should be of interest to planners and administrators and to social scientists who study, research, and teach in these fields, I have not written purely for a professional or academic audience. There is a wider reading public, interested in or involved in public affairs at the local level who, I hope, will find that the book stimulates their understanding of the processes which influence their lives. Planning has been more exposed than most areas of government to public debate. Part of my intention is to reveal the political terms in which that debate is conducted.

It is traditional for authors to express their gratitude to those who have helped them reach the promised land of publication and I do so gladly. Among the many people who have read and criticised my work I would single out David Potter who helped me with the basic problem of trying to achieve coherence in argument. Tony Walton who helped to clarify in my mind some of the methodological problems, and Eric Reade whose perception of the planning process and detailed criticism provided intellectual stimulus and helped me avoid some errors. More generally, my colleagues at the Open University, Paul Lewis, Chris Hamnett, Andrew Learmonth, and Christopher Pollitt, have provided suggestions both of detail and argument which, I feel, have improved my work. John Hunt's ability as a cartographer speaks for itself in the illustrations in the book. To my secretary, Chris Pinches, I owe an enormous debt for patience in typing out successive drafts and coping with numerous corrections. With my wife, Gill, I shared a sense of partnership in the enterprise and without her help and patience I could not have sustained my interest.

Above all, perhaps, I should thank the planners and politicians of Bedfordshire with whom I worked and who are both victims and heroes of the story. I count them as my friends, and from Geoffrey Cowley, Tony Griffin, and Keith Simons of the County Planning Department I learned much about planning and more about politics. My party group provided me with political support over the years covered in the book. There remains one group, only some of whom I know, who made the whole thing possible. To the electors of South Bedford my thanks for providing me with the opportunity in the first place.

Bedford, September 1978

Acknowledgements

Acknowledgements are due to the Ordnance Survey for figures 5.1 Bedford — the shape of the urban area; 5.2 Proposed routes for the western relief road, Ministry of Transport, 1952; 6.3 Luton, the Green Wedge; 6.4 Luton, the Green Wedge, past planning proposals in the area; and 6.5 Luton, the Green Wedge — borough council's proposed development. Also to Bedfordshire County Council for figures 4.1 Minerals in Bedfordshire, as in 1972; 4.2 Fuller's Earth at Woburn — existing and proposed workings; 4.3 The Aspley Heath site: proposed plan of working and modifications imposed after the public inquiry; 5.4 Car parks in Bedford, 1978; 5.5, 5.6, 5.7, 5.8 and 5.9 Bedford Urban Transportation Study; 6.3 Luton, the Green Wedge; 6.4 Luton, the Green Wedge — past planning proposals in the area; 6.5 Luton, the Green Wedge — borough council's proposed development; 7.1 a to g Bedfordshire Structure Plan, Alternative Strategies; and 7.2 Bedfordshire constraints on development. Also to 'Town and Country Planning' for figure 6.1a and b which first appeared in the November 1974 issue of the journal. Finally to the 'Crisis' organisation who supplied the original sketches from which figure 5.3a and b is derived.

CHAPTER 1

The Balance of Power

Three concepts — planning, politics, and power — provide the underlying themes of this book. My intention is to examine the nature of environmental planning and the claims made for it in relation to local government. In doing so I shall reveal a contrast between normative conceptions of planning and the practice of local planning authorities. A second theme is to examine the widely held view that environmental planning is a disinterested activity, based on agreed professional principles and immune from political controversy. This may appear to be attacking a straw man, but it is extraordinary how deeply embedded among professional planners is this view that planning is an apolitical activity. The myth is partly sustained by the degree of consensus that still prevails in many areas of planning policy, but the evidence of increasing conflict confirms the view that planning is political and that choices have to be made which affect the distribution of costs and benefits. To explain the choices made we must understand the values held by those who possess the power to develop planning policy. A third theme is this exercise of power in a local planning authority. I shall demonstrate that the power to *develop* planning policy is concentrated among a few leading politicians and officials, but is not to be confused with the power to *make policy proposals effective*. Leading decision-makers are subject to external influences and they must secure the co-operation of many agencies responsible for implementation. Each of these themes is elaborated in the theoretical and empirical chapters which follow, and from the analysis certain conclusions may be drawn which are identified in the final chapter.

ENVIRONMENTAL PLANNING

Environmental planning[1], is primarily a local government activity, though in certain respects local planning authorities act as the agents of central government from whom powers are derived and by whom their actions are sanctioned. The Secretary of State for the Environment can intervene in planning decisions, he adjudicates appeals and approves strategic development plans, but local authorities are, within these limits, free to determine policy. In this sense environmental planning appears to be more autonomous than other areas of local government activity. Central government wields its influence over such areas as housing, education, and social services both through legislation and through its control over resources. But in another sense environmental planning is weaker than these other activities. There is little control by planning

[1]'Environmental planning' is concerned with those processes and procedures which regulate the distribution of land uses and which are responsible for policies covering the development, conservation, or change of man-made or natural features of the land surface. In Britain it is frequently described as 'town and country planning', 'town planning', or simply planning'.

authorities over the investment required to achieve planning objectives, and considerable dependence on a multiplicity of agencies, public and private, to secure the effective implementation of plans. In other local government services, once government approval has been obtained, the authority and the resources are available to provide the buildings, staff, and other facilities necessary to ensure a defined standard of service. Environmental planning appears to possess freedom, but in fact has little power. It reacts to initiatives from other agencies but it is not capable of determining outcomes without their co-operation. This weakness has been implicitly recognised since, from time to time, attempts have been made to provide planning with the necessary teeth to control development. So far these excursions into 'positive planning' (with the obvious inference that planning is negative) have had little impact on the planning process. Environmental planning continues to reflect and maintain the prevailing values and pattern of power.

Planning suggests rationality, a mode of decision-making that is at once comprehensive, strategic, and synoptic. It is supposedly distinct from the market mode of decision-making which responds to needs and demands as and when they arise. Planning, strictly defined, assumes a knowledge of all the choices available, the selection of specific goals from among alternatives, and the conscious achievement of these goals by prescribed means within a specified time-scale. But, in practice, planning as practised in the environmental field differs little from other forms of intelligent policy-making. Most activities, whether in government or in the private sector, adopt forecasts and objectives and seek to achieve them in some rational fashion. The process is incremental, co-ordinative, and short term. There is thus a distinction to be made between the theory and practice of planning, between rhetoric and reality. An appreciation of what planning is and what planners do must ultimately rest, not on the myths erected by interested parties or assumed by uncritical observers, but upon close examination of the system and the actors within it. A major theme of this book is to demystify some current and widely held conceptions about planning and to contribute to the debate about the future of environmental planning.

POLITICS

One of the more prevalent myths is that planning and politics are related but separate activities. There is the view that politics determines the ends of policy while experts select the appropriate means. Thus politics is involved in value judgement whereas officials are concerned with factual questions about the instruments of policy. This neglects the fact that the choice of means itself requires evaluation among alternatives, but, more importantly, it assumes that means and ends are distinguishable. Fay argues that 'every means is an end relative to the means required to achieve it, so that any given course of action may be either a means or an end depending upon the point of view which one adopts'.[2] In planning the ends defined for some plans may be the means identified to achieve others. An example might be public transport. A better public transport service may be the end of one plan but the means for achieving the end of another plan — a better city centre environment, for instance.[3] The choice of ends or

[2]B. Fay (1975) *Social Theory and Political Practice*, London, Allen & Unwin, p. 51.

[3]A. T. Blowers (1976) Consensus or conflict: a case study in planning, in *Patterns of Inequality*, Unit 30, The Open University, Milton Keynes, p. 75.

means involves some kind of moral commitment, such as whether to support public transport or the private car. Such decisions cannot be reduced to purely technical criteria and to do so involves adopting one set of values in preference to another. But the conviction that it is possible to make scientific judgements without recourse to values is a powerful defence against public discussion of many aspects of planning policy.

Both politicians and professional planners sustain the notion that planning can be treated separately from politics. Many politicians do not appear to recognise planning as a potential vehicle for social change. This displays an instinctive sense of the realities of political power. Politicians are motivated, in part, by the desire to achieve things, and many of them perceive palpable opportunities for imposing their mark in education or social services or housing. Planning appears to many politicians as an esoteric, impenetrable activity. It is often not a matter for party political controversy but a quasi-judicial procedure in which cases are treated on their merits in supposed conformity with certain planning principles. There are, of course, those politicians who recognise the significance of possessing information that may lead to gains from development and those who regard planning committees as an attractive forum for pursuing local constituency interests.

Officials traditionally claim political neutrality. They describe their advice and recommendations as 'departmental' or 'professional' with the clear inference that they are appealing to a substantive and immutable source of wisdom. Such claims provide a powerful defence of their position but also encourage them to avoid conflict and to advocate compromise. It is easy to caricature town planners as content to ensure the continuity of policy, anxious to dissuade politicians from introducing party ideology into policy-making. In my experience planning officers recognise the necessity for politics. They acknowledge the need for political support and initiative to get things done but tend to disclaim any political inclinations themselves. This encourages the idea that politics is a mechanism for decision-making rather than its motivation.

In recent years planning has become more politicised as different interests have been agitated and conflict has penetrated areas where consensus once reigned. Certain planning proposals have been the subject of great controversy (e.g. road schemes, airports, and nuclear plant) and hitherto accepted planning policies have been subjected to scrutiny (e.g. new towns, regional policy) and sometimes attack (e.g. urban renewal). Public pressure for participation has been formally recognised even though its influence so far has been less than was hoped or feared. Planning is increasingly regarded as an activity that has an effect on the quality of life and as a means of distributing costs and benefits among individuals and social groups. At first sight this may appear to contradict the contention that planning is a weak activity. But it is weak in the sense that it does not, by itself, control events. In co-operation with other institutions which control investment and development, planning can react to pressure and contribute to social change. Planning can also contribute to continuity in policy. For example, there has been broad agreement with the need to restrict development on the best agricultural land and on the need to preserve landscapes or townscapes of high amenity.

A second major aim of the book is to explain the conditions under which continuity or conflict in planning policy are likely to occur. Consensus would appear to require either agreement among all participants in a decision, though not necessarily among those not participating; or coalition among decision-makers anxious to avoid conflict; or disagreement over the objectives of policy but agreement over means[4]; or recognition over the inevitability of a certain course of action in the face of external constraints. In such conditions it is possible to achieve continuity over planning policy. Where such agreement is not present, conflicts over policy will occur and the outcome will be uncertain. The greater the conflict the more likely will it be that policy-making responds to short-term pressures rather than long term strategy.

Expressed in more concrete political terms, continuity is most likely to occur where power is secure in the hands of decision-makers sharing common ideological impulses. The absence of competition for resources or finance is likely to strengthen this continuity. Where the balance of power among interests is shifting or fluctuating, or where there is competition for scarce resources, then policy-making is liable to give rise to uncertainty. Both continuity and uncertainty may be present at different times within the same organisation, or at the same time within different geographical areas covered by that organisation, or in different theatres of planning policy. There may, for instance, be continuity in conservation policy but uncertainty in transportation policy.

The studies in this book relate to a local authority where the balance of political power was precarious and liable to shift, where political and professional ideologies were sometimes in conflict with each other, and where external influences (resources, other organisations) were strong. Although such conditions suggest considerable uncertainty (at least in the short run) there still remains a surprising degree of continuity in policy-making. This underlines the significance of factors quite outside the control of the decision-makers. But external factors may now be leading towards a reassessment of planning policies across a broad front. The impact of the economic crisis and the decline of the birth rate in the 1970s had a profound effect on planning generally. Within a few years, planning on the basis of anticipated economic and demographic growth was transformed into planning for a stable population and reduced resources and lowered economic expectations. At the same time there were important institutional changes. The reorganisation of local government and the introduction of new legislation affecting development plans, land, and transportation promoted sudden and disruptive changes. Both the local and the national climate provide a turbulent context in which to examine concepts of conflict and continuity in planning policy.

POWER

The power to make policy and to attempt to effect it is formally in the hands of the elected representatives who constitute a planning committee. In reality this power is confined to a small group of politicians and officials. Politicians are subject to various pressures and influences. The ultimate source of power lies with the electorate; but elections are infrequent and the turn-out low, and results hinge not so much on local actions as on the popularity of the national government of the day. The influence of the electorate may appear to be weak, but the political leadership does pay attention to public

[4]A simple example of this might be where attempts to restrict car parking in a town are supported by one group as a means to improve public transport and by another as a way of increasing parking revenues through higher charges.

opinion, and there is among local politicians the belief that their actions are being observed by the public.[5] Public participation provides a further mechanism for expressing public opinion, though it frequently serves to advance established interests or to endorse the views of the planning authority. The political parties, too, through their control over the selection of candidates, and in devising the manifesto on which elections are fought, will seek to exercise some control over the policy-making of the political leadership. Within these limitations, however, the politicians possess considerable freedom. 'Much research on English local government has argued that there are widespread attitudes in the population which legitimize hierarchical political arrangements in which those who are elected are free to decide the course of public policy.'[6] Access to information and superior knowledge of the constraints and feasibility of policy enables the leaders to influence the manifesto and to interpret its proposals. The tight discipline imposed on the political group enables the leadership to carry its policies. Although leaders are receptive to some of the demands made by their supporters and by the public, they tend to adopt them at a pace compatible with the exigencies of preserving their position. The leading officials in a local authority would appear to be even less susceptible to popular pressure. In theory they are the servants of the political will but in practice they may possess considerable administrative discretion and autonomy. There is considerable debate as to how much power officials do, in fact, wield.[7] The theoretical debate, which is reviewed in the next chapter, seems inconclusive. The case-studies in this book attempt to identify the distribution of power among officials and politicians. What is significant is that leading officials share considerable power to make policy with politicians.

Policy-making can only be effective if it can be carried out. The power to implement policies is dispersed. Before local government reorganisation it was possible, in some authorities, for one political group representing certain interests in the community to enjoy uninterrupted rule and continuity of leadership, while conducting most of the council business in secret without fear of reprisal or public criticism. In the larger counties, the influence of 'county' families had begun to crumble long before reorganisation as party politics began to emerge.[8] Even where power was concentrated among an élite, it was limited to matters over which they had full control. It could not survive reorganisation which introduced larger authorities and which coincided with the emergence of pressure groups and public participation. Above all, the new system split functions, especially in planning, between two tiers of local government — the district and county councils. It has proved increasingly difficult, as later examples will show, for agreement to be reached between the tiers (whether or not party political conflict is also present) and, in many areas of policy, compromises must be forged or disagreements

[5]R. Gregory (1969) Local elections and the 'rule of anticipated reactions'. *Political Studies*, **17**, 13–47.

[6]S. L. Elkin (1974) *Politics and Land Use Planning: the London Experience*, Cambridge University Press, p. 95.

[7]This is, of course, a major point of debate and will be referred to again in the next chapter. Weber argued that 'the trained permanent official is more likely to get his way in the long run than his nominal superior' (*The Theory of Social and Economic Organization*, New York, 1974). Miliband (*The State in Capitalist Society*, London, 1973) agrees, viewing bureaucracy as one of the key elements of state control. Bottomore (*Élites and Society*, Penguin, London, 1966) argues that, despite increasing power, bureaucrats are subject still to political will and dependent on politicians for policy making.

[8]This point is given empirical support by J. M. Lee who analysed power and leadership in Cheshire County Council (*Social Leaders and Public Persons*, Oxford, published 1963).

will persist. It is not just a matter of forging agreement between the tiers of local government. Planning policy relies on various bodies — statutory undertakers, transport operators, nationalised industries, and private industry — for endorsement and implementation. Thus a third theme is to comprehend the extent and limitations on the power exercised by leading politicians and officials.

THE PLANNING POLICY-MAKING PROCESS

The focus of the analysis of planning policy-making is the power relationships of the leading decision-makers of a local planning authority. These relationships are complex and could be described in terms of interlocking networks. Clearly, as one of the participants, I was involved in one set of relationships and only partly related to the networks experienced by other participants. I can only suggest the influence of actors in the process with whom I was not directly engaged. For instance, in the case explored in Chapter 5 I was part of a network which included politicians, local interests, and planning officials. The planning officials, in turn, were part of a network which extended to government departments and the developers, from which I was excluded. Both the officials and the politicians were subject to the various influences which are diagrammatically represented in Fig. 1.1. The diagram is greatly oversimplified and does not attempt to indicate how these influences are transmitted, whether they are direct or mediated. Ideological influences are imparted to politicians through the party organisations, and the politicians in turn influence the officials. Conversely, officials communicate their professional ideology, through which they derive their perception of the function, status, and goals of planning policy, to the politicians. Private interests have a direct channel of communication to officials and to some politicians. Similarly, officials are in direct touch with other officials in government departments and will filter government views by means of reports or verbal comments. Other local authorities have direct links at both political and official level as well as the opportunity to present their views through consultative machinery. Public opinion can express itself through participation, through the media, and through elections. Finally, all decision-makers are influenced by existing policies and by the constraints exerted by the availability of resources. The outcomes in terms of policy will affect the interaction of the actual decision-makers and the political environment within which they are working. The examples later in the book will attempt to unravel the web of relationships and to suggest the significance of the various influences upon the formulation and execution of planning policy.

The central concepts of planning, politics, and power are elaborated in the next chapter and illustrated in the four case-studies which form the main part of the book. In these chapters I shall show that planning, whether called strategic planning or not, is in reality an incremental process responding to immediate pressures from various interests conditioned by resources and the political climate. Viewed as a political process, planning policy-making incorporates both the initiation and the implementation of policy. Power is unevenly distributed, highly concentrated at the formative stages but widely dispersed during implementation. Where interests coincide then consensus may exist, but it is always liable to be broken as conflicts are stimulated by a changing political environment. Conflicts are contained within a pattern of power which planning seems to support. Planning policy-making is conducted within the rules of a game which inevitably reflects the interests of those who possess the information and skill to exploit the process.

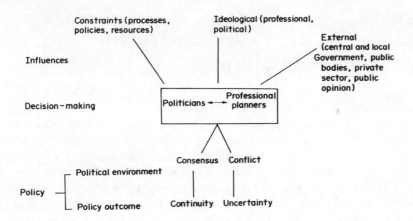

CHAPTER 2

Planners and Politicians

The exercise of power in local government can be observed through its formal manifest-
ations when a vote is taken, but this only reveals the surface, often the last stage of a
long process of negotiation and compromise. In order to reach the formal stage an issue
will have been subject to considerable debate both within the formal framework of the
committee system and, often more crucially, within the informal system of bureaucratic
department, party group, and meetings between certain officials and elected representatives. Informal channels of interaction between the bureaucratic and political processes are of central importance in deciding which issues will be pursued and how and
when they will be exposed for public debate. The informal process of local government
is fascinating yet inscrutable, and the actions and motivations of policy-makers usually
have to be inferred or interpreted from what is visible. Studies of local government
have, by and large, relied on accessible information and surveys of the attitudes of the
actors in the process.

Decision-makers are not likely to reveal information that might damage them and, in
any case, there is a tradition of secrecy in local government which, in my experience,
goes far beyond what is necessary to avoid prejudicing the public interest. Attempts to
expose certain issues may provoke a reaction and intensify the guardedness with which
any information is revealed.[1] Therefore, research into the inner workings of local
government is difficult 'because it is far from easy to provide objective and unam-
biguous evidence on such topics, but above all because social scientists are rarely given
access to the information they need to tackle such questions'.[2]

The evidence on which the case-studies in this book are based is drawn from inside
observation of the process of policy-making in local government. For the four years
under study (1973–7) I was Chairman of the Environmental Services Committee
(planning and transportation) of Bedfordshire County Council and therefore had
access to confidential correspondence and, through informal contacts with politicians
and officials, possessed first-hand knowledge of the development of policy. It can be
said that this provides a biased and partial insight and one that does not allow critical
detachment, since I was a prominent actor in the process of government. That is true,
but a study from the inside, with all its obvious difficulties as an academic enterprise,
does provide a perspective that is lacking in our knowledge of the workings of local
government.

[1]D. M. Muchnik, (1970) *Urban Renewal in Liverpool: A Study of the Politics of Redevelopment*,
Occasional Papers on Social Administration, No. 33, G. Bell, p. 10.
[2]M. J. Hill (1972) *The Sociology of Public Administration*, London, Weidenfeld & Nicholson, p. 14. K.
Newton (1976) *Second City Politics: Democratic Processes and Decision Making in Birmingham*, Oxford,
Oxford University Press, comments, 'it is like trying to get blood out of a red tape', (p. 146).

A major issue in this book is to determine how much power politicians and professional planners possess and how that power is distributed among them. There is a huge literature on the concept of power which need not detain us here.[3] Perhaps one of the simplest definitions is Bertrand Russell's: power may be seen 'as the production of intended efforts'.[4] For Russell, a person or group is powerful to the extent he or it can fulfil his or its intentions. The extent of power in local government planning is, in turn, dependent on the definition, and planning means different things in different circumstances. Those who exercise power — the planners — include both full-time officials and elected representatives. For example, planners have considerable power to determine the patterns of transport provision or the design and layout of housing estates. These detailed functions have profound implications for the lives of many people.[5] Conversely, planners have much less power to effect more comprehensive policies involving social objectives, which may, for instance, assert the need to alter existing patterns of income distribution. As indicated in Chapter 1, the power to implement policies is often weaker than the power to make them. Much depends on the co-operation of other bodies and the need to ensure agreement over future developments. It also requires control over current and future social and environmental processes which, in a mixed economy and plural society like Britain, the planner simply does not have. Opponents of planning policies are often aware of this inherent weakness and, in a Machiavellian way, are content to allow plans to be written which cannot be carried out. But this also invites more trenchant criticism of a process that is taken to be largely esoteric, providing employment for a large number of highly trained specialists but producing little in the way of useful output. 'Planning that disregards the question of implementation languishes as an academic irrelevancy; it may be right but not relevant, correct but not useful.'[6]

The question of whether planning could (or should) be more effective is one I shall consider in the last chapter when some of the evidence can be reviewed. Here I shall examine the nature of planning and its role as an element in the power of the state. Although planning may be relatively ineffective in initiating social change, it has an important role in ensuring the survival and adaptation of the prevailing system of values and distribution of resources. I shall also focus on the political and bureaucratic processes, which are responsible for the development of planning policy. It will be apparent that the power to make policy and take decisions is concentrated among a few leading officials and politicians. The interaction of these decision-makers, and the

[3]Among the interesting debates on power is that raised in S. Lukes (1974) *Power: A Radical View*, London, MacMillan, in which he develops the critique of the one-dimensional view (i.e. that studies should focus on the observable conflict of Factors in the decision-making process). This approach was adopted in R. A. Dahl (1961) *Who Governs? Democracy and Power in an American City*, Yale University Press, and criticised by P. Bachrach, and M. S. Baratz (1962) Two faces of power, *American Political Science Review*, **56**, 947–52 for failing to discriminate among issues and for ignoring the built-in value bias in political systems. Other relevant studies of power include: N. W. Polsby (1963) *Community Power and Political Theory*, New Haven and London, Yale University Press; R. Michels (1959) *Political Parties* New York and Dover. The Free Press, first published in 1915; and M. Meyerson and E. C. Banfield (1955) *Politics, Planning and the Public Interest*, New York, The Free Press.

[4]B. Russell (1938) *Power, a New Social Analysis*, London, Unwin.

[5]A. T. Blowers (1970) Council housing: the social implications of layout and design in an urban fringe estate, *Town Planning Review*, **41** (1) (January) 80–92.

[6]M. Rein (1969) Social planning: the search for legitimacy, in M. Stewart (ed.) (1972) *The City: Problems of Planning*, Penguin, London, p. 440

transmission of ideas and hopes and fears among them, reveals how power is exercised and to what purpose. But their freedom to propose and implement policies is constrained by influences both within the organisation and from outside. These are the themes which will be discussed in general in this chapter and through the analyses of specific areas of policy-making in the chapters which follow.

1. THE LIMITS OF PLANNING

The title of Wildavsky's essay, 'If planning is everything, maybe it's nothing', indicates the problems of definition of planning. 'For if a definition covers all attempts to plan, whether they succeed or not, planning encompasses whatever men do in the world. Since practically all actions with future consequences are planned actions, planning is everything, and nonplanning can hardly be said to exist.'[7] The term is used loosely so that any policy-making may be called planning. In a market or mixed economy, comprehensive planning cannot be the only approach to policy-making. Planning is limited both as a decision-making and as a political process. As a decision-making process it tends to be more incremental than comprehensive, and as a political process it tends to be reactive rather than innovative.

Planning as a mode of decision-making

Comprehensive planning would require an assessment of all the facts, a recognition of all the possible courses of action, and an evaluation of all the possible consequences arising from each alternative.[8] It assumes 'rationality' on the part of planners. In its substantive sense (as defined by Weber) this 'involves a relation to the absolute values or to the content of the particular given ends'.[9] Such an approach would be virtually impossible in an activity such as planning where the ends are frequently given and the consequences of present action on future outcomes cannot be predicted. Furthermore, a comprehensive plan would have to specify the policies by which the plan is to be carried into effect. 'A *plan* is a course of action which can be carried into effect, which can be expected to lead to the attainment of the ends sought, and which someone (the effectuating organisation) intends to carry into effect.'[10]

More limited definitions of planning retain the idea of comprehensiveness but are less assertive about the potential for achievement. Emphasis is placed upon attempts to secure goals for the future, on selecting guidelines, and on choosing among alternatives. For example, Friedmann suggests 'planning is only another name for the application of intelligence to the future'.[11] Dror is rather more definitive — 'a process of preparing a

[7]A. Wildavsky (1973) If planning is everything, maybe it's nothing, *Journal of Policy Sciences* **4**, (2) 127–53, p. 130.
[8]A. Etzioni (1967) Mixed-scanning: a 'third' approach to decision-making. *Public Administration Review*, December, in A. Faludi (ed.) (1973) *A Reader in Planning Theory* Urban and Regional Planning Series, vol. 5, Oxford, Pergamon Press.
[9]M. Weber (1947) *The Theory of Social and Economic Organizations*, edited with an Introduction by Talcott Parsons, New York, The Free Press, p. 185.
[10]M. Meyerson and E. C. Banfield (1955) op. cit.
[11]J. Friedmann (1966) Planning as a vocation, *Plan* **6** (3) 99–124, p. 100.

set of decisions for action in the future directed at achieving goals by optimal means'.[12] Davidoff and Reiner emphasise choice: 'a process for determining appropriate future action through a sequence of choices',[13] and Altshuler suggests that plans should determine 'policy guidelines for public activity'.[14] Yet further dilution of the idea of comprehensiveness is introduced by the stress on the need to monitor, review, and adapt plans to changing circumstances. 'Adaptation to changing circumstances is certainly a virtue of the intelligent man. But it smacks of *ad hoc* decision making.'[15]

Emphasis on flexibility, and the need to adapt and adjust plans, is characteristic of long-range comprehensive land-use planning as practised in the United Kingdom and which has, in recent years, reached its apotheosis in the form of structure plans. Such plans, or bundles of environmental policies, are continuously reviewed and altered if economic, political, social, or demographic circumstances warrant changes. They tend to reflect rather than promote change, as Chapter 7 on structure plans will show. Comprehensive planning policies tend to represent the cumulative effect of a whole series of individual decisions taken at particular points in time and projected into the future. This dependence of the long term upon the short term further reduces the scope for innovation and the consistent pursuit of specified objectives. It leads to the conclusion that long-range comprehensive planning in the sense of a projected future environment being achieved, except in the most vague and general terms, is liable to be vitiated by short-range decisions which are based on the pattern of power prevailing at a particular time. This is the essence of the analysis in Chapter 6.

If comprehensive definitions of planning are too ambitious, the idea that planning can only be an incremental process may seem unduly pessimistic. Lindblom argues that: 'Democracies change their policies almost entirely through incremental adjustments.'[16] He therefore urges that a limited, practical approach based on past experience and awareness of the limited choices available will be superior to a futile attempt at superhuman comprehensiveness.[17] This may be so, but dependence on past practice and emphasis on present constraints may leave concealed other possibilities. Wherever it is assumed that there is agreement about basic social goals, then a strategy of incrementalism, of making small changes individually and sequentially, may exist. The features of such planning strategies are indicated by Dahl and Lindblom[18] — they are close to existing reality; preferences are tested by experience; compromise is encouraged; the effects of making a certain choice can be compared within the previous situation; small changes ensure control; decisions can be reversed; and the established norms of society are not threatened. Etzioni[19] has attacked the ideological premises of incrementalism, suggesting that it serves the interests of the powerful and ignores those of the underprivileged, that it neglects basic innovations in its concentration on short-

[12]Y. Dror *Ventures in Policy Sciences*, 1972, American Elsevior, New York, quoted in M. Burridge (1973) 'Education for urban governance: education for whom?' Centre for Environmental Studies, CES CP10, London, p. 61.

[13]P. Davidoff and A. Reiner (1962) A choice theory of planning, *Journal of the American Institute of Planners* **28** (May), in A. Faludi (ed.) (1973) op. cit., p. 11

[14]A. Altshuler (1965) The goals of comprehensive planning, *Journal of the American Institute of Planners* **31** (August), in A. Faludi (ed.) (1973) op. cit., p. 206.

[15]A. Wildavsky (1973) op. cit., p. 135.

[16]C. E. Lindblom (1959) The science of 'muddling through', *Public Administration Review*, Spring, in A. Faludi (ed.) (1973) op. cit., p. 161.

[17]Ibid., p. 166.

[18]R. A. Dahl and C. E. Lindblom (1953) *Politics, Economics and Welfare*, New York, Harper & Row.

[19]A. Etzioni (1967) op. cit.

run limited changes, and that it reinforces the inertia among decision-makers. In short, the ideology of incrementalism is adaptive and conservative. It leads to the belief, once common among many planners and still held by some, that planning is merely a technical activity from which the necessity to make clear assumptions about intended or prospective social goals is removed since they are implicit.

Planning as a political process

The notion that planning is a technical matter both limits and increases the power of planners. By restricting their focus to issues which can be solved within existing organisational and social arrangements it removes any scope for attempting to change those arrangements. But the idea of planning as a technical matter arrogates to those with the necessary or presumed competence the power to make decisions without challenge. By reducing all judgements to matters of expertise, the planner places himself in a powerful position. But the view that planning is a disinterested technical activity has been contradicted both by experience and by several commentators. The problem of distinguishing ends and means was referred to in Chapter 1. There is a further problem since, by attempting to determine social objectives by employing certain technical means, planners have exposed the lack of congruence between the objectives and the means specified to achieve them The belief that such abstract and ill-defined notions as 'community spirit', or 'social balance', of 'social integration' were merely a matter of housing design, estate layout, and the provision of certain facilities has been rudely corrected by the outcome of post-war housing policies which have provided vast areas of high-density housing in the cities, replacing one set of social problems with another.[20] Of course, planners may have been blamed for things that should not be attributed to them, but the fact is they have been blamed and this has led to a more cautious, less deterministic approach. While this is, in some respects, healthy, there is the danger that a misplaced belief in the success of planning will be replaced by an overdeveloped sense of failure. Such a feeling, if widely shared among the community at large, could contribute to a diminution of the prestige and, consequently, the power conferred on planners. It is difficult, however, to know whether opposition to planners stems from hostility towards them for the power they are thought to have or frustration with them for the power they lack.

It is now widely accepted by academic commentators that planning is a political activity. Although certain decisions are taken automatically without reference to public debate, they have been predetermined by policies already established through the political process. Although many planning decisions may arouse little passion or conflict, they are nevertheless political even if they merely serve the *status quo*. Absence of overt conflict must not be taken for absence of opposition or for general agreement. It may reflect apathy, acquiescence, or alienation. Recently the recognition that planning does involve questions of cost and benefit has become more widespread. Public reaction to some planning projects has intensified, intellectual criticism of

[20]A. T. Blowers (1973) Planning residential areas, *Urban Development*, Unit 29, The Open University, Milton Keynes pp. 91–139.

planning has emphasised its distributional implications,[21] and political conflict over planning policies has become commonplace. In Britain policies for transportation, new towns, the inner cities, urban renewal, office development, and industrial location have given rise to controversy. Planning is not just a remote regulatory device able to assume a consensus of values, but a potential means for influencing the environmental goals of society over which there may be conflict.

The ideology of planning

Planning has a long tradition of radical ideology, but this has always been contained outside the planning process itself. Planning as an organized state activity has been 'practical, incremental, and conservative',[22] There is an important distinction to be made between 'idealistic' and 'realistic' conceptions of planning. The former tends to be radical but ineffectual, the latter conformist but powerful within the limits prescribed by the state. There is a tension between the idea of planning as a technical, instrumental process concerned with the orderly arrangement of the components of the built environment, and that of planning as part of a comprehensive programme of social reform and reconstruction.

From Utopian tradition to servant of the state

Utopianism is the 'occupational disease of planners'.[23] There has always been an ideological strand which has sought to achieve certain social reforms through environmental change. During the nineteenth century, utopian thinkers conceptualised the physical forms in which a reformed society based on the socialist principles of community and equality could be developed. Some, like Robert Owen, Charles Fourier, Jean Baptiste Godin, and Etienne Cabet,[24] attempted to realise their schemes both in Europe and in the more open conditions of the United States. Most of these social experiments were small scale and short lived, though relics of their physical forms survive. They aimed 'at the total reconstruction of the urban and rural landscape in accordance with the emergent social and economic problems'.[25] They were foredoomed to fail, according to Marx and Engels, because they were of 'a purely utopian character' seeking to achieve social change by peaceful means and failing to recognise that town-planning schemes must be a consequence, not the progenitors, of changed economic

[21]There have been a series of recent critiques of the planning process and its distributional aspects. Among these are: D. Harvey (1973) *Social Justice and the City*, London, Arnold; J. G. Davies (1972) *The Evangelistic Bureaucrat: A Study of a Planning Exercise in Newcastle upon Tyne*, London, Tavistock; N. Dennis (1972) *Public Participation and Planner's Blight*, London, Faber; A. J. Catanese (1974) *Planners and Local Politics: Impossible Dreams*, Beverley Hills, Sage Publications; J. M. Simmie (1974) *Citizens in Conflict*, London, Hutchinson Educational; A. T. Blowers (1976) Consensus or conflict: a case study in planning, in *Patterns of Inequality*, Unit 30, The Open University, pp. 55–104.
[22]J. Friedmann (1966), op. cit., p. 100.
[23]P. Self (1976) Strategic planning for quality of life, in T. Hancock (ed.) (1976) *Growth and Change in the Future City Region*, London, Leonard Hill, pp. 32–52, p. 37.
[24]Utopian developments in planning in the nineteenth century are covered in L. Benevolo (1967) *The Origins of Modern Town Planning*, translated by J. Landry, London, Routledge & Kegan Paul.
[25]Ibid., p. 84.

relations.[26] The schemes of nineteenth-century philanthropists such as Salt, Ackroyd, Lever, and Cadbury were far less ambitious in social terms and can be seen, by providing a better living environment for industrial enterprises, to sustain rather than challenge the capitalist system of production of the time. But these, too, were isolated attempts, scarcely influencing the development of the vast industrial towns. More significant, in terms of its physical impact, was the work of Ebenezer Howard and his followers. To Howard is attributed the origins of the new towns movement and the introduction of the garden city concept. Certainly this has had an enormous impact on the thinking of British planners and has been translated into reality since 1945. But, even here, the influence has been limited to a relatively small proportion of total urban development,[27] although the ideas of open space, neighbourhood units, and garden suburbs — often in debased form — have been widely diffused. Howard's scheme, like those of the earlier utopians, was much more than a physical planning concept. It was, as the title of the first edition of his book intimated, a social and political programme, designed to produce 'a peaceful path to real reform'.[28]

What is most interesting is that the more imaginative and visionary planning thinkers have perceived the potential use of planning as a *part* of a programme of social reconstruction. There has been a recognition that ideological inspiration is inseparable from technical developments. When this conception has been allied to a political programme as, arguably, it was in Britain in the early post-war years, then the power and potential of planning becomes very considerable. It is to that short period that we may attribute the most significant advances in town planning and perhaps its only significant innovation, the new town. But it was also the period when planning became transformed into part of the apparatus of government. Herein lies the weakness as well as the strength of planning. As an arm of the state, planning must serve rather than transcend the prevailing pattern of power. While it remained aloof or rejected by the mainstream of political activity, planning could retain its originality and radicalism. Once part of the political establishment it had access to power but only on the terms defined by the powerful.

As a result the limits of ideological conflict within organised planning are circumscribed by what is tolerated by the need to sustain the existing system. Certain changes will be accommodated until they begin to cause strains that threaten established norms, at which point compensating mechanisms will be introduced. For instance, industrial policies to divert industry to depressed areas will continue until they are seen to affect adversely more prosperous areas. Similarly, dispersal of population to relieve congestion will be accepted until it threatens the economy of the major cities. This is not to suggest that ideological conflicts do not occur. They do, but within strict limits. Foley

[26]K. Marx and F. Engels (1848) *The Communist Manifesto*, in K. Marx and F. Engels (1968) *Selected Works*, London, Lawrence & Wishart. Not edited.
[27]There are various estimates of the contribution of the new towns to urban development in Britain. D. Lock, in T. Hancock (ed.) (1976) *op. cit.*, p. 197, estimates that new towns have contributed only 4% of the national house-building programme but have accommodated 30% of those moving from the Greater London conurbation. The GLC, however, estimated that under 10% of the gross outward migration from London was planned overspill (Greater London Council, 'Planned Growth Outside London', December 1975).
[28]E. Howard (1902) *Garden Cities of Tomorrow*, also in Faber Books, 1965, first published 1898 as *Tomorrow: A Peaceful Path to Real Reform*.

suggests that there are three ideologies in British town planning.[29] Two of these — the allocation of land uses among competing interests in order to achieve an orderly arrangement, and the creation of an attractive environment for a healthy and civilised life — merely state the accepted role of town planning as a governmental enterprise. The third — the idea of social advocacy — of planning as part of a broader social programme, is a recurrent idea, but firmly based on the concept that planning's task is to provide for the physical basis of social life. This implies some political commitment to planning as a vehicle for social change. It is this availability of potentially different ideologies which 'has helped to ensure political support from all quarters'.[30] Although historically planning thought has been associated with reformist, not to say revolutionary, programmes, its present position, in Britain at least, is as a legitimate activity of government responsible for the allocation of land uses and the distribution of particular goods and services.

It is the supine service of the state that has led critics to argue the case for action that openly challenges the existing assumptions and political arrangements of planning. As yet their arguments do not amount to a coherent, co-ordinated programme, and have rhetorical rather than practical appeal. The fact is that planning has rarely been perceived and has still more rarely been used as a deliberate method of intervention to alter the distribution of resources in society. Even if it were, it is highly likely that the attempt would prove abortive. Therefore, Harvey pronounces: 'programmes which seek to alter distribution without altering the capitalist market structure within which income and wealth are generated and distributed, are doomed to failure.'[31]

Although planning must be seen as a political activity, it reflects the prevailing values of society and does not seek to oppose them. This provides planning with a carapace of political neutrality which strengthens its position. In the highly political task of arbitrating between competing interests, planning avoids the charge of being partisan by claiming to serve the 'public interest'. 'The political reality is that general public interests are almost impossible to define or articulate.'[32] Meyerson and Banfield contend that something can only be in the public interest 'if it serves the whole public rather than those of some sector of the public'.[33] In Britain there has been a tendency to evaluate issues in terms of utilitarian principles,[34] which implies that gains achieved by some groups are at the expense of others. Choices have to be made, and any appeal to a notional public interest merely helps to obscure that fact. There is a belief that the public interest 'though it is highly complex and does not represent the sum total of simultaneously overt interests, can be defined in terms of coherent social policies'.[35] Very often there are competing interests, overt and concealed, with private and public interests difficult to distinguish. By claiming to act in the public interest planners are able to avoid imputations of bias.

[29]D. Foley (1960) British town planning: one ideology or three?, *British Journal of Sociology*, **11**, in A. Faludi (ed.) (1973) op. cit.
[30]Ibid., p. 87.
[31]D. Harvey (1973) op. cit., p. 110.
[32]A. J. Catanese (1974) op. cit., p. 25.
[33]M. Meyerson and E.C. Banfield (1955) op. cit., p. 322.
[34]This point is discussed in L. Allison (1975) *Environmental Planning*, London, Allen & Unwin.
[35]R. Glass (1957) The evaluation of planning: some sociological considerations, *International Social Sciences Journal*, **11** (3), 393–409, p. 395.

Planning, then, is essentially a reactive process, adapting and adjusting to circumstances. As a vehicle for social change it is weak. The strength of planning lies in its ability to serve the state. It responds to the political climate and does not attempt to transform it. For instance, in the early post-war years planning was embraced by a reforming government and advanced as an element of the state's activity. Once established, planning conformed to the conservative characteristics identified by Michels and Schattschneider[36] as typical of all organisations. Occasionally, planning policies have their origins outside the state machinery. Whereas new towns represent a planning idea developed outside state planning and successfully imported into it, planning has generally been prone to accommodate to market forces and political expediency. It has become accepted as an arbitrator of competing interests and as a co-ordinator of environmental development. More rarely is planning viewed as a promoter of change, though this undoubtedly remains an integral part of the self-image possessed by planners themselves.

2. SOURCES OF POWER

Bureaucratic power

As a state activity planning depends on two sources of power — the bureaucracy and politicians. The relationship between the two is a theme of this book, but it is worth considering the features of each independently first. Much of the following discussion is couched in general terms and relates to local bureaucracies and political groups in general. Planning needs to be seen as a part of the overall organisational and political structure. Planning shares features in common with other services provided by local government as well as having its own characteristics. In particular it possesses a bureaucratic organisation similar to that of other local government activities.

The growth of bureaucracy as an integral part of advanced societies has been described by Weber.[37] According to him the principal features of bureaucracies are their departmental and hierarchical organisation, and the appointment of full-time staff qualified in specific skills to undertake specific tasks. Staff are dependent upon superiors for advancement, and this ensures loyalty and conformity to the norms of the organisation. There is a view commonly held that bureaucracy is not necessarily benign or disinterested. Since bureaucrats are numerous and permanent they can secure considerable control over information and over the evolution or suppression of alternative policies, and are able to work with a degree of anonymity free from public scrutiny. When faced by external pressures from public or political sources which they regard as unpalatable, they can apply tactics of resistance or deferral, or a strategy of adapting policies into a more acceptable form, or they can modify the implementation

[36]Thus R. Michels (1959) in *Political Parties*, New York and Dover, The Free Press, p. 22, states organisation 'is, in fact, the source from which conservative currents flow over the plain of democracy'. E. E. Schattschneider, in *The Semi-Sovereign People: A Realist's View of Democracy in America*, New York, Holt, Rinehart & Winston, 1960, p. 71, argues that: 'All forms of organizations have a bias in favour of the exploitation of some forms of conflict and the suppression of others, because *organization is the mobilization of bias.*'
[37]M. Weber (1947) op. cit.

of policies. It can be argued that bureaucracy acts benignly in the sense that it forestalls extreme measures and concentrates its energies on securing orderly and gradual accommodation of social change. Its very independence of the political and vested interests in society enables state bureaucracies to act in the interests of society as a whole. This line of argument is, of course, open to the serious challenge that powerful bureaucracies acting in secret and removed from public accountability are free to develop their own interests and to serve those who will promote those interests. The motivating force of bureaucracy may be self-preservation and resistance to forces that seek disruptive change. There is a compatibility between bureaucracy and the dominant groups in society. This has led some to suggest that planning officers, in common with other bureaucrats, serve the interests of the powerful. 'Professional planners must serve the interests of the power élite and its political structure if they wish to survive in their jobs.'[38]

Bureaucratic power also issues from claims to expertise and professional status. There has been much discussion as to whether planning has the attributes that enable it to claim professional status.[39] Reade[40] suggests that it is useful to distinguish between two contrasted self-perceptions of role among those who advise government. Those he labels 'experts' appreciate fully that the actual decisions made must rest on political values quite as much as on the technical understanding which they themselves provide. Those he terms 'professionals' and who often employ the ideology of professionalism tend to blur the fact/value distinction. Paradoxically, however, it is often this latter type who are prone to exaggerate the distinction between their own role and the role of the politicians. But while thus *asserting* that it is the politicians who determine 'ends', these 'professionals' in practice often themselves shape policy objectives while denying that they do so. Planners, Reade suggests, belong to this second group. Economists, who are more likely to express their advice in the conditional form — 'If you want x, then it is necessary to do A, B, and C' — are, perhaps a good example of the first type, referred to in his paper as 'experts' as opposed to 'professionals'.

The need to assert professional status on the part of planners may stem from a desire to be recognised, from a need to protect employment prospects, or even, as Davies suggests, from a sense of insecurity. This would account for the 'peculiar intensity of the planners' claim to professional status and for the frequency with which planners proclaim themselves possessed of a charisma which must remain beyond criticism and beyond question'.[41] Be that as it may, the success of the Royal Town Planning Institute in Britain, and other professional bodies elsewhere, in ensuring that entry to the planning job market must be on the terms defined by their peers has placed planners in a powerful position *vis-á-vis* those who would contend their claims to competence. There are certain skills, notably those connected with the legal aspects of development control or those required to deal with such issues as minerals or forestry or conservation, which do require some special training. But the vast area over which planners claim competence requires more than a narrowly based technical training. This is now widely

[38]A. J. Catanese (1974) op. cit., p. 106.
[39]Among the discussions on the role of professionalism in planning are: E. J. Reade (1977) 'Some educational consequences of the incorporation of the planning profession into the state bureaucracy', paper presented to the Conference of Sociologists in Polytechnics Section of the British Sociological Association, April; J. G. Davies (1972) op. cit.; J. M. Simmie (1974) op. cit.; and M. J. Hill (1972) op. cit.
[40]E. J. Reade (1977) op. cit., p. 9. I am grateful to Eric Reade for his elaboration of his thesis in a personal communication.
[41]J. G. Davies (1972) op. cit., p. 95.

recognised, as is clear from the debate on education for planners that is going on inside and outside the profession.[42]

So far professionalism has managed to retain its tight grip, and there are few signs that those who do not acquire the status of chartered town planner will enjoy the same prospects as those who do. Undoubtedly, this professional mystique and protectionism has contributed to the growth in the numbers of planners (though other factors, notably the vast duplication of work inaugurated by the two-tier system of local government, have played their part) and secured for professional planners a powerful and influential position within bureaucracies at local and national level. Politicians are often not in a position to argue with 'professional' expertise marshalled before them. But the growth of professional planning in local government has provoked a reaction. At a time of public expenditure cuts, planning is particularly vulnerable as the necessity for large, apparently non-productive planning departments is questioned.

The strength of highly organised departments is challenged from two sources. One is from within the bureaucracy itself, the other is from the politicians anxious to exert control. Within local government, bureaucracy is organised both vertically in terms of service departments and horizontally in terms of efforts to co-ordinate its functions and control the allocation of resources. The conflict between large spending departments with powerful heads anxious to control expenditure and determine priorities is a feature of both central and local government, and has a political as well as a bureaucratic dimension. The idea of corporate management was introduced in an attempt to overcome conflict and achieve co-operation between the various departments. It became the vogue in British local government, and many new authorities adopted the strong corporate flavour of the Bains Committee's recommendations after 1974.[43] Although Bains laid considerable emphasis on the importance of the elected representative in the new authorities, this could only be achieved by a change in his role in which party political conflict would be subdued and replaced by a co-operative effort to agree on long-term goals and priorities for the organisation. In reality Bains was asserting the predominance of a managerial system which socialised and depoliticised elected members, and encouraged them to identify with the organisation rather than with the short-term demands of political expediency or the predilections of party ideology. They were to become 'co-opted as a kind of administrator into official decision-making'.[44] That corporate planning essentially serves bureaucratic needs was long ago perceived by Meyerson and Banfield. '*Corporate* planning seeks to attain ends which pertain to the organization as such and are not substantially directives to attain the ends of some public.'[45] After the initial flush of enthusiasm it appears, in several authorities, that commitment to corporate planning is becoming nominal. The superstructure remains (Policy and Resources Committee, Chief Executive, Management Team) but, at a time

[42]Among the contributions to this debate are D. Diamond, and J. B. McLoughlin, (1973) *Education for Planning*, Progress in Planning Series, Vol. 1, Oxford, Pergamon Press; D. Eversley (1973) *The Planner in Society; The Changing Role of a Profession*, London, Faber; and (1976) The education of planners, in T. Hancock (1976) op. cit., pp. 221–55: Centre for Environmental Studies, London (1973) *Education for Urban Governance*, CES CP 10, Conference Papers; Royal Town Planning Institute (1976) *Planning and the Future*, Discussion Paper, November.

[43]The Bains Report (1972) *The New Local Authorities: Management and Structure*, London, HMSO.

[44]D. M. Hill (1974) *Democratic Theory and Local Government*, The New Local Government Series, No. 12, London, Allen & Unwin, p. 87.

[45]M. Meyerson and E. C. Banfield (1955) op. cit., p. 313.

of retrenchment in spending, its functions are no more than the budgetary control which has always required trade-offs between various departments. Any further encroachment on the policy-making autonomy of the departments has been vigorously resisted by heads of department in alliance with their elected chairmen. Although corporate management may have failed to reduce the powers of departmental heads, it is indicative of a trend towards more sophisticated managerial and budgeting systems which some feel will further erode the power of the elected members

'As things are, indeed as trends go, policy information is becoming more and more the property, not of the public, nor even of the councillor, but of the officer and specialists within urban government. Intelligence within the bureaucracy calls for countervailing intelligence without and raises questions about the working of contemporary urban democracy.[46]

It is, however, possible to exaggerate the power of the bureaucracy.

Political power

In theory, politicians are responsible for policy and can exert their authority over the administrative system. This power is rarely exercised and when it is it tends to be sporadic and sometimes unpredictable. 'Political activity is like lightning, in that it may suddenly strike into any corner of the administrative system, but only rarely does so. The great bulk of administrative operations continues in political obscurity, and the main interactions between politics and administration occur at the top levels of government.'[47] The customary distinction between elected politicians who are responsible for policy-making and officials who administer policies[48] does not fit the experience of local government. The roles of both officials and politicians vary and they frequently overlap, with politicians concerning themselves with matters of administrative detail and officials engaged in the development of policy. The interesting questions are to what extent politicians are able to assert their control over the bureaucracy, and which individuals are mainly responsible for the direction of policy in a local authority.

Party politics is now the characteristic feature of political organisation in almost all local authorities. With the arrival of the parties has come a changed conception of the role of politics. The idea that politics is merely a matter of administration based on commonly agreed goals has had to be abandoned. Such a view may have been prevalent in the days when local politicians tended to describe themselves as independents. It is an alien concept to today's politicians who seek election through their allegiance to a political party which purports to represent specific interests. There is still a tendency to play down the importance of party in decision-making, but political cleavages at local level appear to be increasing and involving areas of policy where consensus previously prevailed. Although all parties claim to represent the interests of the electorate, Conservatives tend to stress the interests of constituents as ratepayers while Socialists

[46]C. Cockburn (1974) Urban Government, in G. E. Cherry (ed.) (1974) *Urban Planning Problems*, 213–42, Aylesbury, Leonard Hill Books, p. 229.
[47]P. Self (1972) *Administrative Theories and Politics*, London, Allen & Unwin, p. 151.
[48]The relationship between administration and politics is discussed in P. Self, (1972) op. cit., Ch. 5; and M. J. Hill (1972) op. cit., Ch. 10.

make claims on behalf of constituents as consumers of services provided by the authority. Different emphasis, marshalled by party discipline, introduces conflict into local government. But conflict polarises around particular issues. The annual budget is the centrepiece of the party struggle in many authorities. Ideological conflicts occur over education, housing, and the social services. Increasingly, party conflict has appeared in transportation policies as parties tend to give different weight to the needs and demands of the private motorist against the user of public transport[49] (see Chapter 5). There are other areas where conflict over objectives may be resolved through agreement over means; areas where general agreement prevails; and areas where, through ignorance or indifference, conflict has not become apparent. Much of planning policy seems to fall into this category. Although party differences occasionally flare up, conflicts in planning are often between organisations (Chapter 5), or between different interests rather than along party lines. The view of planning as a passive, reactive activity, which I discussed earlier in this chapter, may encourage politicians to disregard its potential as a source of social conflict and change. But there is growing evidence that politicians, partly in response to growing public interest and awareness, are beginning to introduce party political values into planning policy and to subject debates to the constraints of party discipline.

It is a moot point whether the increase in party activity has enhanced or diminished the power of politicians over the bureaucracy. In any case it is difficult to distinguish the increase in party activity from other factors, such as the increasing complexity of legislation and management.

Officials will often confess to a preference for organised party government since this reduces the uncertainty enabling them to anticipate events and guide the authority in an atmosphere of relative security. Newton argues that 'the party system has contributed to a wider spectrum of members, a clearer choice of issues and greater awareness of public opinion as expressed through the parties'.[50] The variations among local authorities in party discipline, in political balance, and in the significance of party policy make any generalisation difficult. Bulpitt's survey of a number of councils in the north-west of England demonstrates the different degrees to which parties attempt to impose their will on local government.[51] His general conclusion is that party differences are more apparent than real, and that, on the whole, parties are restrained. Conditions of permanent one-party rule provide the potential for 'strong' government such as Dearlove found in Kensington and Chelsea.[52] Continuity of control (as in a number of shire counties with Conservative control and in a few urban authorities with Labour control) provides an atmosphere of political certainty enabling members and officers to work in close co-operation. But large majorities can also lead to drift, insularity, and, at worst, corruption. Absence of effective opposition (and, given the swings in many local elections, opposition groups can be reduced to risible numbers) can have the consequences spelled out by Sharpe from his survey in Greater London. There is nothing

[49]A. T. Blowers (1976) Transport planning: a new direction? *Town and Country Planning Summer School, Report of Proceedings*, Nottingham, pp. 16–20.
[50]K. Newton (1976) op. cit.
[51]J. G. Bulpitt (1967) *Party Politics in English Local Government*, London, Longmans.
[52]J. Dearlove (1973) *The Politics of Policy in Local Government*, Cambridge, Cambridge University Press.

'to keep the majority party on its toes and provide an additional source of scrutiny and enquiry to meet the inevitably persuasive voice of the expert. Nor can it be doubted that an opposition helps to clarify the broad issues of policy and generally renders the work of the Council more stimulating. It has also been argued that the party system helps to maintain a neutral bureaucracy operating under a known code of formalized procedures'[53]

Overwhelming majorities can also lead to a loss of political direction. Various factions may develop and officials may step into the vacuum or, conversely, become reticent for fear of becoming identified with a particular, and potentially unstable, faction. Where an organised opposition has a firm base, though in a semi-permanent minority, as was the case found in surveys of Sheffield,[54] Leeds,[55] and Newcastle under Lyme,[56] then the majority was encouraged to organise itself effectively in order to succeed with its policies. Where political control was weak, divided, or altogether absent, as, for example in the rural area of Newcastle under Lyme,[57] then officials could initiate policy. Where shifts in control are possible or likely, the authority of the politicians may be undermined and their will may weaken, especially when elections are imminent and officials are concerned lest policies acceptable in the short term may be reversed at a later stage. They may therefore adopt a cautious strategy in the hope that a violent reaction will not be provoked.

In Bedfordshire, where during the period of this study no party achieved overall control, there was no certainty that any policy could be carried, though in the early years the organisation, initiatives, and confidence of the Labour group enabled them to achieve part of their programme. As confidence ebbed and energies flagged, and as an election which was likely to result in a Conservative victory approached, so the Conservatives increased their resistance to Labour policies and officials become increasingly reluctant to recommend courses of action that had appeal to one or other party. But even in Bedfordshire the party conflict was often confined to specific issues. The work of the council was in the hands of the leading members and officials. Although their attitudes were tempered by the general political climate they were still responsible for much of the policy-making.

The rule of the few

Although it is difficult, on the basis of the available studies of local authorities, to reach any useful conclusion about the significance of the party system in the relative balance of power between members and officials, most research points towards a growing concentration of power at the top. In other words, the leading members of the authority, together with the chief officers, wield the power to direct its affairs. Lee, from his observations of Cheshire County Council, attributes this tendency to changing

[53]L. J. Sharpe (1960) The politics of local government in Greater London, *Public Administration*, **38**, 157–72, p. 169.

[54]W. Hampton (1970) *Democracy and Community: A Study of Politics in Sheffield*, London, Oxford University Press.

[55]H. V. Wiseman (1967) *Local Government at Work*, London, Routledge & Kegan Paul.

[56]F. Bealey, J. Blondel and W. P. McCann (1965) *Constituency Politics*, London, Faber.

[57]Ibid.

economic and social circumstances leading to the development of a professional bureaucracy and the rise of the political parties. All these changes made it clear that the responsibility for county government rested upon a combination of chief officers and the leading councillors, who formed a kind of ministerialist party or 'inner ring'. 'The vitality of the administration depended upon the vigour of the few.'[58] The published research analyses the situation prior to local government reorganisation, and most of it considers cases of single-party rule whether permanent or liable to change. This book deals with an authority which experienced minority government during the three years after local government reorganisation. It examines the relative influence over policy of officials and politicians and considers some of the pressures to which they were subject. Fears were expressed at the time of reorganisation that the size and complexity of the new system would reduce the ability of politicians to cope and that the new authorities would become increasingly remote from the public. Buxton argued that the power of officials would be enhanced and that part-time amateur councillors would be unable to act effectively either as policy-makers or as representatives. It will be possible to assess, from the evidence presented for one authority, whether these fears have been borne out.

Political leadership

The emergence of the political leadership in local authorities is a product of the personality, calibre, and predilections of individual members. From time to time there are comments about the relatively poor quality of councillors. But, as several studies have pointed out,[59] councillors, whatever their party, tend to be better educated than the population as a whole. The working class is underrepresented, and Hindess regards this as a reason for the disappearance of class politics at local level and the emergence of a prevailing consensus over many issues.[60] The demands of complex organisation require leading politicians with time, energy, and intellect if they are to debate on level terms with full-time professional officials. There is some evidence that the relative abilities of officials and members in general have altered in favour of the officials.[61] This has added to the concern that members are unfitted and unable to control the bureaucracy. Hindess refers to this problem in planning: 'it may be thought that what is wrong is the calibre of the men in public life, that men of higher calibre would be able to stand up to their advisers and bureaucrats and to keep the planners under control.'[62]

[58]J. M. Lee (1963) *Social Leaders and Public Persons*, Oxford, Clarendon Press. A follow-up study, which considered the effects of local government reorganisation, discovered certain changes in organisation and attitudes, but no fundamental transformation in the basis of recruitment or power structure in the authority: J. M. Lee, B. Wood, B. W. Soloman, and P. Walters (1974) *The Scope of Local Initiative: A Study of Cheshire County Council, 1961–74,* London, Martin Robertson.
[59]Among the studies of councillors are: The Maud Committee, (1967) *Management of Local Government,* Vol. 2, *The Local Government Councillor,* by L. Moss and S. R. Parker, London HMSO, L. J. Sharpe (1960) op. cit., and (1962) Elected representatives in local government, *British Journal of Sociology,* **13** (3) 189–209. Details of the social background of councillors are provided in most of the case-studies in local government which are cited at various points in this chapter.
[60]B. Hindess (1971) *The Decline of Working-class Politics,* London, MacGibbon & Kee.
[61]This is suggested from a historical survey in Wolverhampton by G. W. Jones (1969) *Borough Politics,* London, Macmillan.
[62]B. Hindess (1971) op. cit., p. 160.

Much, therefore, depends on the quality of political leadership. Lee showed that the leaders of Cheshire were able, by virtue of the time they devoted to their council work (some made it virtually a full-time occupation) and the experience gained over the years, to acquire the necessary skills for the job. Undoubtedly continuity of one-party control and leadership contributed to the authority of the relatively small group of members who held the important offices. Where the informal rules of the political groups encourage fairly brief tenure of committee chairmanships, the overall knowledge of the leading councillors may be widened,[63] but there is less likelihood of individual members holding the reins of power in one area of the council's work long enough to counteract the influence of the permanent official. The problem is compounded in authorities which experience a high turnover of membership, combined with changes in political control. In Bedfordshire, for example, in 1977, 56 new members were returned out of a total of 83.

Since local government reorganisation, modest payment for council work has been introduced but rarely compensates for the enormous amount of time expended by some members on council work.[64] There have been calls for the introduction of full-time councillors and, in some isolated cases, leading politicians have given up their ordinary work to devote themselves exclusively to council affairs. The job is still bound to attract those who, by virtue of flexible working arrangements or undemanding jobs or retirement, can find the time. It is from such members that the leadership will have to be recruited. The hopes of some observers that council work will attract 'a wider and more capable cross-section of the public' are, it is claimed, ill-founded since 'the burden of service will almost certainly prove too great for the vigorous men, holding down responsible jobs elsewhere in the community, whom the reformers seem to have in mind as the new generation of councillors'.[65] The working class and business managers, for example, will be largely excluded, leaving councils to be run by the retired, small businessmen, trade unionists, housewives, those with a special interest in its affairs (estate agents, builders, professional workers, etc.), and those who find the work a stimulating antidote to routine occupations. It should be said that, though there is much criticism of this state of affairs, there is very little evidence that changes in the composition of councils would introduce greater efficiency or more control by members.

Although political leadership is a function of ability, and the time that can be given to the job, it also reflects the different roles adopted by members. Basically there are two types of member — those who regard the representation of the needs and interests of their constituents as the principal function, and those who concern themselves primarily with policy-making and the management of the authority. These roles are, of course, not mutually exclusive. All members are involved to a greater or lesser degree in the probems of their ward. They are also expected to spend time on party work, attending meetings, and contributing to the humdrum but vital work of party organisation generally. Such work is essential if the councillor is to maintain his party identity and to stand

[63] As was the case in Kensington and Chelsea surveyed by J. Dearlove (1973) op. cit.
[64] The workload of local councillors is described in H. H. Helco (1969) The councillor's job, *Public Administration* 47 185–202; also in The Maud Report (1967) op. cit. The question of payment for members was fully discussed in the *Report of the Committee of Enquiry into the System of Remuneration of Members of Local Authorities* (The Robinson Committee), 1977, Cmnd. 7010. Among its recommendations were £1000 basic annual payment to all members and a special responsibility allowance for leading members. The recommendation did not receive much support from the local authority organisations.
[65] R. Buxton (1973) *Local Government*, Harmondsworth, Penguin, 1st edn., 1970.

a good prospect of being reselected to fight his seat. Those who devote themselves largely to case work may contribute less to the policy-making activities of the council. But they are involved in committee work and thereby gain specialist insight into parts of the council's work and its policy-making. Those who seek positions on the council where they can possibly direct its affairs may also be able, through their influence, to deal with large amounts of case-work for their own and other members' constituents.

It is difficult to identify the criteria for the selection of the leadership, who are elected by the members of the group. Clearly seniority and experience are important. Where turnover is high then the criteria are less easy to define. In 1973 reorganisation combined with a swing to the left brought together groups of councillors unfamiliar with the authority's area and functions and largely unknown to each other. Not surprisingly, geographical influences, old loyalties, and first impressions generated a leadership of mixed ability. Even so, in Bedfordshire County Council there was a surprising stability of leadership in the years after reorganisation. Of the 6 leading members of the Labour group elected in 1973, 5 remained, though some were in different posts,[66] in 1977. The leadership of the Conservative group was also remarkably stable, though the group did contain more members with previous experience of council work. The tradition of selecting leaders from among those with experience and seniority was maintained after 1977 when all the chairmen of the main committees were selected from among the 21 Conservatives (out of a total of 75) who remained from the previous council. Thus, even during times of political and administrative upheaval, the leadership of political groups tends to be stable. Either by chance or intuition, or by a recognition of the qualities that make for leadership, the party groups are able to select those with the inclination, stamina, and ability for the job. It is an iterative process. Those elected develop the qualities necessary to ensure they keep the job.

Despite the high turnover among local government politicians, the casualty rate among the leadership between elections seems to be low. Although some leaders retire from the council or to the back-benches, and some are deposed for reasons of inability or failure to perform the party's wishes, the majority hold on to their positions provided they can maintain their membership of the council. On those councils where elections take place on an all-in/all-out basis once every four years there are considerable losses of members, including leaders, who have no immediate prospect of return. County councils are more vulnerable to the loss of continuity of leadership than either district councils, where elections may be held on an annual basis, or than national parliament where high turnout usually prevents the enormous political swings that have been experienced at local level in recent years. In Bedfordshire the elections of May 1977 reduced the Labour group from 38 to 5. Of the 6 leading Labour members of the former council, 4 had decided to retire, 1 was defeated, and 1 was re-elected.

Although experience, long tenure of office, and political security can enhance the power of leading members, even those with none of these advantages but who have

[66]The six leading Labour members may be defined as the group leader and the chairman of the county council and chairmen (or 'shadow' chairmen) of the major committees. The group leadership changed once when the leader became chairman of the county council. The spokesmen for Education, Environmental Services and Leisure remained throughout the four years, while those for Policy and Resources (the new leader) and Social Services changed once. Changes in the leadership group were brought about by illness. The disposition of chairmanships during the life of the council is described in A. T. Blowers (1977) 'Checks and balances: the politics of minority government, *Public Administration*, Autumn, 305–16.

ability and interest in the work can exercise considerable influence. The power of the political leaders, even in the reorganised system of local government, is frequently underestimated. Their grasp of policy and of its relationship to technical issues and

> 'their awareness of the potential power of bureaucrats together with the tactics and strategies which they can use to get their own way, make the most senior of committee members quite formidable in their own areas of interest. . . . Politicians may not be all-powerful, but they are far from powerless in the face of technically expert, full-time professionals.'[67]

The source of their power is the party group. Although the back-bench members of the group can, through their weight of numbers, overrule the leadership, they rarely do so. This may reflect both the leadership's interpretation of what is acceptable as well as the back-benchers' lack of interest or contentment with the policies being followed. Blondel and Hall[68] discovered a political modesty and lack of perception of the power structure among the members they surveyed which would account for the lack of aspirations to powerful positions of many councillors.

The various rules, procedures, and sanctions adopted by party caucuses in different local authorities have been covered in detail elsewhere.[69] The coherence and discipline of party groups varies according to the type of authority, the political balance, the issues at stake, and the conventions that come to be adopted. They vary from the highly organised groups typical of the former county boroughs (Leeds, Sheffield, Birmingham, and Wolverhampton are among the examples which have been studied), through the highly organised one-party boroughs (Kensington and Chelsea, and Newcastle under Lyme) to the looser framework of party rule found in Cheshire, and the faction-ridden situation in the rural area of Newcastle under Lyme. Overall, there seems to be an increase in the degree of party organisation as the party system becomes prevalent and as issues become polarised on party lines.

In Bedfordshire, the precarious political balance from 1973–7 made a highly disci-plined organisation essential if the largest group, Labour, were to be able to carry their policies. During the early part of their four years (the first year was a period of 'shadow' government as the new council prepared to take over in 1974) the group maintained a high attendance record and adherence to group decisions. They controlled the main chairmanships (with the notable exception of education) and held a casting vote on most of them (again education with its co-opted members was exceptional). But they were in a minority when the full council met. This situation led to considerable uncertainty, since policies had to be maintained as they moved through the various committee stages leading to the meeting of the full council. Since little power had been delegated to committees, the full council actually took important decisions instead of, as is more usually the case, providing the imprimatur for decisions already agreed by committees and the ruling party caucus. There is no doubt that the precariousness of their position stimulated the Labour group to maintain its solidarity in the face of

[67]K. Newton (1976) op. cit., p. 235.
[68]J. Blondel and R. Hall (1967) Conflict, decision-making and the perception of local councillors, *Political Studies*, **15** (3) (October) 322–50.
[69]The organisation of party groups is discussed in most of the studies of individual local authorities cited in this chapter.

powerful opposition. Over time, by-elections, falling attendances, occasional defections, and failing confidence sapped the group's strength, but it maintained the political initiative throughout the four-year period.

The differences between Labour and Conservative groups in their attitudes towards group discipline are more apparent than real. Conservatives appear to adopt a more deferential attitude towards their leaders, but less seems to be known about their group organisation. 'The internal workings of the Party are generally well concealed from public scrutiny and the Party is, in the main, less helpful in providing information than the Labour Party.'[70] In the past, Conservative groups appear to have been less disciplined than their rivals. The approach of party groups would seem to be as much determined by the political situation as by party attitudes. For instance, the Bedfordshire Conservative group, when in a minority, tended to be loose knit unless there was the propect of attracting Liberal support to defeat Labour policies. After its massive victory in 1977 the Conservative group was in a position to tolerate some defections or absentees and still carry the policy of the leadership. Five months after the election in Bedfordshire, conflict over the extent of expenditure cuts led to the resignation of the most senior Conservative, the Chairman of the Education Committee, though this event did not disturb the underlying unity of the group since he was not a member of the leadership. When the leadership itself is divided then a façade of unity may become impossible.

It is at the party caucus meetings that the back-bencher is able to challenge the policies of the leadership. Usually the superior knowledge and information possessed by the leaders, combined with the status they have secured, is sufficient to achieve the backing of the group as a whole. All members are expected to adhere to group decisions (the degree to which free votes are permitted varies widely) whatever attitudes they have expressed within the group or publicly. Group decisions may limit the freedom of action of the individual councillor, but they provide the necessary muscle for the leadership to attempt to achieve its ends.

Administrative politics

We have seen that the majority of local politicians exercise only a peripheral influence on policy-making, leaving most of it to the leadership. Similarly, within bureaucratic departments most officials are remote from the policy-making process. It is the chief officers with their chairmen who carry the greatest responsibility. At this top level there exists what Self calls a zone of 'administrative politics'.[71] It is here that policies are chosen and decisions taken. Knowledge of this process is of far more significance than the sterile debate about the degree to which bureaucrats or politicians exercise power. The questions are: How do these leading figures exercise their power? What limitations do they impose on each other? What are the constraints which influence their decisions? Some general answers are given in the rest of this chapter which is largely based on the findings of various surveys of local government. More specific insights into the exercise of power in planning policies by officials is a major theme of the chapters which follow.

[70]K. Newton (1976) op. cit., p. 232.
[71]P. Self (1972) op. cit.

Chief officers

Chief officers require political skills. Even if they merely saw their role as that of adviser and implementer of the will of politicians, they would still need to present and defend the policies put forward. Some chief officers, notably planning officers, see their role as much wider than this, playing a crucial part in the initiation and development of policy. The tendency is for planning officers to play what Catanese describes as a 'covert-activist' role: 'the covert-activist planner will give the appearance of being a value neutral but will make his true beliefs clear to those special interests that are most likely to be useful in the implementation of these values.'[72] Over a whole range of issues the planning officer will seek to convince his political masters of desirable courses of action as he sees them. The growing complexity of planning procedures and techniques [e.g. the introduction of transportation studies (Chapter 5) and the Community Land Act (Chapter 6)] place greater influence in the hands of the planner who has the time, expertise, and staff at his disposal to comprehend the detail and its policy implications. Unless the politicians are able to match officers, with their departmental back-up, in skill and understanding, they may be increasingly at a loss to perceive the political content and potential choices which are embraced within the decisions they are asked to take. In dealing with politicians, planning officers act politically. 'Thus, only if the profession's image includes the picture of the planner as rightfully a political actor will the planner attain both professional rewards and the completion of concrete programmes.'[73]

The power of the chief officer stems from his control over a department. His subordinates achieve their promotion through him and it is to him, not to the politicians, that they owe their loyalty. The chief officer is therefore able to direct the work of his department and to decide what information or recommendations are revealed to the politicians. He possesses 'an almost complete control over the chief sources of information'.[74] In Bedfordshire, some of the more 'extreme' suggestions from junior officials for the structure plan were suppressed before they reached the committee agendas (Chapter 7). The chief officer can, therefore, decide whether a policy directive is practicable and, if the politicians insist upon it, he can attempt, if he wishes, by various means, to amend or dilute it. It is he, not the politician, who decides what recommendations to make. Of course, his recommendations can be ignored, but if this is done it is the politicians, not the chief officer, who will bear the responsibility. The power to make recommendations enables a planning officer to address an audience beyond the committee room. As we shall see (Chapter 4), a planner's recommendation may be turned down by his committee but the evidence of conflict between officer and member may weaken the politician's position if the issue has to be resolved by appeal to a higher authority. In effect, the chief officer can invite the politicians to ignore his advice at their peril. In general, the planning officer's appeal to 'planning merits' or 'principles' is sufficient to discourage politicians from challenging his recommendations unless there are obvious party considerations or outside pressures which urge them to do so. Over a whole range of items which are, on the face of it, not contentious, the chief officer will have his way.

[72]A. J. Catanese (1974) op. cit., p. 145.
[73]F. F. Rabinovitz (1967) Politics, personality and planning, *Public Administration Review*, March, in A. Faludi (ed.) (1973) op. cit., p. 267.
[74]J. M. Lee (1963) op. cit., p. 213.

There are a number of devices at the disposal of a planning officer to ensure the success of his policies.[75] He can present long reports which are difficult for the hard-pressed politician to absorb, or short reports which present inadequate information on which to base a considered decision. Reports can be exceedingly technical, and their impenetrable language may reduce the politician to virtual impotence. The planning officer may present only one alternative when others could be considered, or at least fail to reveal all the options. He may appeal to past policies or potential objections in order to prevent a particular course of action. He may oversell a policy in order to ensure its downfall or undersell it to attract support. He may accept a policy but claim that manpower or resources are insufficient to ensure its implementation. Where policies are likely to be keenly contested he may informally lobby political groups or individual councillors to ensure that his preferences are carried. His control over the resources of his department, over the agenda reports and minutes, and over the timing of issues,[76] gives him enormous influence if not final authority over policy-making. The chief officer will resist any interference by members in the affairs of his department. Indeed, members are usually content not to interfere since to do so would lose them the confidence and co-operation of the bureaucracy. This does mean that much of the inner workings of local government are hidden from the public gaze and even from that of elected representatives.

The chief officer's views are public knowledge. Whereas in central government all policies are enacted in the name of the Minister, in local government the chief officer is explicitly responsible for reports and recommendations and participates in the public debate of the committee (though not of the council). The chief officer is a clearly identifiable public figure and in many cases is more well known than his chairman. Although he will jealously guard his independence of the politicians, the chief officer recognises that ultimately the success of his policies, and, by implication, the image of his department, rests on his ability to carry his chairman with him. Much of the detail of policy comes from the department, much of it in response to applications for development. But broad policy directives can and should come from the politicians, and it is the chairmen of the council committees who are largely responsible for setting the political guidelines of the authority.

Chairmen and chief officers

Judgements as to what is, or is not, feasible are made at the top. Before judgements are made by chief officers and chairmen of committees, a sifting process will have occurred both within departments and within the party caucus. The development of policy requires an ability on the part of chief officers to assess the political atmosphere and on the part of political leaders to understand whether policies are practicable in

[75]Some of these are covered in K. Newton (1976) op. cit.

[76]The chairman of a committee is formally responsible for the agenda and can scrutinise the minutes before they are published. In practice the agenda is arranged by the officials. Some of the items, especially planning applications, must be considered within a certain time period but over much of the agenda (especially on strategic planning matters) officials can influence the timing of issues. They also write and present reports. Politicians, through the chairman, can initiate agenda items (though they rarely do so) and, of course, they vote on the issues discussed. Normally the chief officers and chairmen take the crucial decisions on timing and presentation of issues.

administrative terms. Leading officials and politicians play entrepreneurial roles. From their study of Coventry, Friend and Jessop observed: 'A competent Chairman, combining a shrewd political insight with a clear sense of understanding of managing a public service for which he was responsible, could therefore provide a crucial link between the departmental process, the political process, and the community at large.'[77] Similarly, it is the chief officer's job, 'to be able to translate the politician's requirements into practical policies and to be able to handle all the pressures upon him from the public, from pressure groups and from his own colleagues'.[78] The chairman's links are with his party, his group, and the electorate; the chief officer's with his department, with other departments, with his professional colleagues, with other authorities and central government ministries, with pressure groups, and with developers. These different sets of external relationships can lead to conflict between officers and members, as Chapter 4 demonstrates.

A great deal depends on the capability and compatibility of chairman and chief officer. Although this relationship will differ in every case, the most creative relationships seem to occur where there is mutual respect and an awareness of the strength and limitations of the role of each partner. Where this does not occur the tensions between officer and chairman can lead to mistrust.[79] Problems occur when officers are politically innocent or chairmen administratively inept.[80] Although a chairman will want to get his way, he needs the support of his chief officer. This support is likely to be more vigorous if it results from an equal partnership than if the chief officer adopts a fawning, sycophantic role.

Both chairmen and chief officers must avoid too close an identity with each other. Chairmen cannot afford to be branded as officers' men, and chief officers need to remain detached from the political process. Inevitably, some chairmen will lose touch with their party's grass roots,[81] and some chief officers, forced to concentrate on their administrative and political roles, cannot keep pace with knowledge and developments in the field for which they are responsible, and so 'expertise resides primarily in the lower ranks of a hierarchy'.[82]

Although chairman and chief officers possess considerable influence over the development of policy, particularly in the stages before it reaches committees, there are a number of limitations on their power. During the various committee stages (possibly working group, sub-committee, full committee, and council), policies can be amended. Items such as development control, which fall within general policy guidelines, require a simple decision of acceptance or rejection, although there is always the possibility of appeal if an application is rejected. The development of strategic policy, however, is a less straightforward process and does not depend on a decision being taken at a single moment in time. The longer-term strategic transportation and planning policies are capable of continuous evolution, adjustment, and amendment to suit changing political

---

[77]J. K. Friend and W. N. Jessop (1969) *Local Government and Strategic Choice*, London, Tavistock Publications, p. 56.
[78]M. J. Hill (1972) op. cit., p. 146.
[79]This point is made by A. J. Catanese (1974) op. cit., J. K. Friend and W. N. Jessop (1969) op. cit., p. 66, and R. C. Lucking, K. Howard, and M. J. Greenwood (1974) Corporate planning and management: a review of their application in English local government, *Town Planning Review*, **45** (2) (April) 131–45.
[80]J. M. Lee (1963) op. cit., p. 134.
[81]See K. Newton (1976) op. cit., ch. 7.
[82]M. J. Hill (1972) op. cit., p. 18.

and economic circumstances. They are also areas where external influences impose considerable constraints on the actions of policy-makers.

3. THE CONSTRAINTS ON POWER

Among the constraints on the power of the leading members and officials of local authorities are the electorate, political parties, special interests, other authorities and central government, resources, existing processes and policies, and the problems of implementation.

Electoral influences

It is generally acknowledged that the influence of the electorate on the policies of local authorities is weak. This view is derived from the fact that elections for county councils are infrequent, that turnout is low, and that the elections are regarded as a test of opinion about the national government of the day. Generally, local elections are subject to large swings (mainly brought about by the differential abstention rates of supporters of the political parties) and, when they occur during the mid-term period of national government, the unpopularity of the party in power is reflected in the fortunes of its representatives at local level. In Bedfordshire, the unpopularity of the Heath government in 1973 enabled Labour, for the first time, to capture more seats than the Conservatives (though the amalgamation of Luton, with a large Labour majority, with the former administrative county was a determining factor here). The 1977 elections took place at a time when the Labour government was unpopular and consequently Labour suffered heavy defeats in the council elections. Some would conclude that local issues have virtually no influence on the outcome of elections,[83] and that claims made by the parties of popular support for particular policies are a 'confidence trick'.[84] 'In reality most governments rest on a bed of apathy and acquiescence rather than on anything as active and enthusiastic as is suggested by the term "support".'[85] This suggests that officials and councillors have a virtually free hand to do as they please without fear of electoral reprisal.[86]

While it may be true that the actions of local government have little effect on the outcome of local elections, it does not necessarily follow that councillors acknowledge this. The essence of the system of representative democracy is the belief that elected representatives are accountable for their actions and that they possess a mandate for particular programmes. Constant invocation of the wishes of ratepayers for expenditure restraint, or of the demands of the public for certain standards of services, indicate that councillors are seduced into the belief that their actions are being observed and that they will receive rewards for thrift or for improving standards of service. They behave according to the 'law of anticipated reactions'.[87] Perhaps more important than purely electoral calculation is the relationship councillors seek with their electorate. This may

[83]R. Buxton (1973) op. cit., p. 91.
[84]B. Hindess (1971) op. cit., p. 14.
[85]J. Dearlove (1973) op. cit., p. 80.
[86]K. Newton (1976) op. cit., p. 7.
[87]R. Gregory (1969) Local elections and the 'rule of anticipated reactions', *Political Studies*, **17**, 31–47.

occur through public meetings, petitions, the press, surgeries, or visits to constituents. Through such contacts councillors expect to be able to gauge public reaction to certain issues and to articulate the needs and demands of the public they represent. Politicians do not, therefore, act in entire immunity from the pressures of public opinion which can act both as a restraint and a spur to their policies. To some extent this pressure from the public is filtered through the political parties and pressure groups which also act as a constraint on power.

Political parties

Political parties consist of a number of different bodies, each of which can exert a restraining influence on the activities of elected members. Usually the party organisation is responsible for the drawing up of a panel of candidates and endorsement of those candidates eventually selected.[88] It is also responsible for the manifesto on which the election is to be fought, and may from time to time draft policies which it exhorts the councillors to follow. Although it cannot enforce its will on the elected members, it does possess the sanction of refusing to endorse the candidature of recalcitrants in a future election. Selection of candidates is usually through the branch party based on the electoral division to be contested. Unlike MPs, sitting members must submit themselves for reselection before every election, though usually (but not always) they are readopted. The need to satisfy both the constituency (or county) party as well as the branch can therefore loom large in the calculations of the individual councillor. It encourages him to look after the interests of the ward and to avoid adopting political postures that may endanger his chances of reselection. Although there are always examples of councillors who neglect their party duties or pursue policies not favoured by their party (some of whom pay the penalty), the vast majority accept that they are representatives of the party and understand the limitations this imposes on their actions. The local councillor is thus restrained by his party at ward, constituency, and group level.

Special interests

The influence of pressure groups on the policy-making of local authorities appears to have increased in recent years. Groups representing particular interests or areas have become more organised and articulate. Partly in response to this and partly to encourage it, public participation has been developed as an element in the decision-making process, notably in planning. The effectiveness of this and the questions it poses are

[88]The conventions of group behaviour vary (see pp. 25–6). In Bedfordshire, policy for the manifesto was the responsibility of the county party, and annual conferences were held during the life of the administration. The Labour group were responsible for interpreting and implementing party policy and held policy meetings from time to time. Group meetings were held before council meetings and committee members also met to decide their attitude to various items on the agenda. Members were expected to adhere to group decisions (though several felt there should be more 'free votes' than were allowed). Discipline was fairly tight, though only in two cases were persistent offenders against group decisions reported to the county party and reprimanded by the group. In no case was the whip withdrawn, though defections occasionally lost the group crucial votes.

considered later (Chapter 7) and have been a major theme of a number of studies.[89] In the planning field public interest and organised protest have been stimulated by proposed action by planning authorities. Those pressure groups which are aroused by a specific issue may succeed in deflecting the authority from its intended course. Other groups have wider aims and may be instrumental in shifting the direction of policy in general. Thus amenity groups have been partly responsible for the increasing emphasis on conservation, though economic factors have also played a part. In the field of transportation the 'roads lobby' has helped to achieve considerable investment in road building and car parking, though more recently the reduction in public expenditure, combined with the growing influence of other transport lobbies, has succeeded in switching the emphasis more towards users of public transport and cyclists.[90]

There are other interests that play a less overt role and seek to achieve their objectives through informal contacts with decision-makers. The influence of industry in securing land for expansion is considerable. Various private interests requiring planning permission have direct access to the bureaucracy and often to the elected members. This may give them considerable advantage in the decision-making process (Chapter 6). Such interests are able to initiate decisions, and in doing so to influence the general direction of policy. The pressures exerted by various interest groups upon officials and members may be considerable and occasionally lead to charges of corruption. Quite aside from venality is the informal pressure exerted upon decision-makers as a result of their membership or contacts with a wide range of interest groups.

The influence of special interests on the leading decision-makers should not be exaggerated. Appeal against planning decisions is only possible in the event of a planning permission being refused, and public inquiries on applications are restricted to the specific case and may ignore alternatives (Chapter 6). The advent of formal public participation and the examination in public of structure plans provide greater opportunity for the public to express opinion on the wider issues of planning policy. But, as Chapter 7 will show, the process is limited and controlled by the planning authority. The views of participants are likely to be ignored if they contradict or question the parameters within which the plan has been conceived. Participation tends to be used by planning authorities to resolve a conflict or to confirm the philosophy being pursued. It provides further limitation on the actions of the planning authorities. It has become a co-optative process effectively incorporating or circumventing potentially dissident elements in the population.

Participation rarely surrenders any power to the participants. Where active involvement of the community is encouraged to guide the development of a plan, it is usually achieved through representative organisations. These tend to be pressure groups for specific interests, are predominantly middle class, and are able to make their point in the manner required by the planning process. Even so, they may not secure the action they advocate; 'it is only when officials act because they fear the consequences of not

[89]Among the studies of public participation are the Linked Research Project into Public Participation in Structure Planning, Department of the Environment, which has produced thirteen reports; N. Dennis (1972) op. cit.; C. Hague and A. McCourt (1974) Comprehensive planning, public participation and the public interest, *Urban Studies*, **11**, 143–55; J. M. Simmie (1971) Public participation: a case study from Oxfordshire, *Journal of the Royal Town Planning Institute*, **57** (4) 161–2. A review of the theory and practice of participation is given by M. Fagence (1977) *Citizen Participation in Planning*, Oxford, Pergamon Press.

[90]Department of Transport (1977) *Transport Policy*, Cmnd. 6836, London, HMSO.

acting that a group may be considered politically influential and a participant in the decision.'[91] Usually issues are too complex or too remote for the public at large to become actively interested. The growth of pressure groups, paradoxically, may have increased the tendency for planners to become insulated from awareness of the competing demands and needs felt by the population at large.

Participation as presently practised leaves out of account the least articulate and most materially disadvantaged groups in the community. Their prime concerns are such services as housing, social services, and public transport. Other environmental issues which would quickly bring protests from better-off groups are of little interest to those who lack basic services. Occasionally, when their interests seem directly threatened, opposition may be aroused, though it is frequently too late to alter the decision. Unable to mobilise and organise in their own defence, they are particularly dependent on the ability of politicians to articulate their grievances for them. The case-studies will demonstrate in what circumstances pressure from various interest groups is likely to affect the policies being pursued by the planning authorities.

Central and local government

It is frequently asserted that local government is little more than an agency of central government. Central government sets the legislative framework for local government, imposes certain mandatory levels of service, and keeps a tight rein on local government expenditure through the allocation of the rate support grant which amounts to about two-thirds of total local expenditure. Through white papers, circulars, and other forms of communication, central government departments attempt to establish policy guidelines which they expect local authorities to follow. It may be argued that central control has intensified over the years as increasing legislative demands are imposed on local government. The economic crisis of the 1970s led to cuts in local governments expenditure. Although the 1972 Local Government Act created larger and therefore theoretically stronger local authorities, by reducing their numbers the government may have made it easier to exert central control. Buxton provides this interpretation of the implications for planning of the Act:

'All in all, this rather cumbersome system of theoretical local autonomy overlaid with strong elements of central control must give rise to the suspicion that the new system has been seen by central government as a good way of transferring much of the detailed work of supervising local planning from Ministry officials, whilst at the same time keeping in reserve powers that will make it easy to control divagations by local authorities from ministerially approved procedures.'[92]

The new development plans (discussed in Chapter 7) must be approved by the Minister after a lengthy, not to say interminable, period of consultation, participation, and examination in public. Local plans do not have to be referred to the Minister but he retains his panoply of quasi-judicial powers such as the right to 'call-in' applications and to hold public inquiries.

[91]G. A. Almond and S. Verba (1965) The sense of civic competence, in *The Civic Culture*, Little, Brown, in F. Castles *et al.* (eds.) *Decisions, Organisations and Society,* Penguin, London, p. 210.
[92]R. Buxton (1973) op. cit., p. 179.

Governments have long recognized the problems of central–local relationships and continue to stress their desire to encourage vigorous and independent local government. This theme has been reiterated in a series of white papers[93] and ministerial pronouncements. 'The dilemma which faces central government is to secure and promote an effective local democracy with genuine political choice and at the same time fulfil their responsibilities for the management of the economy and for the standards of public services.'[94] This dilemma, on a broader scale, is at the heart of the devolution debate, and of discussions about the prospect of further local government reform introducing regional authorities.[95] While it may be true that local government, in certain respects, enjoys little independence, there is some evidence pointing in the other direction.[96] Local authorities have considerable discretion in the local implementation of government policy. The power of government to control expenditure in detail is insufficent to prevent quite different policies being pursued. In public transport, for example, county councils adopted quite different attitudes, varying from Oxfordshire's dependence on market forces,[97] referred to disparagingly by critics as a 'rural pedestrianization policy', to South Yorkshire's deciding to refuse to accept any increases in fares and foregoing any support from the government to pay for the heavy subsidies this policy requires. Considerable variation occurs in the levels of services provided among the local authorities. For instance, some have concessionary bus passes for the elderly, some have higher pupil/teacher ratios, and so on. Even when statutory obligations are imposed, local authorities with sufficient political willpower can hold out against the government for a considerable time, as the refusal to implement comprehensive education by several authorities illustrates. In planning there is considerable freedom to pursue independent approaches, encouraged by the absence of any statutory regional planning machinery. As Chapter 7 indicates, county councils have produced quite different philosophies in their structure plans, leading to incompatibility between neighbouring counties. There is, of course, a difference between proposals on paper and ability to implement them, which I shall come to in a moment, but the freedom from central control is greater than is often thought.

Central–local tension is also felt within local government, especially in those areas where powers relating to a particular service are shared between county and district authorities. The two-tier system, with its rather muddy sharing of planning powers, and the agency arrangements entered into whereby district councils implement certain county services, notably transportation, have exacerbated political, bureaucratic, and geographical divisions. Members, especially those with 'dual membership' of district and county authorities, may take up postures based on geographical loyalties. In Bedfordshire, pressure from district councils, especially applied on those members with dual allegiance, was sufficient to ensure generous agency functions being granted to the

[93]Among these are *Local Government Finance*, Cmnd 6813, London, HMSO, 1977; *Department of Transport (1979)* op. cit., and the 'green paper', a consultative document; *Housing Policy*, Cmnd. 6851, London, HMSO, 1977.

[94]*Local Government Finance* (1977) loc. cit., p. 3.

[95]*Report of the Royal Commission on the Constitution, 1969–73*, Cmnd. 5460 and 4560–1. London, HMSO (The Kilbrandon Commission, 1973); *Devolution: the English Dimension,* A Consultative Document, London, HMSO, 1976; The Labour Party, London (1977) *Regional Authorities and Local Government Reform.* A Consultation Document, July.

[96]This argument is asserted by J. Stanyer (1976) *Understanding Local Government*, Glasgow, Fontana/Collins.

[97]Oxfordshire County Council (1976) *Local Transport in Oxfordshire.*

district authorities. Theoretically there is a case for a plurality of powers. Davidoff and Reiner argue, somewhat airily, that it can contribute 'to that higher synthesis . . . arising from conflict of ideas and values',[98] a point that is echoed by Grauhan.[99] But experience with the new system has led many to support the view of Lock that it causes 'wasteful duplication of staff and effort and much delay in negotiation and political competition'.[100] Energy is absorbed by the need to protect one authority's interest against that of another, demarcation disputes are frequent, and the distinction between the powers of the two tiers has become blurred. Removal of the two-tier system, especially where parts of the same function are shared, would not prevent conflict and the need for consultation, but it would make it clear where the power to take decisions lies and reduce the scope for procrastination by one authority which opposes the policies of another. The conflicts, compromises, and delays inherent in the two-tier system, especially when combined with agency powers, is a major theme of Chapter 5 and is also considered in Chapters 6 and 7. In essence it reduces the powers of individual authorities and may also serve to prevent rather than promote implementation of policies.

Existing policies and resource constraints

Quite apart from the restrictions imposed by central government and other authorities, the powers of a council are also bound by past policies. This is less evident when there is political continuity, but a change of political control brings the expectation of change. Given the influence of central government, changes at national level may have more significant impact than those introduced by changes of administration locally. Part of the reason for the general continuity of policies is the ability of the bureaucracy (as observed earlier) to restrain political initiatives, to modify policies in the light of impending political change, in short to provide stability in the administration. This stabilising influence of the bureaucracy leads to ambivalent attitudes among politicians. Hill confessed that when his party was in power 'he resented curbs on policy development imposed by officials who refused to regard certain suggestions as feasible, but in opposition was grateful for the limitations imposed on the potential 'excesses' of the dominant party'.[101]

Another reason for continuity is the consensus among political groups on a whole range of issues. We have noted the tendency for increasing division, and few authorities would today confine their disputes purely to matters of patronage, as Bulpitt found in some north-western authorities he observed, but the party battle does not impinge on all areas of activity. Rates, comprehensive education, public transport, social services, and housing are among the areas where the set-piece ideological battles take place. Over a whole range of planning matters there is broad agreement (sometimes for different reasons), and where conflict occurs it is not necessarily on party lines. The Bedfordshire Structure Plan illustrates this principle (Chapter 7). In this case the need to get agreement over a long-term strategy that would be acceptable to the myriad of bodies involved, that would be approved by central government, and that would survive

[98]P. Davidoff and A. Reiner (1962) op. cit., p. 36.
[99]R. R. Grauhan (1969) Notes on the structure of planning administration, in A. Faludi (1963) op. cit., p. 309.
[100]D. Lock, (1976) New towns in the future city region, in T. Hancock, (ed.) (1976) op. cit., p. 207.
[101]M. J. Hill (1972) op. cit., p. 202.

political change, was a strong inducement to continuity. The fact that the changes insisted on by a new administration were minimal confirmed this approach.

Nonetheless, political change can create the climate for significant, if not fundamental, changes in direction. When the gunfire of party conflict dies away much may remain. Political initiative is always at its height after an election. The winners can claim public support and can take the initiative with the bureaucracy by establishing the political climate for future action. But the zeal of a new administration wanes over time. Initially, the manifesto commitments will be honoured, polemically if not in practice. Eventually, the administration will accommodate their policies to the prevailing circumstances. Bureaucratic influence increases over time, and the officials' support for the ruling party may diminish as a new election approaches if a change in political control seems possible. Bedfordshire during 1973–7 shows this pattern. In 1974 the Labour group introduced a concessionary fares scheme, cut the roads programme, boosted public transport, and introduced a nursery education programme and a consumer advice service, all within a few months of taking office. In 1977 the Conservatives threatened to cut the nursery schools, to reduce public transport subsidies and introduce charges for the bus passes, and applied a series of cuts on service levels as a whole, again within a few months of the election. The changes were abrupt in both cases, but neither party sought to alter fundamentally the range and level of services provided. Politics at the local level tends, for much of the time, to be practical and pragmatic. Rhetoric needs to be distinguished from action.

A further limitation on power is imposed by the level of available resources. This is particularly so during times of financial crisis such as were experienced during the period studied in this book. But it works in both directions. Those who would impose severe cuts may be less enthusiastic when this would mean rejecting available finance from the government or when it would imperil services. Those who would spend beyond the level of resources are restrained by the heavy burdens this might impose on ratepayers. Local councils tend, whatever their political flavour, to work to certain standards and to adopt certain priorities. That these standards and priorities vary is the essence of local politics, but the differences in approach should not blind us to the broad similarities and the continuity that is the typical pattern of local government.

Implementation

Resources are one of the keys to the ability of a council to implement its policies. In planning especially, resources are often in the hands of other authorities and in the private sector, and this reduces the control over future development that can be exercised. Indeed, planning policies can only be implemented with the co-operation of other bodies. 'Positive planning,' which implies a conception of future development, in contrast to 'reactive planning', where a response is made to an immediate demand, must be based on assumptions and forecasts about the future. Since these are apt to change — and indeed the need for flexibility is a keynote of many plans — control over implementation cannot be assured. This brings us right back to the earlier discussion about the theoretical weakness of planning. It can lead to the conclusion that 'plans are meaningless documents unless implemented.'[102]

[102]D. M. Muchnik (1970) op. cit., p. 81.

Certainly the evidence from Bedfordshire is that much of the planning effort was abortive and esoteric. There is evidence of a growing dissatisfaction with planning, and this partly stems from the delays, duplication, and ineffectiveness of the present system, a topic to which I shall return in the final chapter. On the other hand, planners are also criticised when they do succeed in implementing schemes, as the history of urban motorways, tower blocks, etc., testifies. It also has to be recognised that implementation is not synonymous with development. At times of slow population growth and a need to conserve resources, plans calling for restraint, conservation and maintenance of the built environment, and protection of the countryside and agriculture can be implemented by preventing development. Just because a plan does not achieve its outcomes does not mean that planning has been ineffectual. To judge that, we would need to know what would have happened in the absence of a plan. Thus while planners cannot always implement their plans, and frequently cannot implement them within the time-scale or terms originally projected, planning is not so powerless as is sometimes supposed. But neither is it as powerful as some would have us believe.

CONCLUSION

Although town planning had its origins and inspiration in the work of Utopian thinkers, social revolutionaries, and reformers, it is today firmly entrenched as part of the panoply of state powers. Although part of the vision of the 'founding fathers' of town planning has been realised, the concept of town planning as an integral part of a fundamental social transformation has little influence on present planning thinking and still less on planning practice. That is not to say that many professional planners eschew the potential of their craft for improving the environmental conditions of society, and some indeed view it as one means of attaining the redistribution of real incomes and wealth. But, apart from a minority, some of whom are engaged in community action, planners assume that such changes must be achieved within the established framework of planning, not from without. To this end they are prepared, in order to exert some influence, to accept the constraints of bureaucratic organisation. Their skills are therefore employed in the service of the state. One of the primary, if implicit, aims of government is to ensure its own survival. To do so it must arbitrate between the various claims made for resources, to avoid social conflict, and to anticipate change. Planning, as part of the state's organisation, mediates various interests, seeks to achieve consensus, and attempts to co-ordinate and guide activities to avoid future conflicts.

Planning is a dependent activity, subservient to the needs of the state, and therefore the potential for independent action is severely limited. But, within the limitations prescribed by the necessity to ensure the maintenance of the prevailing pattern of social relationships, planners exert considerable influence and power. And it is a power that is unequally distributed, being concentrated among a few officials and politicians who control large bureaucracies and political parties. The distinction between administration and politics becomes irrelevant; what matters is the relationship between those leading politicians and officials who are responsible for the development of policy and its implementation, and their interaction with the powerful interests in society at large.

The sources of power of bureaucrats and politicians are different. Bureaucrats can command the loyalty of subordinates, can control the flow of information, can assert professional values that they consider (and may be accepted by others) as incontestable, and can profess the technical expertise and political neutrality that enable them to appeal to such persuasive notions as rationality and the public interest. Politicians can claim the support of a popular mandate, the ability to represent particular interests, and the backing of an organisation which can deliver (on most occasions) a decisive vote. Each has need of the other's skills and support. Together they form a powerful combination, substantially free from electoral pressures and able to co-opt or assume popular support for their policies.

Policy-making is not, however, achieved in a vacuum. Much planning activity is in response to pressures for development. Although planners cannot prevent such pressures, their reaction to them is expected to relate to general principles of policy. Each decision should be seen in the context of the whole. Freedom to set general policy guidelines is limited by many factors — by existing and future resources, by the policies and attitudes of central government and other authorities, and by the anticipated reactions of other groups or the electorate as a whole. Given the various influences to which planning policy is subject it is not surprising that overall planning policies are couched in general terms, flexible, and subject to change. At best they may be seen to be sufficiently robust to accommodate change; at worst to become a series of *ad hoc* reactions to events leading to a form of pre-emptive decision-making. It is difficult to make generalisations since the conditions vary in each planning organisation. In some areas of policy, planners have secured a measure of control and consistency, in others planning is little more than a simple reaction to events. The examples which follow investigate different areas of planning policy- and decision-making, and focus especially on the degree of control which is exercised by the leading decision-makers within the planning organisation – in this case a county council. From these examples we should gain some insight into the limits of power which condition the development, maintenance, and change of planning policy.

CHAPTER 3

Profile of a County

TOPOGRAPHY AND ECONOMY

The four case-studies which occupy Chapters 4–7 are each based on the same area, Bedfordshire. This chapter describes the geographical and political environment in which policy-making developed in Bedfordshire during 1973–7. Bedfordshire lies in that indeterminate part of the country between East Anglia, the East Midlands, and the Home Counties (Fig. 3.1). It straddles the main north–south railway routes and trunk

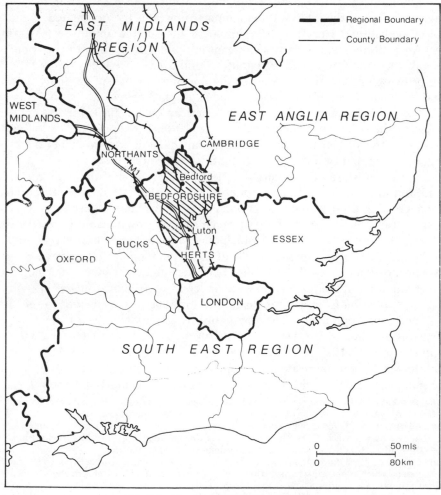

Fig. 3.1. The location of Bedfordshire.

roads to the Midlands and the North. Many people pass through it but, apart from Woburn Abbey and Luton Hoo, there is little to make them dally. The landscape is unremarkable, consisting of a succession of vales and scarps. The Marston Vale stretching south westwards from Bedford across the centre of the county provides the most distinctive and familiar landscape, the brickfields, a wasteland where the Oxford Clay is worked by the London Brick Company. In the north there is the undramatic but pleasant lowland of the Ouse valley. The wooded Greensand Ridge stretches across the county from west to east and is, in the planners' terminology, an area of 'Great Landscape Value',[1] although vulnerable to mineral extraction (Chapter 4). In the south of the county the chalk downs around Dunstable and Luton form a part of the Chiltern area of outstanding natural beauty.[2]

Economically the county has nationally significant manufacturing activities and a considerable area of high-grade agricultural land. About half the employed population in 1971 worked in manufacturing industry, well above the national (34.5%) and south-east regional (31.9%) averages. In the Luton/Dunstable area two-thirds of male employment (55% of the total) was in manufacturing industry, dominated by car firms (mainly Vauxhall and Chrysler) who employ a fifth of the employed males in the county. Agriculture is particularly significant in the north and east of the county and nearly half the agricultural land is in grades 1 and 2.[3] Service industries are the most rapidly growing but remain, in terms of employment levels, substantially below the national average. Unemployment has tended to stay below the national average, though the dependence on a few largely American-owned firms renders the future prospects of the county's economy somewhat brittle. Proximity to London and the expanding centres of Hertfordshire has encouraged commuters to live in the county, but in general the county is still very self-contained in employment terms.

In area Bedfordshire is the third smallest of the non-metropolitan counties of England, but there are eight English counties with smaller populations. Its population has been growing until recently at about 2% per year, more than three times the national average. Although in the past much of this growth came from net inward migration (70% of the total 1951–61), including substantial numbers from outside the United Kingdom who accounted for 10% of the population in 1971, more recently the greatest proportion of growth (60%) has been accounted for by natural increase. In 1971 over a quarter of the population were under 15 years of age, suggesting consider-able future expansion from natural increase despite the trends towards lower fertility being experienced nationally. The population is predominantly urban (72%), and about two-thirds live in the two major urban areas — Luton/Dunstable/Houghton Regis in the south (44%), and Bedford/Kempston in the north (18.5%). Apart from these major settlements there are several smaller towns such as Biggleswade, Ampthill, and Leighton-Linslade, which account for about 10% of the total population (Fig. 3.2).

[1] Areas of great landscape value were defined by the county planners and included the area south of Luton (Luton Hoo), various areas along the Greensand Ridge, and the Upper Ouse Valley.
[2] The Chilterns Area of Outstanding Natural Beauty was designated by the Countryside Commission in 1964. The four counties in which it lies (Bedfordshire, Buckinghamshire, Hertfordshire, Oxfordshire) estab-lished the Chilterns Standing Conference to co-ordinate policies for the area.
[3] The Ministry of Agriculture, Fisheries, and Food classifies agricultural land in five grades according to the degree to which its physical characteristics impose long-term limitations on agricultural land use. The highest grades (1 and 2) grow a wide range of crops, and produce high yields. The lowest grades (4 and 5) are severely limited. Almost all Bedfordshire's agricultural land is within the first three grades.

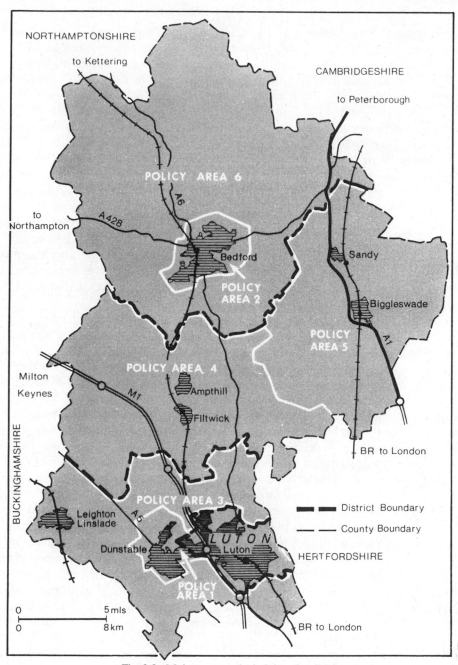

NORTHAMPTONSHIRE

to Kettering

CAMBRIDGESHIRE

to Peterborough

POLICY AREA 6

A6

to
Northampton

A 428

Bedford

Sandy

POLICY
AREA 2

Biggleswade

POLICY
AREA 5

A1

Milton

Keynes

POLICY AREA 4

M1

Ampthill

Flitwick

BUCKINGHAMSHIRE

BR to London

POLICY AREA 3

Leighton
Linslade

A5

District Boundary

County Boundary

Dunstable

L U T O N
Luton

HERTFORDSHIRE

POLICY
AREA 1

0   5 mls
0   8 km

BR to London

Fig. 3.2. Main towns and administrative divisions.

COUNTY POLITICS

The mixture of manufacturing and agriculture, urban and rural is reflected in the political structure of Bedfordshire. Until local government reorganisation in 1974, Bedfordshire, like most of the so-called 'shire counties', was predominantly Conservative. With the incorporation of Luton County Borough in the county, swelling its population by a third, the political balance was shifted and, for the period 1974–7, with which we are concerned in this book, Bedfordshire was one of several counties with minority government.[4] In the elections for the new county council, which took place in 1973, Labour took 39 seats, Conservatives 32, Liberals 9, and Independents 3. The relative strengths of the parties only changed marginally as a result of subsequent by-elections with the Conservatives gaining 1 seat from Labour and 1 from an Independent. The balance of the parties at the end of the period was, therefore, Labour 38, Conservatives 34, Liberals 9, and Independents 2. Labour was an overwhelmingly urban party taking 25 seats (1 of which was subsequently lost) out of 37 in the Luton/Dunstable/Houghton Regis area and 9 out of 14 in Bedford/Kempston. Of the other 5 Labour seats, 3 came from the small towns (Biggleswade and Leighton-Linslade) leaving only 2 from rural seats. By contrast the Conservatives were predominantly a rural (19 seats) and suburban (12 seats) party, holding only 3 seats in the inner urban area of Luton. The Liberals took 7 suburban and 2 rural seats.

Lack of overall control by one party resulted in a delicate political balance. In contrast with some authorities no alliances – formal or informal – were negotiated between the parties, and fewer powers were delegated to standing committees than often occurs with majority government. As a result the full council of 83 members was considerably more than 'a body whose major function, in terms of agenda content if not in importance, is to rubber-stamp decisions which have effectively been taken elsewhere'.[5] It could, and frequently did, overturn recommendations of programme committees. The political balance ensured that debates were open and meaningful but it also lead to uncertainty in decision-making on many issues.

The Labour group managed to secure, at least in theory, control over most of the programme committees. Five of the seven committees had 21 members, the exceptions being Education with 29 plus 13 co-opted members, and Police with 18 plus 9 magistrates. The 21 places on the 5 committees were distributed among the parties giving Labour 10. Conservative 8, and other groups 3. However, the chairman of the council was also a voting member of each programme committee. Since Labour held that office throughout the life of the council, the Labour group could achieve political equality with the other groups combined. Where Labour held the chairmanship of a committee they could secure control through the chairman's casting vote. Although absentees and the role of the minor parties could prove decisive in certain circumstances, Labour, on the whole, was able to initiate and carry its programme at least on those committees over which it had effective control.

[4]A. T. Blowers (1977) Checks and balances; the politics of minority government in Bedfordshire, *Public Administration*, Autumn, 305–16.
[5]The Bains Report (1972) *The New Authorities, Management and Structure*, London, HMSO.

THE ENVIRONMENTAL SERVICES COMMITTEE

One of these five committees was Environmental Services whose activities are discussed at various points in this book. Although the membership of the committee varied during the four-year period with which we are concerned, its balance of political and geographical interests remained substantially the same. Taking the membership of the committee for the final year of the council (1976–7), then its 11 Labour members (including the chairman of the council) were urban, 7 from the Luton/Dunstable/ Houghton Regis area and 3 (including the chairman of the committee) from Bedford, the remaining Labour member representing Biggleswade. Of the 8 Conservatives 5 were rural members. In terms of policies and interests, the focus of the committee was on the two major urban areas from which 13 of its 22 members were drawn. Rural interests were not neglected and were successfully articulated to the committee through powerful interest groups which tended not to be present in the more deprived urban areas. On election in 1973 the committee was lacking experience. Only 3 Labour members had served on the previous county council although only 2 had had no previous experience of any council work. The Conservatives, as was to be expected of the majority party on the previous council, were more experienced, with 6 having been on the previous council while all had served previously on a local authority. Two of the three Liberals were serving on a council for the first time.

Although there was a distinct social difference between the two major groups in terms of occupations, neither was particularly representative of the electorate as a whole. The Labour group in 1976 included four skilled manual workers, a postman, a prison officer, two clerical workers, a housewife, a retired miner, and a lecturer. Among the Conservatives were four managers or directors, a haulage contractor, an optician, a retired banker, and a housewife. The Liberals included a systems analyst, a social worker, and an insurance inspector.

In establishing an Environmental Services Committee the county council has espoused the concept, promoted in the Bains Report,[6] of few committees each covering broad though related fields. In particular they were anxious to integrate, at least at the political level, strategic planning and transportation. At the same time, this was achieved at national level through the Department of the Environment though subsequently (in 1976) the former division into Departments of Environment and Transport was resurrected. Any attempt to establish a sub-committee structure separating highways from planning functions was resisted, and although policy advisory groups were set up, the multifarious functions vested in the Environmental Services Committees resulted in its meeting more frequently (monthly) and longer (meetings usually took a whole day) than any other council committee. Among these functions were transportation, including highways construction and maintenance, traffic management, and public transport co-ordination; waste disposal; county planning matters, including the preparation of transport policies and programmes (TPPs) and the structure plan; and a variety of other matters such as urban conservation, historic buildings and archaeology, countryside protection, and gipsy caravan site provision. Although the committee enjoyed certain delegated functions notably as county planning authority on

[6]Ibid.

matters of development control deemed to be 'county matters (including minerals),[7] there was reserved to the county council power to approve or amend any scheme declared to be 'a major scheme',[8] notably the annual transport policies and programme (TPP),[9] and the structure plan.[10] In common with all committees, Environmental Services was subject to financial control exercised through the budgetary process determined by the county council on the advice of the Policy and Resources Committee.

The powers of the Environmental Services Committee were further limited by external bodies. These included statutory bodies such as the water authorities, and also central government, especially the Departments of Environment and Transport. Through advice in the form of circulars, and through its control of finance and notably the allocation of transport supplementary grant (TSG),[11] central government is able to exert considerable persuasive and fiscal power over local authorities. Moreover, central government possesses important planning controls. It adjudicates, at planning appeals and public inquiries, through its planning inspectorate reporting to the Minister. Government approves TPP submissions and bases its allocation of TSG upon them. Structure plans (see Chapter 7), once approved by county councils, must be endorsed by the Minister after an examination in public has been held at which the Department of the Environment acts as both judge and jury. This role has been questioned by the planning profession. 'Some people argue that a departmental Inspectorate, and a decision-making system based in a Government Department which has originated a particular proposal or scheme, cannot fairly judge such a scheme.'[12] Structure plans must be compatible with those of other authorities and 'interpret national and regional policies'.[13] Although there are no executive regional planning bodies, the government takes advice from its regional planning councils and standing conference of planning

[7]'County matters' include those development proposals (for instance car parks) which may affect the county councils as strategic planning and transportation authorities. Proposals which are in conflict with county policy must either be refused or referred to the county council before the district council — as the local planning authority — determines them.

[8]Bedfordshire County Council, Schedule of Committee Functions, Environmental Services Committee, p. 102, II 1.

[9]Transport policies and programmes (TPPs) are submitted annually by each transportation authority (county councils) and provide an analysis of transportation problems, proposals, and priorities for the area, together with a programme of investment.

[10]Structure plans are written statements of the county council's 'policies and main proposals for change on a large scale' (Ministry of Housing and Local Government, *Development Plans, A Manual of Form and Content*, 1970, p. 4). They were introduced by the Town and Country Planning Act 1968 on the recommendations of the Planning Advisory Group (PAG) as a more comprehensive form of planning to replace the previous land-use plans. The functions of this new planning system can be summarised: 'the aims of the plan should be designed to satisfy social and economic aspirations as far as possible, through the creation of an efficient physical structure, and a good environment; the policies should be set out to provide a framework for the continuous process of making planning decisions' (ibid., p. 5). The Bedfordshire Structure Plan is discussed in Chapter 7.

[11]The Transport supplementary grant is the means by which central government provides extra finance to support expenditure from rates and rate support grant on transport projects. It is based on transport policies and programme and gives borrowing approval for capital projects. It enables the government to keep a fairly tight control over both the amount and type of transportation expenditure and ensures that government priorities are met.

[12]Royal Town Planning Institute (1976) *Planning and the Future*, discussion paper prepared by a working party established by the RTPI.

[13]Department of the Environment (1974) *Structure Plans*, Joint Circular 98/74, London, HMSO.

authorities,[14] and local policies are expected to have regard to regional objectives as expressed in regional strategic plans. Thus there are obvious legal and practical limits to the objectives exercised at local level. The relative authority of central and local government already discussed in the previous chapter will be discussed in relation to specific examples.

DISTRICT COUNCILS

Conflict between the two tiers of local authority has already been discussed in general terms. It arises from the sharing of local planning powers between the two tiers created by the Local Government Act 1972. The second tier, the district councils, is responsible for the preparation of local plans within the framework of the structure plan. Of greater significance, in terms of the balance of power, is the districts' responsibility for development control.[15] Apart from the few matters referred to the county councils, districts deal with all planning applications, and accept, modify, or reject them through their planning committees. This control over day-to-day implementation of planning policies provides the district councils with effective power, as it is up to them to interpret strategic and local plans. It can be argued that it is at the detailed local level that the important planning decisions are taken which condition the development of an overall strategy. Where conflicts occur between the two tiers of local authorities it proves difficult for the county council to impose its wishes on the district. Conversely, the district council may, through a series of decisions, pursue policies that ultimately contradict county council strategy. Even where county councils possess ultimate authority, as, for example, over transportation, districts may be able to delay or thwart the implementation of county policies. They can achieve this through the exercise of their planning powers, through the process of consultation, and through the agency arrangements[16] that may exist. Where powers overlap, and where conflicts arise opposing authorities are able to neutralise each other's initiatives. The allocation of planning and transportation under the Local Government Act 1972, quite apart from the duplication and increased manpower it may have produced, has, in many cases, contributed to the uncertainty and inconsistency which is a feature of planning practice if not of planning policy. This point will be underlined in the case-studies which follow.

Conflict between local authorities serving the same territory has geographical, political, and bureaucratic origins. Geographically, there is resentment of interference by one authority in what are regarded as the legitimate affairs of another. This is particu-

[14]Eight economic planning councils covering the regions of England composed of appointees from industry, trade unions, local government, and academics, who advise. Until 1979 there were the government on regional matters. The South-East Economic Planning Council includes Bedfordshire. The planning authorities of the South-east have established the Standing Conference for London and South East Regional Planning (SCLSERP) which co-ordinates planning policies and advances regional views to the Minister for the Environment. These two bodies, together with the Government, commissioned the *Strategic plan for the South East* (1970) and its subsequent *Review* (1976) which are discussed in Chapter 7.

[15]'Development control' is the process by which applications for planning development are passed or refused by a locally elected planning committee receiving advice from professional planners and assessing applications in the light of its current development plan or policies.

[16]Under the Local Government Act 1972 the new county councils were empowered to grant functions to be carried out by the district councils acting as their agents. These include road improvement and maintenance and traffic management functions. Agency arrangements in North Bedfordshire are discussed in Chapter 5.

larly evident where a former county borough (such as Luton) or a borough previously enjoying considerable delegated powers (such as Bedford) loses some of its authority to a county council, as happened throughout the county in 1974. This resentment may cut across party political lines especially where some members represent both authorities (as was especially the case with Luton). It tends to become entrenched where the two authorities are under different political leadership (as was the case between the county council and Bedford). Officials owe their loyalty to the authority they serve, and may both inspire and respond to geographical and political conflicts between authorities. County officials experience frustration at being unable to implement their policies, while district officials resent what they regard as interference in their affairs from the county council.

Bedfordshire possessed during the period under consideration all the ingredients for conflicts of this kind. There are four district councils within the geographical county (fig. 3.2). Luton Borough Council (the former Luton County Borough, an all-purpose authority) is the largest, with a population of 161,000, entirely urban and Labour-controlled until 1976 when the Conservatives came to power. North Bedfordshire Borough Council (124,500) covers the northern part of the county focused on Bedford. Until 1976, when the Conservatives won overall control, the borough council experienced minority government, with Labour just ahead of the Conservatives although the substantial independent group prevented Labour from exercising much influence except over housing matters. South Bedfordshire District Council (88,500) comprises Dunstable and Leighton-Linslade and the intervening rural area, and, like North Bedfordshire, had no overall control (although the Conservatives were the largest group) until the Conservative victory of 1976. Finally, Mid-Bedfordshire District Council (90,000) is the largest in area and mainly rural with two small towns — Biggleswade/Sandy and Ampthill/Flitwick. It was Conservative-controlled throughout the period under discussion.

Geographical conflicts were especially prevalent between Luton and the county council and tended to frustrate party allegiances. Such conflicts tended to diminish with time both within the county council and between it and the borough. Conflicts on planning and transport matters continued throughout the period between the county council and North Bedfordshire (see Chapter 5). Conflicts were less overt between the other two districts and the county council, perhaps because controversy tended to focus around the urban areas. This experience of powerful urban authorities challenging the county council was evident at both the political and bureaucratic level.

The conflicts that occurred arose partly out of different ideologies, and partly through competing organisations. They were constrained also by the availability of resources and by existing policies and processes. Conflict was especially evident over transportation and land policies, which will be dealt with in the case-studies (Chapters 5 and 6). There were other conflicts, notably over environmental issues, that were internal between politicians and planners, and one of these is discussed in Chapter 4. Finally, there were many issues over which a consensus was generated, contrived, or assumed, or which were wholly excluded from the decision-making process. These are, by their very nature, difficult to analyse, but their existence must be recognised, and was responsible for the degree of unanimity that existed over many of the policies in the county's structure plan. In each case the interaction of politicians and planners provided the fulcrum around which the policy-making process turned.

CHAPTER 4

Politicians versus Planners — the case of fuller's earth

A central — some would say the most important — task of planners is to allocate land among competing uses. Conflicts over use tend to be present in three types of area: areas where land is highly accessible and in consequence in short supply relative to potential uses (e.g. central parts of cities); areas of transition where existing uses are subject to change of use (e.g. areas of decay); and areas where pressures for growth require land to be acquired for different purposes (e.g. urban fringe areas). But over much of the land surface there is broad agreement over use, and existing uses are expected to remain — in the planners' phrase — 'largely undisturbed'. This does not suggest that the landscape is unchanging; indeed, the lack of planning controls over agriculture has enabled far-reaching and fundamental changes to occur in the appearance of rural areas as large-scale mechanised agriculture and factory farming have swept away field boundaries and hedges, introduced large agricultural buildings, and generally transformed the rural environment.[1] Rural settlement patterns are changing slowly, too, partly under the influence of planning policies which concentrate on key villages. Such strategies common in areas of population growth or decline, may have contributed to the increasing inequalities of mobility and accessibility experienced in the rural areas.[2]

Within rural areas conflicts over land use tend to arise sporadically, for instance when developers wish to build in a particular village, or an industrialist wishes to expand at an existing site. In such cases the long-term strategy adopted by the planning authority may be challenged and, in cases where permission is refused, an appeal can be made to the Minister. Usually the conflicts are over local interests, the need to protect the amenity and environment against the need to accommodate population or employment. Occasionally the conflict involves national interests; for example, the introduction or development of an airport or the mining of a strategic mineral. Such issues cannot be contained simply within the framework of local planning policies — though clearly these are relevant — but must be judged on their individual merits. They are of intrinsic interest since they involve such a variety of interests and demonstrate the limits of power of the decision-makers involved. Such an issue is the subject of this chapter.

At the local level the decision whether to grant or refuse a planning application is made by the members of a planning committee who constitute the local planning authority acting on the advice of professional planners. In most cases this advice is

[1]G. Wibberley (1974) The proper use of Britain's rural land — a critical view, Royal Town Planning Institute, Diamond Jubilee Conference, 13–15 June; Countryside Commission (1974) *New Agricultural Landscapes*.
[2]A. T. Blowers (1978) Future rural transport and development policy, in R. Cresswell (ed.) (1978) *Rural Transport and Country Planning*, Glasgow, Blackies.

accepted. The process is, however, not a straightforward matter of planners exercising professional judgement in the public interest which is legitimised by democratically elected representatives. 'There simply cannot be any objectively correct answer to the question of how resources should be allocated. It is a question for politicians, not experts.'[3] The professional planner, especially the chief officer, has considerable administrative discretion and access to information from a wide variety of sources, and makes his own recommendation to the committee. Of all the areas in local government, planning expresses 'the dominant role of the official who has the initiative in administrative bargaining and consults with a wide range of interests'.[4] In attempting to arbitrate conflicting interests and applying his judgement to them, albeit against a background of planning policy, the officer plays an essentially political role. He may, as was suggested in Chapter 2, appeal to such notions as the public interest.

> 'Elected representatives in both central and local government are thus advised by bureaucrats (among them are town planners) to follow certain specified policies which are said to be in the public interest — a normative concept which overrides criticism on sectional and political grounds — and which are supported by an apparently functionally rational battery of techniques over which only the planners have professional mastery.'[5]

But in those areas where explicit judgements between interests have to be made, and where techniques are inapplicable, in other words where the planner occupies a more overtly political role, his judgement may be more open to question. Where the consistency of the advice received is open to doubt and where opposing interests are able to organise and gain access to politicians, then his advice may not be heeded, and a conflict between the political and professional decision-makers may arise as it did in the case about to be analysed here.

Local politicians may see their role in deciding applications in various ways. Occasionally development control decisions are taken on party political lines. In many cases politicians will accept the advice they are given. Where there are disputes between authorities, a conflict of advice, or an expression of local opinion, politicians will undertake consultations, often through a small group of members who will visit the site and listen to the various views. They will then try to interpret the issue in relation to general planning policy in order to justify any decision they make. Planning policies are rarely so watertight as to be incapable of supporting several interpretations. It is necessary to appear to achieve consistency between policy and decisions based upon it if appeals against decisions are to be upheld.

The role of public opinion has increased as demands for greater participation have been met and as local interests have been mobilised to oppose certain proposals. 'In case planners have not noticed it, they are far more often, and more viciously attacked, for doing something, than for doing nothing, because opponents of action are educated, articulate, single-minded, and successful, and those who would gain from action are

---

[3] E. J. Reade, (1976) 'An attempt to distinguish planning from other modes of decision making', seminar paper, Department of Town and Country Planning, Manchester University, November, p. 8.
[4] D. M. Hill (1974) *Democratic Theory and Local Government*, The New Local Government Series, 12, London, Allen & Unwin, p. 87.
[5] J. M. Simmie (1974) *Citizens in Conflict*, London, Hutchinson Educational, p. 121.

cowed, under-privileged, unorganized and poor.'[6] Where the amenity of relatively affluent areas is threatened then it is almost inevitable that hostility will be aroused, fanned by a pressure group, and that local resources of money, expertise, and organisation will be deployed in an effort to resist the proposal. Even if the local interests cannot stop the proposal, they may often succeed in having it modified, or accepted with stringent conditions applied. There is considerable investment of time, expertise, and money made by applicants and opponents to ensure the success of their case and to bring pressure to bear, by various means, upon the decision-makers.

The decision-makers tend to respond to these pressures in different ways. Planning officers, who purport to make disinterested judgements, tend to consider cases 'on their merits', weighing up strategic against local issues. However, they receive advice from central government departments and attempt to anticipate the probable outcome of an inquiry if an appeal against a decision is likely to be made. Applicants often have direct access to officials and thus have the opportunity to influence them. It would be surprising if the weight and balance of opinion and advice received did not affect judgement. But planning officials are also aware of local interests whether transmitted through the politicians or more directly. The planning officer is, in fact, the recipient of information from all sources and, theoretically at least, in the best position to weigh up the conflicting issues. Local politicians are 'at the interface between the arguments going on within political bodies and within the administrative machine'.[7] Though politicians may be regarded in some quarters as the mere mouthpieces of the planning officials, voicing the arguments of received planning wisdom, there are occasions when local pressures to which they are highly sensitive cause them to reject official advice. In cases where national and strategic issues may appear in conflict with local and environmental considerations, there exists the possibility that planning officials and local politicians will lean in different directions. Although we might expect politicians to support local interests and officials to be prepared, on occasion, to submit to national interests, this is not always so, as later examples given here will demonstrate. We need to comprehend the channels of communication to which the decision-makers are exposed. It would be difficult, if not impossible, to gain a comprehensive picture of the varying information, advice, and pressures to which each decision-maker is subject. Nonetheless, careful study of particular cases can provide insight into the decision-making process.

THE EXPLORATION OF MINERALS

Minerals, unlike most other forms of development, are not footloose, they must be worked where they occur. The location of mineral deposits in areas of great amenity, on valuable agricultural land, or in other sensitive areas frequently gives rise to conflict between strategic and local interests. Unlike the bulk of planning applications which are matters for district councils to resolve, the exploitation of minerals is a matter reserved

[6]D. Eversley, (1976) The education of planners, in T. Hancock (ed.) (1976) *Growth and Change in the Future City Region,* London, Leonard Hill, pp. 241–2.

[7]R. R. Grauhan (1973) Notes on the structure of planning administration, in A. Faludi (ed.) *A Reader in Planning Theory*, Urban and Regional Planning Series, Vol. 5, Oxford, Pergamon Press.

to the county councils.[8] District councils may submit to the county council their own observations or recommendations. The procedure adopted in Bedfordshire was for a Minerals Sub-committee, consisting of three members of the Environmental Services Committee, to visit the sites of minerals applications, to meet with local interests, to consider the consultations with various authorities and bodies, and to make recommendations (whether unanimously or not) to the parent committee. The Environmental Services Committee would then consider all the information at its disposal and the recommendation made by the County Planning Officer before making its decision. In rare cases where national and local issues are involved the Secretary of State may 'call in' the application for his decision after a hearing or public inquiry. In 1973 only 160 out of a total of two-thirds of a million applications were called in. Minerals applications are, however, among those likely to be called in. They 'often raise problems of more than local importance and the national need for particular minerals has to be balanced against planning issues. Such matters cannot adequately be considered by local planning authorities and, in any case, involve technical considerations requiring expert opinion of a character more easily available to the department [of the Environment]'.[9] Where the local planning authority decides to refuse the application, an appeal against the decision by the applicants and a subsequent public inquiry is almost inevitable in the case of minerals exploitation. Although a decision to accept a minerals application may be determined by the local authority, a refusal usually results in the final decision being taken by the Secretary of State. This was the case with an application to mine fuller's earth, a rare mineral in Bedfordshire.

Though a small county, Bedfordshire possesses several minerals of local and national significance, and their exploitation has resulted in large areas devoted to mineral workings (see Fig. 4.1). A survey in 1972[10] estimated that 1824 ha (4507 acres) had been affected by mineral workings and that a further 2166 ha (5352 acres) remained likely to be affected out of a total acreage for the county of 119,130 ha (294,369 acres). The most significant of these was Oxford Clay worked for the brickmaking industry of the Marston Vale in central Bedfordshire producing nearly a fifth of national production, with planning permissions covering 1678 ha (4146 acres), and with a reserve sufficient to last well into the next century. So far only about a third of the available land has been worked. In addition a small area of Gault Clay is worked near Leighton–Linslade. Sand and gravel permissions covered 819 ha (2024 acres) in the Ivel and Ouse valleys, and sand was extracted from the Lower Greensand mainly around Leighton–Linslade (642 ha, 1739 acres). Of the other minerals there are small workings for Great Oolite and Cornbrash for building stone in the Upper Ouse Valley and for chalk in areas on or close to the Chilterns in the south of the county (499 ha, 1233 acres with permissions). 'Many of the county's most important minerals coincide with attractive landscapes,'[11] and

[8]'Applications relating to the winning and working of minerals or the erection of buildings or plant for that purpose, prospecting for minerals, and disposing of waste. The decision on such applications, whether to grant permission or refuse, is one for the County planning authority.' Bedfordshire County Council, Environmental Services Committee, 29 April 1977, Agenda Item 21, 'County matters: a note on the functions of the local planning authorities in Bedfordshire.'
[9]J. B. Cullingworth (1976) *Town and Country Planning in Britain*, 6th edn., The New Local Government Series, No. 8, London, Allen & Unwin, p. 50.
[10]Bedfordshire County Council (1972) *County Review*, Minerals Aspect Report, Consultation Draft, March, p. 7.
[11]Bedfordshire County Council (1976) *County Structure Plan, Report of Survey*, p. 173.

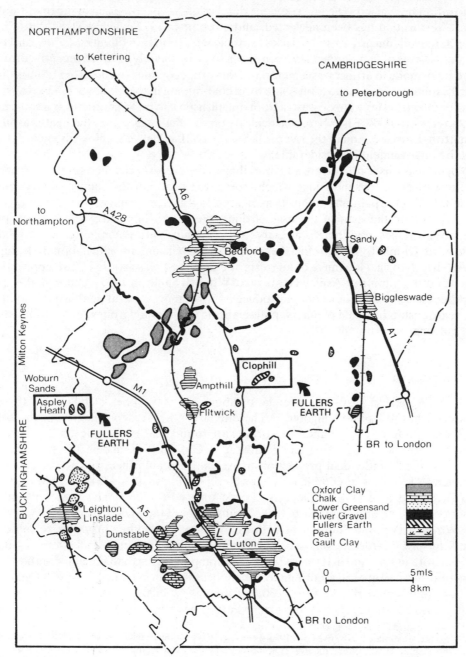

Fig. 4.1. Minerals in Bedfordshire, as in 1972.

restoration has varied. The most obvious dereliction has been caused in the brickfields, where restoration has been neglected, and a report in 1972 concluded that 'little has been achieved, due in part to the lack of sufficient quantities of filling materials, and the area of what is in fact derelict land continues to grow steadily.[12] More recently, efforts have been made to attract waste materials from other counties (refuse from London and Northamptonshire, and possibly shale from coal-mining in the Midlands). The decision to allow the transfer of toxic wastes from one disused claypit to another was a source of controversy in 1978. Elsewhere, particularly on the chalk scarps, on the heaths around Leighton–Linslade, and in the river valleys, the conflict between minerals exploitation and the environment is considerable.

Nowhere is this conflict more apparent than in the area where fuller's earth is located, on the Lower Greensand Ridge which crosses the centre of the county and has been designated by the planning authority as an area of great landscape value. Extraction has taken place on the west of the ridge around Woburn Sands and Aspley Guise, two attractive villages, and there is a reserve with planning permission in the centre of the county at Clophill. The conflict between local environment and national strategic needs, involving a wide range of interests and attitudes, was aroused by an application to extend the mining at Aspley Heath near Woburn Sands in 1975. Although the case has specific characteristics it does introduce issues of more general significance, notably the relationship between planners, politicians, local pressure groups, private industry, and national government.

FULLER'S EARTH

Over the period 1970–4 an average of about 175,000 tonnes of fuller's earth was produced in the United Kingdom.[13] The only areas where deposits are known to be thick enough to justify commercial working are found near Bath, at Redhill in Surrey, near Maidstone, at Baulking and Fernham in Oxfordshire, and in the two sites in Bedfordshire.[14] Individual production figures are not published, but the largest UK producer is Laportes, predominantly from Redhill, with smaller workings at Maidstone and Bath and a reserve at Clophill. At the time of the application the only other producer was the applicant, Berk Ltd., a subsidiary of the Steetley Co. Ltd., working the Woburn deposit. Subsequently an application by another producer to mine at Baulking in Oxfordshire was successful after a public inquiry. Production was thus limited both in area and in terms of producing companies, and had remained static while consumption had grown, according to the applicant, to an average of 208,000 tonnes in 1970–4, and would rise to about 250,000 tonnes by 1980.[15] Fuller's earth varies in quality and consequently to some extent in the uses to which it may be put. 'No two

[12]Bedfordshire County Council (1972) op. cit., p. 4.
[13]This is the estimate for the five years 1970–4 given by W. C. Gilpin in evidence on behalf of the applicants at the Aspley Heath Public Inquiry. It is substantially the same as that given at the public inquiry at Baulking in Oxfordshire of 174,000 tonnes for the period 1969–74. Production in 1974 was 166,000 tonnes. The source for statistics is *United Kingdom Mineral Statistics, 1975*
[14]Proof of Evidence, Aspley Heath Planning Inquiry, Prof. W. Davies.
[15]Statistics of consumption vary. W. C. Gilpin produced a five-year average (1970–4) of 208,000 tonnes at the inquiry. This is somewhat higher than the estimate of the Institute of Geological Sciences (and given at the Oxfordshire inquiry) of consumption rising from 133,000 tonnes in 1967 to 203,000 tonnes in 1974 at an annual average rate of 5.4%.

fuller's earths are exactly the same in properties nor in the range of applications they can satisfy.'[16] Fuller's earth is a type of clay which has a purifying and decolorising property and which swells or gels in water. When chemically treated, fuller's earth attains similar properties to 'bentonite', which occurs naturally in the United States and which has a wide range of industrial applications.[17] It is used as a binding, bonding, dispersing, and suspending agent, and for reducing the permeability to water of earth and rock formations. It is difficult to gain precise estimates of its consumption in different uses. By far the most important is as a binding agent in foundry moulds taking about 130,000 tonnes per year, 100,000 from UK producers. One-third of this total was from the Woburn deposit. Other uses are in decolorising and purifying oils (40,000 tonnes, all UK); in drilling muds on North Sea oil rigs (15,000 tonnes, 80% from the Woburn deposit); in civil engineering (10,000 tonnes); for pelletising iron ore (a new use for which the Oxfordshire deposit was required); and a variety of other uses including plasticisers and catalysts (25,000 tonnes).[18] The Woburn deposit was used mainly for foundry work (60%), in drilling muds (24%), and in civil engineering (10%).[19]

Of the various UK deposits, that at Redhill 'would suggest a reserve life at present extraction rates of 10–15 years'.[20] At Woburn, where production was at an annual rate of 50,000 tonnes, unless permission to extend the working were granted, the existing working would be exhausted by 1979. When the application was submitted in 1975 the UK industry was facing the prospect of a substantial decline in production after the existing Woburn working closed, at a time when consumption of fuller's earth appeared to be increasing at a rate of about 5% per year.

FULLER'S EARTH AT WOBURN

Although there is evidence of earlier workings for fuller's earth at Woburn, modern production began in 1949 on a small site (20 acres) north-west of that applied for in 1975. This was worked until permission was granted for a much larger site east of the road between Woburn Sands and Woburn (Fig. 4.2) covering 48.2 ha (120 acres) in 1961 and subsequently extended to 55.58 ha (137.35 acres) including a processing plant. It is an interesting commentary on the growing concern to regulate mineral workings and to achieve protection for the environment through restoration to note that only two conditions were attached to the 1949 permission, 7 to its extension in 1959, and 16 to the 1961 permission, whereas twenty-four were proposed in the event of the 1975 appli-

[16]R. H. S. Robertson (1976) 'Report on aspects of the fuller's earth industry to Bedfordshire County Council' 3 August, 2.1.

[17]Fuller's earth is a calcium montmorillonite clay. When treated it can be converted to sodium montmorillonite. This form, known as Wyoming bentonite, occurs naturally in the United States.

[18]These estimates of amounts used in various applications are drawn from W. C. Gilpin using his company's (the applicants) figures and government statistics for 1975. Similar figures were given at the Baulking inquiry and included an estimate of a new demand for bentonite for iron ore pelletising of 20,000 tonnes.

[19]These estimates of the proportion of Woburn fuller's earth entering different markets were given by D. J. McVittie on behalf of the applicants at the public inquiry.

[20]Letter from D. E. Highley, Institute of Geological Sciences to County Planning Officer, 2 December 1975.

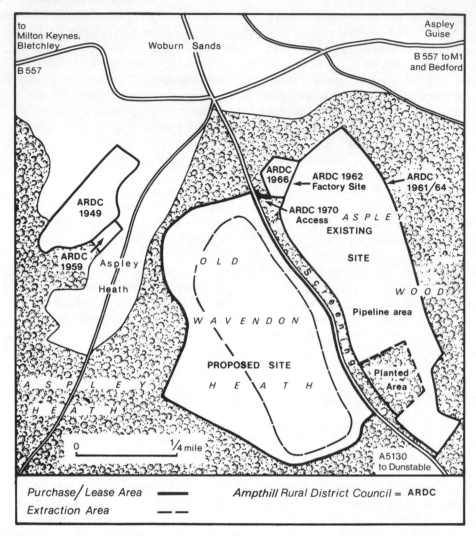

Fig. 4.2. Fuller's earth at Woburn — existing and proposed workings.

cation being granted.[21] The 1975 application was for an area of 56.5 ha (139.4 acres) of which only 34.6 ha (85.65 acres) would be worked, immediately to the west of the road and the existing workings. This would enable the company to continue their annual production of 50,000 tonnes at Woburn using the processing plant already installed.

The site is ¾ mile south of Woburn Sands, 1 mile south-west of Aspley Guise, and 1½ miles north-west of Woburn. Immediately to the west is Aspley Heath, and the nearest dwelling is 200m away. The site consisted of undulating ground sloping south-

[21]Only one condition had been imposed on the permission granted at Clophill in 1952. It was a general condition requiring a detailed programme of working and restoration to be submitted to the authority before development began. The county council had to seek to translate that condition into a satisfactory plan of working when the company decided to begin working twenty-six years later in 1978.

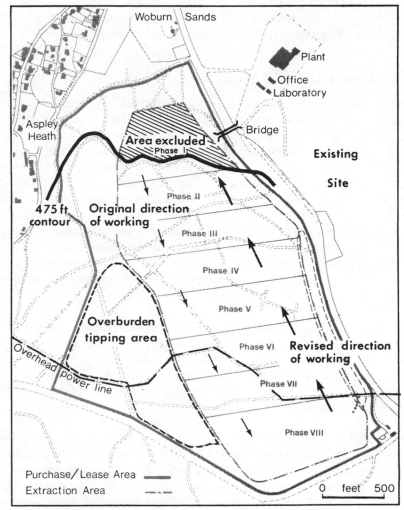

Fig. 4.3. The Aspley Heath site: proposed plan of working
and modifications imposed after the public inquiry.

wards from a scarp and covered by a coniferous woodland owned by the Bedford
Estates at Woburn, which was crossed by a number of footpaths. It is situated within the
area of great landscape value which was the part of the Brickhills recreation area.[22] The
working of the site would take place over ten years, moving southwards and
progressively backfilling, restoring, and reafforesting the land. The whole area would
be restored to woodland within twelve years. (Fig. 4.3). The depth of working would be
between 18 m and 47 m, and the fuller's earth would be transported across the road to

[22]The Brickhills recreation area had not been formally designated. Bedfordshire and Buckinghamshire
County Councils (1973) 'The Brickhills Recreation Area', Draft Consultation Document, January.

the processing plant by means of a bridge.[23] The decision whether to allow the application or not rested upon 'the need to work this rare and valuable mineral against the damage that may be done to the environment and local amenity'.[24]

EXISTING PLANNING POLICIES

Planning policy regarding minerals is couched in broad and general terms and has to be interpreted in the light of circumstances surrounding each individual application. In the case of rare minerals such as fuller's earth, policies tend to stress the conflict between environment and national need. Although there is no national policy to secure reserves, as far back as 1951 the government set up regional conferences to ensure that suitable reserves were available to meet production requirements. The Strategic Plan for the South-East stated that 'Fuller's Earth will continue to make a small but useful contribution to the export market. Strictly limited supply and relatively high value of this mineral demands priority for its extraction despite possible conflicts with amenity, environment and agriculture.'[25] The county council's policy understandably placed considerable emphasis on the environmental problems caused by mineral workings. The 'Handover Plan', which was the policy in force at the time of the application, stated:

'The working of Fuller's Earth generally involves considerable conflict with amenity in areas of great landscape value and is accepted only because of the national significance of the mineral. As further deposits could be discovered anywhere in the Lower Greensand, no specific control policy has been adopted and any future application can only be treated, as those in the past, entirely on its merits, balancing national needs against local disadvantages.[26]

The proposed and subsequently adopted policy in the structure plan was more succinct but similar: 'Any future application for the working of Fuller's Earth will be treated entirely on its own merits, weighing national need against environmental and other considerations.'[27] Various policies covered the environmental issues. Among them were policies to conserve woodlands, to protect areas of great landscape value, to promote recreational facilities in the Greensand Ridge, and to ensure the restoration of any workings.[28] With such an armoury of policies the local planning authority could defend either an acceptance or a rejection of an individual application to mine fuller's earth in Bedfordshire.

[23]Some means of connection between the site and the processing plant was necessary if the plant were to be used after the adjacent workings were exhausted. A bridge was found to be most economic although it raised further problems of amenity and consequently would have to be the subject of a separate planning permission.

[24]Environmental Services Committee, 20 February 1976, Agenda Item 15 (20).

[25]South-East Joint Planning Team (1970) *Strategic Plan for the South east,* Vol. 2, 5.77–5.81.

[26]Bedfordshire County Council (1974) *The Handover Plan*, January, p. 26.

[27]Bedfordshire County Council (1977) *County Structure Plan*, Policy 70, p. 54.

[28]Ibid., Policies 55–57, 59, 62–64, 79–81.

THE STRATEGIC ISSUE

The case for extracting fuller's earth at Woburn relied on the importance of the material to the national economy. It was claimed that failure to maintain production at Woburn would reduce UK production by almost a third and would leave production in the hands of one supplier. (When the application was made, the appeal decision on Baulking was unknown.) The Department of Industry was anxious to avoid any shortfall in production, which would have to be made good by imports with a consequent effect on the balance of payments (estimated to amount to a loss of more than £1 million per year at 1975 prices if production at Woburn ceased). In a letter to the County Planning Officer the department stated: 'We would certainly wish to avoid this and hope that the council will be aware of the national interest when deciding the company's application.'[29]

The Mid-Bedfordshire District Council and the local interests declared their doubts about the national need for the mineral. The district council resolved 'that this application be refused in view of the considerable doubt as to the strategic need for Fuller's Earth'.[30] The local interests argued that substitutes were likely to be available for several of the uses of fuller's earth in the long run, that some domestic production was exported,[31] and that use of the material in certain luxury and cosmetic trades hardly constituted a national need.[32] In particular they argued that North Sea drilling rigs (for which Woburn is the major UK supplier of bentonite for drilling muds) 'are changing to a synthetic substance rather than using fuller's earth'.[33] Another aspect of this market was expressed by a representative of the Institute of Geological Sciences: 'I am now not so sure that bentonite consumption in the North Sea will necessarily continue to rise, particularly as it seems likely that smaller amounts of drilling mud are required for a production well rather than an exploration well.'[34] A similar situation was true in some foundry uses and in ore pelletisation. It appeared, too, that some production was used

[29]Letter from the Department of Trade and Industry to the County Planning Officer, 8 December 1975. In the letter the word 'wish' had replaced the original word 'seek'.

[30]Mid-Bedfordshire District Council, Planning and Development Committee, 16 December 1975.

[31]Estimates of exports and imports vary. W. C. Gilpin in his statement on behalf of the applicants at the inquiry estimated the five-year average, 1970–4, as imports 50,000 tonnes per annum and exports as 17,000 tons per annum. The Oxfordshire inquiry gave an import total for 1975 of 45,000 tonnes. The applicants, in a letter to the County Planning Officer (27 January 1976) using statistics of the Institute for Geological Service and HM Customs and Excise, gave an import total of bentonite materials of 73,000 tonnes (61,000 Wyoming bentonite) and exports of 21,000 tonnes. Clearly there are problems of definition of the relevant material.

[32]Mr. D. E. Highley of the Institute of Geological Sciences estimated that in 1974 26,000 tonnes of material, mainly for floor absorbents and pet litter, was imported from the United States of which 10,000 was fuller's earth. He commented: 'Natural fuller's earth granules are also used for this purpose but I suspect it is indigenous fuller's earth which is substituting for imported sepiolite and attapulgite and not the other way round.'

[33]Letter from M. Kemp to the chairman of the Environmental Services Committee, 15 January 1976.

[34]Letter from D. E. Highley, Institute of Geological Sciences, loc. cit. According to one of the opponents only about 5000 tonnes of Woburn material was being used in oil muds. 'Although more than four times this amount of bentonite is produced at Woburn, the Company prefers to export the difference and also imports bentonite from off-shore drilling,' (letter from the Clerk to Aspley Heath Parish Council to the County Secretary, 14 January 1976). In the light of the estimates of 24% of Woburn production (50,000 tonnes) being used for drilling muds, and the estimate 80% of the drilling market (about 15,000 tonnes per year) being supplied from Woburn, the estimate of 5000 tonnes per year appears rather low. It does indicate the problem of obtaining statistics and the likelihood of discrepancies arising which can satisfy opposing arguments.

in such applications as cosmetics and cat litter and 'that if the Government is serious as to this substance being of strategic need and in limited supply, it would hardly allow 35,000 tons to be used in this way'.[35] The local interests concluded, 'Prediction of future consumption cannot be based reliably on past consumption, mainly because of the pace of change in related technologies and competition within the chemical industry from the various commercial interests for new product markets and shares of existing markets.'[36] It was pointed out that imports had recently declined. The local interests regarded the application as 'profit motivated' and 'the real issue is whether a small effect on the trading activities and profits of only one section of an already highly profitable, broad-based, multinational group of companies' should take preference over all other interests. Finally, they argued, the existence of the reserve at Clophill made the exploitation at Woburn unnecessary.

This hard-hitting attack on the strategic need for fuller's earth proved difficult to sustain against the massed expertise deployed by the applicants. It appeared that most of the experts on fuller's earth were already employed in the industry or associated with it in some way. The county council's search for an independent expert who would be able to cast doubt on the strategic need and indicate the prospect for substitutes, proved fruitless. Although a specialist adviser was retained, no witnesses on the strategic need could be called against the applicants 'since their views would not support the case against working the mineral at Aspley Guise'.[37] The local county councillor for the area observed: 'In the nature of things, advice on substitute materials from a Fuller's Earth expert can never be disinterested.'[38] The applicants were able to call on their Director of Research, a senior drilling engineer, the Director of the Mineral Products Division, an expert on foundry materials and a professor of applied geology, all of whom were involved in the use of fuller's earth.

The applicants argued that there were few areas where the material could be commercially exploited,[39] that the areas held in reserve, together with Woburn, were essential to maintain production, that substitutes were either not available, expensive, or unlikely to supplant bentonite in the near future, that the investment already present at Woburn would be wasted if an extension to the workings was not granted, and that failure to maintain production would adversely affect the balance of payments. As far as North Sea drilling muds were concerned, a switch from exploration to development would increase the number of wells drilled. The substitution of polymers would occur in certain drilling operations but it was a complex and very costly process. Bentonite would be required in the foreseeable future and, if not supplied from domestic sources, would be imported.[40] A similar conclusion was true for the foundry moulding industry which accounted for a third of the national demand. There were no substitutes immedi-

[35]Letter from M. Kemp, loc. cit. His figure of 35,000 tonnes was taken from the *Sunday Times*, 19 October 1975, an estimate of the amount of sepiolite and fuller's earth used as cat litter.
[36]Letter from the Clerk to Aspley Heath Parish Council, loc. cit.
[37]Letter from the County Secretary to the chairman. Environmental Services Committee, 29 September 1976.
[38]Letter from Councillor Chapman to the Chairman, Environmental Services Committee, 10 October 1976.
[39]Prof. W. Davies in his statement on behalf of the applicants described geological explorations and concluded that although a full assessment was not available the resources to undertake it would have to come from the industry. 'A hiatus in production could, of course, put an end to further exploration of fuller's earth resources.'
[40]Statement on behalf of applicants by G. H. Smith.

ately available and 'A large number of firms all over the country making an essential contribution to the economy would be profoundly and adversely influenced in their operations by any failure to maintain supplies of the correct type of clay.'[41] Consequently: 'It is clearly in the National interest to secure the maximum benefit from the orderly exploitation of these reserves.'[42] If further working was not permitted the existing processing plant would have to be scrapped (worth £1 million), the industry would be reduced to one supplier, expertise would be lost, imports would increase, and thirty-six employees would be made redundant. The Clophill deposit should be regarded as part of the national reserve and, even if Baulking were to be developed, Woburn would still be needed since its 'product quality and markets are firmly established through 15 years of production'.[43] This conclusion was largely confirmed by the county council's adviser who stated: 'I should say that if a major supplier were to cease production suddenly there would be no time to develop the use of substitutes and suppliers of substitutes would be unable to supply the hungry market.'[44]

ENVIRONMENTAL CONSIDERATIONS

The main opposition to the proposal was based on the environmental impact it would have. In particular it would harm the landscape and forestry of the area, conflict with recreational needs, and impose excessive noise on a quiet residential area. Other potential grounds for opposition such as traffic and agriculture were not applicable in this case.

The site was in one of Bedfordshire's areas of greatest landscape value, at one time considered as a potential Area of Outstanding Natural Beauty. It was considered in the regional plan to be of regional significance for the conservation of fine landscapes. In such areas the county council was adopting a policy that 'will pay particular attention to proposals for development to ensure that the character of these areas is not adversely affected in any way'.[45] The destruction of the landscape was bound to be in conflict with this policy. Conservation of existing woodlands was another policy being pursued by the county council. At any one time about a third of the area would be devoted to mining operations, which would be bound to destroy the 'quietness and tranquillity' of the woodland. A consultation study proposed the improvement of recreational facilities, although it noted the possibility of demands for extracting fuller's earth. The area was close to the expanding new town of Milton Keynes and could relieve the pressure for recreation from the Chilterns area to the south. A survey in the summer of 1976 by the county council revealed that between 79 (Saturday) and 177 (Sunday) people used the site for recreation, half of them living within walking distance and using it mainly for walking.

The local opposition to the mining proposal stressed the loss of recreational potential and the problems of restoring the site after mining operations had eased. They claimed that the area possessed facilities for informal recreation which were 'at their most

[41]Statement on behalf of applicants by A. D. Morgan.
[42]Statement by D. F. McVittie, p. 12.
[43]Ibid.
[44]R. H. S. Robertson (1976) op. cit., 3.6.
[45]Bedfordshire County Council (1977) *County Structure Plan*, Policy 59.

accessible and most charming throughout the ridge'.[46] It was accessible by car from several surrounding centres of population, offering a variety of attractions — walking, wildlife, and picnics. Though it formed only a small part of the proposed Brickhills recreation area it was the most accessible, since other parts were confined to golf courses and woodland with limited access. The local interests had conducted their own survey covering the Bank Holiday period to gain an appreciation of maximum use of the area. At that time four-fifths of the visitors came from outside the immediate vicinity and from a total of 301 comments elicited about the area only 4 had no objection or supported the proposal to mine there. The area, opponents concluded, was 'crucial as an amenity; without it, the Brickhills Recreation Area is a name, not a reality'.

Although the mining proposal included a complete restoration of the site, opponents pointed to the failure of the company to restore the land on the existing site from which fuller's earth had been extracted. Mining had commenced in 1961, but by 1975 only part of it had been grassed and attempts to establish trees had failed. The contours had been levelled. The record of the company led the district council's Planning Officer to fear that 'it is a very difficult matter to restore such a site, after excavation, in this area, to anything like the character and condition that existed prior to the works, however experienced and well-intended the applicants may be'.[47] Some doubts were cast on the ability and intentions of the company to restore the site according to any conditions attached to a permission. The leader of the local opposition commented 'It is a personal view and, sadly, one which I find it disappointing to record, that conditions are so meaningless to applicants, and difficulties of enforcement such a problem'[48] that he had concluded the application should be rejected outright.

The company did not deny the damage that would be done to the amenity and recreational potential of the area, but stressed that the woodlands would require some felling in any event and that the area would be fully restored within twelve years. They had appointed landscape architects to advise on the restoration of the area. The owners of the land, the Bedford Estates, stated that given the age of the trees there would probably have been a decision taken within the period proposed for the excavations 'to fell a large proportion of the areas concerned and to replant'.[49] The company argued that the site covered only 4% of the Brickhills recreation area,[50] a manmade landscape over which there were no viewpoints. They regarded planning policies as recognising the importance of mining despite the acknowledged environmental value of the area. They proposed to retain tree-cover as screens, to relocate the footpaths during operations, and through restoration 'to provide a similar landscape structure to that at present pertaining'.[51] 'It is not possible to show that any permanent harm would be caused by mineral working.' Indeed, the restoration proposed enabled them to claim 'that the land surface will be improved following workings of the mineral'. Attempts to plant trees on the pastoral part of the existing workings had been disappointing owing to drought.

[46]D. A. Sturdy and J. E. Duckworth (1976) Statement on behalf of the local interests, 'Aspley Heath, the importance of the amenity to the public', p.1.
[47]Statement by the Planning Officer, Mid-Bedfordshire District Council, pp. 2–3.
[48]Letter from M. Kemp, loc. cit.
[49]Letter from the Steward of Bedford Estates to the County Planning Officer, 3 November 1975.
[50]Opponents claimed that 18% (the 'largest and best') of the area available for general public recreation (i.e.) excluding game reserves, shooting rights, golf courses, farming, and other uses) would be lost. (statement by Sturdy and Duckworth (1976) op. cit.).
[51]Statement on behalf of applicants by J. B. Clouston, p. 10.

While the environmental and recreational issues were clear cut, though interpretations differed, the evidence on noise was confusing. Noise can be simply defined as
'unwanted sound'. Assessment of noise is subjective and measurement is given in terms
of decibels (dB) and the scale is logarithmic not linear. Thus 'a difference of 10 dB
approximates to a subjective doubling or halving of the loudness sensation'.[52] The
measurement attempts to assess the average experience of loudness. The dB(A) is a
means of reducing the effect of both high- and low-frequency noises to produce a unit
which roughly corresponds to the frequency response of the human ear. The critical
measurement is the dB(A) L_{10} level, that is the dB(A) level which is exceeded for 10%
of the time. It thus relates mainly to peak noise levels rather than ambient levels.

A major problem in relation to noise is the absence of any legally accepted standard
of noise level. Local authorities are empowered to control noise on construction and
demolition sites under the Control of Pollution Act 1976. Certain codes of practice have
been set which apply to the sound made by machinery at construction sites. Little
definitive advice beyond an exhortation in a circular seems to have been given about
noise levels in mining operations. 'The need then is to take every precaution to ensure
that noise emitted by the development does not on the whole make the area a less
pleasant place to live in.'[53]

The company appealed to a standard recommended by the Wilson Committee[54] of an
indoor level of 45 dB(A) L_{10} for a suburban dwelling. They claimed that with silenced
machinery and with corrections for topography the worst sound levels experienced for a
short period with machines working at surface level would be within the standard. 'My
predictions indicate that, when there is no physically solid barrier between the houses
and machines, the recommendations of the Wilson Committee . . . will be met even
with the windows open.'[55] As excavations moved away and became deeper the noise
would be very considerably reduced. The consultant for the local interests suggested
that other corrections, such as for temperature and wind, could also be made which
could increase or decrease the measurements. He argued that the Wilson standard was
both out of date and intended for traffic noise. He appealed to a different standard
which, using the applicant's predictions on noise level, suggested the proposed enquiry
could constitute a nuisance to residents. Using the Wilson standard and the same
measurements as the company, the district council argued that a level at the nearest
dwelling with a window open of 44 dB(A) $L^{10}$was above the 40 dB (A) recommended as
the level that should not be exceeded in a *rural* area.

The debate on standards, corrections, and measurement of noise was esoteric and
inconclusive. The local interests argued that average measurements failed to account
for individual variations in susceptibility to noise levels. Residents in the area were
liable to be sensitive to any new noise intrusion. The consultant for the local interests
made the somewhat gratuitous observation that: 'There is no doubt, therefore, that the
only way to reduce the possibility of noise nuisance from the proposed workings to zero,
is to refuse them.'[56]

[52]Report for applicants by K. Ratcliffe, 'Predicted environmental noise levels from extraction of bentonite at Aspley Heath', February 1976.
[53]Department of the Environment, Circular 10/73, *Planning and Noise.*
[54]Committee on the Problem of Noise (1963), Final Report, Cmnd. 2056, London, HMSO.
[55]Proof of evidence on behalf of applicants by K. Ratcliffe, November 1976.
[56]Technical report on potential noise nuisance on behalf of local interests by K. Attenborough.

The noise issue was not part of the county council's case at the inquiry. Noise pollution was, in any case, a district council responsibility and the County Planning Officer had accepted his district colleague's view that the working would not cause a great nuisance.[57] Their Environmental Health Officer argued that 'Whilst the proposal is obviously an intrusion into a high amenity area . . . I can find no objection'[58] on grounds of noise. However, the district council's Planning Committee decided to reject the application on the grounds that its effect 'would be intolerable by reason of noise and disturbance'. Thus at the inquiry both the district council and the local interests presented evidence on the noise issue while the county council did not. Confusing as much of the evidence on noise appeared, it did have an impact on the outcome of the enquiry.

THE COUNCIL'S DECISION

The application to excavate fuller's earth at Aspley Heath was made on 15 July 1975. The Mid-Bedfordshire District Council recommended refusal on two grounds — doubt about the strategic need for the material and the noise and disturbance it would cause, drawing attention to the proximity of a primary school, two preparatory schools, convalescent homes, and 'the unique physical features of the site'. The county council's Minerals Sub-committee met on the site with representatives of the local parish councils and the district council early in 1976. The report prepared for them by the County Planning Officer appeared to lean in favour of the application. It pointed out that the working was for a ten-year period 'and no permanent damage to the Landscape will be done'.[59] It would only affect a small part of the Brickhills recreation area and there were no access rights in the area other than the footpaths. Restoration would be to a high standard and 'could ultimately be of benefit to the public bearing in mind the existing topography which in some parts is difficult for walking'. At the site meeting the county officers emphasised that if the application were granted it would be easier to control the workings through stringent conditions than if it were left to the results of the inevitable public inquiry if permission were refused. However, the officers required further information before they were prepared to make a recommendation to the Environmental Services Committee. The local interests had the opportunity of presenting their objections informally to the three members of the sub-committee.

Before the Environmental Services Committee met on 29 February 1976 to determine the application, attitudes began to harden. In particular the local interests pressed their case with the chairman of the committee. In a letter to him the leader of the local protestors confessed 'when I first considered this matter I took the view that the application ought to succeed, with conditions'.[60] He had since changed his mind. The County Planning Officer had three choices available to him — to recommend for, or against, or to leave it to the committee to decide. He intimated to the chairman that it had been a hard choice to make but that he felt the permission should be granted.

[57]This view conveyed in a memorandum from the Planning Officer, Mid-Bedfordshire District Council, to the Minerals Officer, Bedfordshire County Council, 26 January 1976. On 22 January he had stated that noise levels of 52–58 dB(A) during the first three months of operations '*will not* constitute a nuisance'.

[58]Memorandum from the Senior Environmental Health Officer to the Planning Officer, Mid-Bedfordshire District Council, 26 September 1975.

[59]Report to the Minerals Inspection Sub-Committee, 6 January 1976.

[60]Letter from M. Kemp, loc. cit.

Accordingly, the members of the committee were faced with a detailed report and a recommendation to accept the application with conditions.

Extensive consultations had been undertaken. The three local parish councils affected by the proposal were opposed to it though one, the least affected, was strongly opposed unless investigations show 'that this deposit must be exploited to meet the national need'.[61] The local amenity society registered its 'categorical objection'. Of course, the leading figures in these various groups were closely in touch with each other, and some were members of more than one body. The Department of the Environment forbore to comment specifically since it had a quasi-judicial role in the adjudication of planning appeals. But it did refer to the strategic plan for the south-east (see above p. 56) and added somewhat ambiguously: 'No doubt, however, you will consider what is said [i.e. about priority for extraction of fuller's earth] in the light of the current supply of and demand for the material and the extent to which these factors may have altered.'[62] The Department of Trade and Industry's concern to sustain production has already been noted. Other consultations had not provoked support or opposition to the proposal but had sought to protect specific interests (e.g. recreation, forestry) if the permission was granted.

Objections were received from thirty-three residents. The main concerns were noise (mentioned 21 times), amenity loss (20), doubts as to strategic need (10), depreciation of residential values (8), proximity of workings (8), and visual impact (4). Some also pointed to the profit motive inherent in the application. The company wished 'to maintain its own profits apparently regardless of other interests'. 'This product is being exported at a vast profit to the Company and presumably to the Woburn Estates also.'

The Committee had before them the results of these consultations but only an indication of the number and type of the objections. They also had to depend on the officer's interpretation of the evidence as given in his report. 'Whilst it is properly the function of Central Government to consider the question of national need nevertheless it is necessary, in my opinion, to obtain as fully as possible the facts relative to this aspect in order to balance this against the environmental damage that may be done to the site and its environs.'[63] Having considered the facts the County Planning Officer concluded that need 'is a determining issue and must weigh heavily in favour of granting a planning permission.' On the environmental issue, felling of trees was inevitable in any case and no permanent damage would be done, therefore the proposal should not be resisted on these grounds alone. The recreational loss would be 'of little consequence' and the proposal would be 'unlikely to constitute a noise nuisance nor would the workings on the whole make the area a less pleasant place in which to live'. Although the temporary loss in the area would be 'regrettable', overall the County Planning Officer felt the objections 'are not so great as to warrant refusal of the application'.

The opposition to the development was presented in a highly effective speech by the Conservative Member for the area in question who was not a member of the committee. He played on the export of the material, its use in luxury products, and its relative insignificance as a product. To suggest that the price of oil would be affected by an increase in the price of bentonite was tantamount to suggesting that the price of meals

[61]Letter from the Clerk to Aspley Guise Parish Council to the County Planning Officer, 16 October 1975.
[62]Letter from the Department of the Environment to the County Planning Officer, 16 October 1975.
[63]Bedfordshire County Council, Environmental Services Committee, 20 February 1976, Agenda Item 15 (10).

would be adversely affected by an increase in the price of pepper and salt. Any conditions imposed were likely to be ignored and the potential felling of trees on the site would not have anything like the same effect as its destruction by mining operations. Profits for the company and the landowners were at the heart of the issue. He urged the committee to follow Oxfordshire's recent example and reject the application on environmental grounds. His speech was applauded by all the members, a quite unprecedented occurrence. Despite its evident hyperbole and deliberately one-sided attack, it drew a sympathetic response. Other members were quick to point out that planning officers constantly chided them for not giving sufficient weight to environmental considerations. The committee unanimously rejected their officers' advice and opposed the application on the grounds that it would do demonstrable harm to the appearance and character of this high amenity area and its environs'; that it 'would conflict with the aim of maintaining and improving this area for public recreation and would reduce, to an unacceptable degree, its tranquillity and charm'; that they were 'not satisfied that the national need for fuller's earth outweighs the environmental damage which would be caused to this high amenity area'; and that alternative reserves of fuller's earth existed with the benefit of planning permission elsewhere in the county at Clophill.[64]

BEFORE THE INQUIRY

The company appealed against the decision and a public inquiry presided over by an Inspector of the Department of the Environment results. The planning officers maintained that the appeal was certain to succeed but the local interests increased their determination to resist it. A Fuller's Earth Liaison Committee (FELIC) was set up, and the local interests made separate representations at the inquiry. The local interests employed a consultant on noise and had a recreational survey undertaken. The Environmental Services Committee, prompted by the local councillor, decided to back their decision by employing a counsel at a cost of £3000 to defend their case.

As the inquiry approached, the local interests intimated their misgivings about the role of the County Planning Officer in this case. The local county councillor wrote to the chairman of the Environmental Services Committee expressing his concern as to whether the County Planning Officer 'is wholeheartedly pursuing the county council's objectives or his own'. He spoke of a lack of confidence and the conviction of FELIC that the officer 'is working against us, not for us. This is not to suggest that there is any venality about this. I am sure that if you or I had been such implacable supporters of the application we would feel it equally impossible to oppose it wholeheartedly now'.[65] As evidence of his mistrust he instanced the fact that consultations were taking place between the officers of the council and the applicants. This was explained by the County Secretary as the common practice in order to agree detailed conditions to be attached to the permission in the event of its being granted by the Secretary of State. At a meeting between the local interests and the chairman of the Environmental Services Committee

[64]Environmental Services Committee, 20 February 1976, Minute 76/k/54. In the Oxfordshire case the planning committee had similarly rejected the officer's recommendation to accept the application by 8 votes to 2.
[65]Letter from Councillor Chapman to the chairman, Environmental Services Committee, 26 September 1976.

further points were raised. FELIC complained of the lack of liaison over the recreational surveys, the inadequacy of the county council's survey, the council's acceptance of the company's statistics on noise, and a general lack of vigour in searching for adequate evidence to oppose the application.

A further difficulty was the obvious difference between the view of the County Planning Officer and that of the Environmental Services Committee. The Assistant Planning Officer working on the case had suggested to his chief that either a recommendation to accept be given or the matter be left for the committee to decide. The County Planning Officer took the view that he should recommend acceptance. According to his Assistant, the County Planning Officer might have weighed the national interest too heavily. The idea that more stringent conditions could be imposed if the county council decided to accept the application rather than having acceptance imposed by the Minister suggested that his recommendation was based on the view that an appeal would succeed. In any case, stringent conditions were acceptable to the applicants and could be negotiated as part of the terms for an acceptance by the Minister. Fear of defeat at an inquiry was hardly an argument in favour of recommending acceptance.

The County Secretary conceded that the Planning Officer could not 'conceal the fact that his own views differ from those of the Committee on what may be termed the political issue involved in weighing environmental considerations against the need to work the mineral'.[66] The QC briefed to represent the council had argued that no attempt should be made to hide this difference of view 'which can be accepted openly since such an issue is not really a matter for specialist opinion in any case'.[67] But he did not feel that the chairman of the committee should attempt to explain his Committee's decision on the grounds that he might 'very easily create the impression that some of the matters which the Committee considered in reaching its decision do not, when examined, support the correctness of that decision'. In sum: 'a limited case presented solidly and well is usually more effective than a case presented on a broader front, some salients of which are too weak to withstand pressure.'[68] It would be up to counsel to justify the committee's decision and it would be better to avoid damaging cross examination by exposing a 'policy' witness. This view seems to confirm Elkin's conclusion that ' "political" considerations were not thought to be relevant points of discussion at an inquiry'.[69] Although there was a conflict it was the committee's decision, not the officer's recommendation, that formed the county council's case. Thus it was in an atmosphere of some mutual suspicion between the local interests and the County Planning Officer, and an open disagreement of view between the County Planning Officer and the members of the Environmental Services Committee, that a united front in opposition to the application was deployed at the public inquiry.

[66]Letter from the County Secretary to the chairman, Environmental Services Committee, 29 September 1976.
[67]Ibid.
[68]Letter from the County Secretary to the chairman, Environmental Services Committee, 22 October 1976.
[69]S. L. Elkin (1974) *Politics and Land Use Planning: The London Experience*, Cambridge, Cambridge University Press.

THE PUBLIC INQUIRY

The public inquiry was held in Aspley Guise in November 1976. The local campaign against the application was visible in the profusion of protest notices, in the wide coverage in the press and on TV, and in the crowded parish hall throughout the inquiry. Most of the arguments concerning the strategic need for the mineral and the environmental harm that would result were well known. The noise issue provided a highly technical and sometimes hypothetical debate, but the opponents managed to stress the lack of concern about the effect of noise on those using the area for recreation. However, the county council's objection on the grounds that there was an adequate reserve elsewhere in the county at Clophill brought an interesting statement from Laportes, the company who held the reserve there. It had previously been anticipated that the Clophill deposit was a long-term reserve intended for use when the Redhill area had been exhausted. It was revealed at the inquiry that working there could commence within three to five years. The extraction would be combined with the working of the aggregate overburden for which there was considerable demand. The fuller's earth would be sent to Redhill for processing. However, the revelation on Clophill was heavily qualified, and the Inspector concluded that its future depended on the economic situation.[70]

The information could be interpreted both for and against the Woburn application. The appellants could argue that there was sufficient national need to justify both Clophill and Woburn, and that, without Woburn, production would be substantially in the hands of one producer. The use of the Redhill plant would mean writing off the valuable asset at Woburn. Conversely, the county council could argue that earlier extraction at Clophill would make good the shortfall resulting from the exhaustion of the existing Woburn site, that two major sites in fairly close proximity in the county would be excessive, and that, by agreement, the Clophill material could be processed at Woburn, thus extending the life of the plant there. Certainly, the early opening of the Clophill site removed any lingering doubts about the correctness of the county council's decision in the mind of the Assistant Planning Officer giving evidence on their behalf. In the event the Clophill deposit appeared to have little influence on the mind of the Inspector who felt 'there is some degree of uncertainty whether the alternative material would be available at a time when the existing workings come to an end'.[71]

The decision of the Minister in favour of mining at Baulking in Oxfordshire, announced in October 1976 (a month before the Woburn Inquiry), appeared to have a bearing on the decision at Woburn, although, as with Clophill, it was possible to argue either way. There were certain obvious parallels between the two cases. The production rates (50,000 tons per annum) and the length of working were similar; there would be a detrimental effect on the environment; and in both cases the members had turned down the application against the advice of their officers. But there were also differences. The Baulking deposit in Oxfordshire was of very high quality; indeed the company claimed 'The exceptional quality of the Baulking deposit merits it being regarded as unique in

[70]In fact Laportes announced eighteen months later that they proposed full-scale working at Clophill by the end of 1978.
[71]Extraction of fuller's earth, land at Old Wavendon Heath. Aspley Heath. Woburn Sands, Inspector's Report, August, 1977, para. 277.

Britain.'[62] It would be used partly in a new process of pelletising iron ore. Although Baulking was not in an area of great landscape value, workings would be detrimental to the village and would affect the amenity of the Vale of White Horse area of outstanding natural beauty.

The case for mining at Baulking was similar to that at Woburn, namely that increased production was needed to meet the shortfall in indigenous supplies in an expanding market. If mining at Woburn ceased, the balance of payments position would be worsened, but production at Baulking 'whether or not extraction continues at Woburn, would make a valuable contribution to the totality of home demand, exports and import savings'.[73] Against this, the Oxfordshire County Council argued that production could be maintained at Woburn; but if not, then the possible alternatives were the opening of the Clophill deposit, an increase in imports, or a new discovery of a substitute less damaging to the environment. Although the Baulking bentonite was of superior quality for most uses, this was not a critical factor. There was some doubt over the future growth of the industry with changes in processing, the use of substitutes, and economic stagnation. The Oxfordshire County Council had also argued the case for mining at Woburn, with its existing plant, labour force, and expertise, rather than at Baulking. Although the Inspector, in reaching his recommendation, acknowledged that mining at Baulking 'would unquestionably have a detrimental impact on the local landscape and on local residents' lives',[74] he considered 'the balance of public advantage lies in allowing the present appeal'.[75] The Minister confirmed his Inspector's view and allowed the appeal. Thus, although Woburn had been cited in the evidence at the Baulking inquiry, the decision had been made on the evidence presented at the time when the issue at Woburn was in doubt.

It is difficult to be certain whether the Oxfordshire decision had any bearing upon that (to be) made at Woburn. At the Aspley Heath inquiry the Inspector did no more than note the successful appeal at Baulking. It may be inferred that he accepted the argument that sinceBaulking could contribute to a new and expanding market, whereas Woburn would maintain an existing one, they were not likely to impinge closely on each other. The interest lies in the similarity of timing, arguments, and outcome of the two inquiries. In principle the decision was the same, but at Woburn the opponents won a minor but not unimportant victory.

THE RESULT

The Inspector, in presenting his conclusions in August 1977, was clearly persuaded by the economic arguments in favour of mining the material. He rejected the claims that substitutes could be readily used and felt that 'the savings to the national economy by using home produced materials would be significant and cannot be lightly discounted'.[76] He dismissed the arguments for Clophill as an alternative, and did not feel that loss of recreational use was sufficient grounds for refusal. However, on the question of noise he had serious reservations, particularly about the levels that would be

[72]Extraction of fuller's earth at Baulking, Oxfordshire, Inspector's Report, para. 39.
[73]Ibid., para. 8.
[74]Ibid., para. 145.
[75]Ibid., para. 149.
[76]Extraction of fuller's earth, land at Old Wavendon, Inspector's Report, 2 August 1977, para. 276.

experienced during the period of the first cut (see Fig. 4.3) when excavations would be at or near surface level and closest to the dwellings. He seized on an alternative direction of excavation suggested by the local interests at the inquiry and proposed that the area nearest the dwellings be excluded. As a result he recommended that the appeal in its submitted form be refused. His summary statement was:

'I appreciate the importance attached to this comparatively scarce mineral and its role in the national economy, but I am of the opinion that the effect of the excavations upon the local community and the landscape would be greatly ameliorated if the operations were to be made in the reverse direction from those expressly sought and the area to be excavated amended in the northern part of the site'.[77]

The Minister allowed the interested parties to make further observations on the possible change in the direction of working and the proposal to stop the workings on the northern part of the site where they would break through the steeper part of the escarpment. The representations did not affect the outcome as proposed by the Inspector. In his decision letter in March 1978 the Minister was satisfied that 'a strong case on economic grounds' had been made and that no alternative materials were readily available. However, he did accept the Inspector's proposition to change the direction of working and to limit its northern extent on the grounds that this would not affect views from the north, and would 'ensure that the disturbance from noise to nearby residents is not such as to outweigh the need to exploit the fuller's earth on the site'.[78] He allowed the appeal, subject to twenty detailed conditions which were substantially similar to those originally proposed by the county planner. Thus the claim that conditions imposed by the Minister would be less stringent than those of the planning authority were not upheld by this decision. The mining interests were victorious on the general principle of excavation, but local opposition had secured a not insignificant victory in the actual terms of the permission. But in the longer term the modification might prove less attractive. Working from south to north meant that residents would experience working moving towards them rather than away from them as originally intended, and this might affect property prices. Given the topographical details of the site it was not inconceivable that a case could later be made out on economic grounds to extract fuller's earth from the northernmost area excluded from the accepted scheme.

Obviously the Inspector had been impressed by the arguments and weight of opinion gathered together by the opponents of the scheme. He seems to have attached considerable importance to the noise issue which was not pursued by the chief antagonists, the county council, and which the local interests' noise consultant confessed he would not have considered 'as important an issue as the preservation of amenity'.[79] Although the local interests were unable to resist the general principle of mining in the area, they were sufficiently persuasive to protect their residences from the worst potential effects of the workings. The issue had aroused local passions and given rise to a highly visible campaign. The local interests had fully exploited their influence with local councils and their expertise in the formal process of the inquiry. They had ensured packed meetings

[77]Extraction of fuller's earth at Old Wavendon, Inspector's Report, 2 August 1977, para. 287.
[78]Department of Environment, Land at Old Wavendon Heath, Aspley Heath, Appeal by Berk Ltd., 3 March 1978.
[79]Personal note from K. Attenborough dated 12 August 1977.

throughout the inquiry. It would be difficult to ignore such a protest and satisfying to reach a conclusion that could bring some consolation to both parties.

IMPLICATIONS OF THE DECISION

Any explanation of the differences of view which emerged between professional planners and the elected representatives over the fuller's earth issue must recognise the ideological and external pressures to which each were subject. Thus the simple model outlined in Chapter 1 becomes more complex when we investigate a specific decision. The various influences on the decision-makers in fact have varying impact, and we may conceive of networks of relationships. The network experienced by the planners will be different but will overlap that experienced by the politicians. Each network will provide the environment in which the issue is considered and judged. The environment within which the planners were working generated different impulses and perceptions to those received by the politicians.

In short, the information available to the planners, and the relationships they enjoyed with central government departments and the mining industry, influenced them to favour the application. The pressure of local interests and the desire at least to appear to weigh environmental issues caused them to stress the problems of reconciling the conflicts. The local politicians, less directly under the influence of government or the mining industry, but more exposed to the pressures and apprehensions of local interests, were swayed in the opposite direction. In justifying their decision they emphasised their role as protectors of the environment and tended to accept arguments which minimised the national need for the mineral. Thus we have a situation where the mining company with reasonable access to the professional planners are in conflict with local interests with clear channels of communication with the politicians. The resulting conflict is left to be resolved at a higher level with the Inspector making recommendations to the Secretary of State. The role of each of these groups of actors — the applicants, the local interests, the professional planners, the local politicians, and the adjudicators at the public inquiry — reveals the ideological, economic, environmental, and political influences which contributed to the decision-making process.

The mining interests

The applicant had a single-minded interest in securing permission to continue extraction of fuller's earth. His economic arguments were clear-cut — he would remain in business as a main competitor to the largest producer, he had guaranteed market outlets, and could maximise the use of the plant and expertise concentrated at Woburn. While acknowledging the damage to the environment he could claim it was short term and would be fully restored, that change in the area was inevitable anyway, and that every effort would be made to reduce the nuisance caused by the extraction. Since fuller's earth was a rare mineral, deposits that offered prospects of viable extraction were restricted.

The applicant had the advantage that statistical information on the reserves, production, trade, and uses of fuller's earth and its future potential were largely the property of the industry itself. It was therefore difficult to contradict his arguments on national strategic need. Experts on fuller's earth were themselves involved in the industry, a fact the county council had discovered when attempting to gain suitable independent evidence to challenge the claims made by the applicants. The mining industry also had the opportunity of access to central government and to the local planning officials. It is obviously very difficult to establish how significant this was since, by its very nature, such access tends to be informal and confidential. But clearly the Department of Industry, sensitive at a time of economic difficulty to the claims of industry, were impressed with the case made out for mining at Woburn. It is a moot point whether the negotiations with the county planners trespassed beyond discussion of appropriate conditions in the event of the application being granted. All one can say is that the county planners, too, were satisfied that the strategic case had been made. At the inquiry the Inspector accepted the force of the economic argument and accepted the application in principle.

Local interests

There has been a reaction to the activities of well-heeled, articulate pressure groups who are seen to stand in the way of 'progress', whether it be in the form of a road proposal, an airport, or an industrial enterprise. The planning system has yielded to the demands for public participation and this has been taken advantage of by highly organised groups who have succeeded in preventing various planning proposals. Whether their success is to be attributed to organisation or to a change in public opinion generally and a downturn in the economy is arguable. But there is a feeling that the pendulum has swung too far and has benefited the well-off rather than the unorganised underprivileged groups. No better testing ground of the power of local interests could have been found in Bedfordshire than at Aspley Heath, a highly attractive area containing a wealthy population intent on safeguarding their environment.

The local population contained those who were prepared to object, to back their objection financially, and to organise their protest drawing upon their political contacts and the local legal and environmental expertise. They were able to apply their muscle on a sympathetic district council to recommend refusal of the application, to orchestrate an impressive series of local objections, and to persuade, through contacts and the well-briefed appearance of their local county councillor, the county councillors to reject their officers' recommendations. They carried their opposition to the point of marshalling a detailed and comprehensive case at the public inquiry. In local decision-making terms the force of Simmie's assertion that 'those groups with most information, education and finance in British society will dominate localised decisions'[80] seemed to be borne out. Their activities, combined with both the planners' and the applicants' compliance, were sufficient to ensure that the application was contingent upon a whole series of conditions. They were also able, by voicing their fears about the potential hostility of the county planners, to maintain the pressure on the county council to make as effective a case as possible. In the event they gained a significant modification of the application.

[80] J. M. Simmie, (1974) op. cit., p. 136.

The professional planners

In Chapter 2 the various ideologies to which planners subscribe were identified. Among these are the desire to reconcile competing land uses in order to achieve an orderly arrangement, and the desire to provide a good environment for healthy and civilised life. Judgements, where ideologies are seen to be in conflict, tend to be made by recourse to the ambiguous notion of public interest. In the case examined here public interest could be construed as the need to protect the environment for the benefit of the local population and those wishing to use it for recreation, or as the need to secure for the country the economic benefits from the winning of a rare mineral. Planners are quite prepared to subjugate local specific interests to the idea of the elusive public interest.[81] Although their pronouncements in the form of recommendations are supposedly grounded in professional judgement, the criteria they use are often open to interpretation and do not point to any definitive conclusion. In other words, planners, knowingly or unwittingly, make political choices.

In the case examined here there was no explicit policy upon which a recommendation could be based. Like many policies of a strategic nature, those relating to mineral workings in general and to fuller's earth in particular offered no firm guidance, leaving individual cases to be treated on their merits. This feature supports the contention made in the opening chapter that decisions tend to be responses to the balance of power existing at particular points in time. They are incremental rather than related to any consistent long-term strategy. Nor was there any useful precedent to lean upon since previous applications had been decided many years before in different economic and environmental circumstances. There does seem a willingness on the part of the planners to be convinced by the force of the applicant's arguments. Little effort was made to challenge the statistics (understandably in the absence of independent experts) and the arguments that substitutes were unlikely to affect the market went largely by default (whereas in Oxfordshire this point was advanced by the county council). Similarly, the existence of fuller's earth elsewhere, notably at Baulking and at Clophill, was not used as an argument against the application by the planners in the report to committee. This seems strange since Clophill was also in the county. The planners accepted the view that Clophill should be regarded as a long-term reserve. But the committee used it as grounds for objection, and their view was, to some extent, upheld by the revelation at the inquiry that production at Clophill could begin if the economic climate was propitious. It was later substantiated by the decision to develop Clophill in the short term. The planners tended also to minimise the environmental damage that would result — stressing, like the applicants, the short term, the restoration, and the lack of disturbance that would occur.

It is, perhaps, inevitable that some rationalisation should be made in a report to justify the planners' decision. It is also possible that the informal pressures applied by central government and by the mining interests should cause them to lean in favour of

[81] A characteristic noted in general terms by A. J. Catanese (1974) *Planners and Local Politics: Impossible Dreams*, Beverley Hills, Sage Publications; 'The planners seek to form an argument that refutes special interest groups in favour of benefits to the elusive public interest' (p. 24). J. G. Davies, (1972) *The Evangelistic Bureaucrat*, London, Tavistock, commenting on the case of Newcastle upon Tyne, states: 'There was, furthermore, friction implicit in the encounter between those who are (or consider themselves to be) the guardians of the public interest and those whose sectional or individual interests have to be subordinated to that public interest' (p. 163).

the application. There seemed to be a prevailing view in the planning department that the application would succeed anyway and that refusal would be costly and futile. In such an atmosphere it is not surprising that the planners were impressed by the pressures they perceived from above, and were resolved to transmit that pressure to their committee. Although the County Planning Officer had no power to take the decision he had the discretion of being able to make a recommendation. At the time he could only have guessed at the committee's reaction but was determined to exercise his right to choose. One may applaud him for courageously deciding to risk rejection by the committee, or condemn him for his foolhardiness and for potentially weakening the county council's stand against the application. Much depends on how the role of a planning officer is viewed, whether it is to offer expert advice or to make political judgements. The case studied here had to be decided on the basis of political judgement, not expert opinion.

Local politicians

The planning committee were clearly vulnerable to pressure from local interests. Although the committee was politically mixed and represented all parts of the county (with no member actually representing the specific area in question) there was a tendency to accept the local view when it was not in conflict with other county council interests. It is difficult to summarise the views of individual members. The decision had no party political overtones, though Labour members were presumably impressed by the idea that the application was profit-motivated and would benefit both the company and the landowner, and destroy the local environment. The Conservatives held similar views in this case and were also sympathetic to the local interests who provided both support and votes for their cause. The applicant had no direct access to the committee and his case was transmitted by the planning officers. Arguably this counteracts the ability of private interests to secure direct access to officials, though in some cases (see Chapter 6) they do have clear channels of communication with influential members.

It might be said that the planning committee did not have before them the full facts of the case, that they had to decide on the basis of evidence distilled by officers and pressure applied by local interests. Some members, the Minerals Sub-committee, and the chairman, had more detailed knowledge through their site visits and briefings by officers. In the committee room, members are liable to be swayed by an argument put with emotion and evident conviction though based on selected and sometimes questionable evidence. This was the case with this application. But they are also aware of their function as the protectors of the interests of their constituents. If any single explanation is possible for the members' unanimous decision, it lies in their conviction that Bedfordshire's interests should be given priority over any others. They felt that it was up to the Minister, if necessary, to overrule them on grounds of national interest.

Herein lies a clear distinction between the planners' view that national interests must be weighed against local ones and that of the politicians who give primacy to local interests. The politicians felt there was a certain inconsistency in the advice they were receiving from their officers, and this reinforced their belief that the application should be opposed. Some time before the fuller's earth issue arose, another part of the

Greensand Ridge near Ampthill had been threatened by an application to extend a chemical works. Although it was on the clay plain it was adjacent to the ridge and next to Houghton House, a classified ancient monument. A previous application to extend the plant had been refused on appeal, though the Inspector had clearly indicated that refusal was on technical grounds of access, siting, and scale, rather than on the principle of the development. The company made a new application late in 1975 which the Planning Officer recommended the committee to refuse on the grounds that it was close to an area of great landscape value and that its scale would 'do demonstrable harm to the visual character of this high amenity area'.[82] Although the principle could not be challenged, given the appeal decision, the new application was, in terms of its height and scale, likely to prove 'an environmental disaster'. Before they took a decision the committee took the unprecedented step of meeting the applicants. Nevertheless, the committee accepted the recommendation adding that they would assist in the relocation of the factory elsewhere in Bedfordshire on land zoned for industrial use.

There were some obvious differences between the two cases. The principle of extending the factory had already been established and an industrial development certificate had been granted. Although the company claimed that expansion at their existing works was the only development they were prepared to contemplate, industry is more footloose than mineral workings, and the applicant was not as restricted as the company wishing to extract one of the few known fuller's earth deposits. The factory would be permanent, the mineral working temporary. But to the committee — and this is the important point — the two applications, which were almost contemporaneous, had evident similarities. Both implied the destruction of a visual and recreational amenity, and both pitched national need against local environment. The factory would be the only UK producer of a particular chemical and could therefore make claims similar to those of the fuller's earth producers. The chemical company claimed that refusal of permission would cause them to invest outside the United Kingdom, implying a detrimental effect on the economy. Government pressure to allow the application was strong in both cases. What the committee could not comprehend was why the planners should accept the national case in one instance but assert environmental values against industrial needs in the other. To the planners the cases might have appeared quite different (as, in many respects, they were), but the members were more sensitive to the similarities and felt there was an apparent conflict in the recommendations put to them by their officers. In both cases the members had attempted to uphold the interests of the community they represented.

THE ROLE OF THE INSPECTOR

The Inspector must attempt to weigh up the balance of arguments. In the case examined here he felt he had to balance the importance attached to the mineral and its role in the national economy against the impact that the working might have in both the short and long run on the area and its residents. The question arises as to what are the criteria upon which he makes a decision, what is in effect a political decision in favour of

[82]Bedfordshire County Council, Environmental Service Committee, 5 December 1975, Agenda Item 11 (10).

one and against the other. Allison portrays the role of an Inspector as follows:

> 'To help make his recommendations, the inspector carries with him a rather light conceptual tool kit, the main items in which are "amenity" and the "public interest". He must first decide whether the interests of "amenity" are threatened by a development. If he considers that they are, he must then decide whether the probable economic gains are sufficient to outweight the loss of amenity. If they are, the development is in the "public" interest"; if not, not'[83]

Although an inspector must apply his subjective judgement it is expected that he will not be partisan. He is, nonetheless, bound to reflect the pressures and influences brought to bear on a case, and the best he can do is avoid disturbing that balance. In this case he was able to find a formula which gave some recognition of the power of local interests while not fundamentally altering the decision in favour of the applicant. On occasions it is not possible to effect a compromise, and an inspector has to choose between competing parties, possibly two local authorities. His choice and the eventual decision of the Minister in such cases may well disturb the balance of power and have clear political implications, as Chapter 6 will show.

Although an inspector makes a recommendation for ministerial approval, the cases are rare when his recommendation is rejected (though one such case is examined in Chapter 6). The planning inspectorate fulfils two important functions. One is as a point of appeal for parties aggrieved by a refusal of planning permission. The other is as the arbiter of local and national interests. It is in this role that the Inspector can be seen quite clearly as a servant of the state maintaining the balance (a word frequently used in his reports) between conflicting interests, an agent for the maintenance of the *status quo*.

CONCLUSIONS

The power to take and to implement decisions of the type considered here is concentrated. Though conflict may occur, it has to be resolved and once taken the decision is final. Development control decisions are supposed to relate to strategic policies, but, as we have seen, these may give little guidance as cases are treated incrementally on their individual merits. Although the power resides in the first instance with the local planning authority, the applicant can resort to appeal, in which case the Minister makes the final judgement. Thus the applicant has two opportunities — the first to gain acceptance at the local level, the other to appeal to a higher authority. The local interests, by contrast, must ensure that they succeed at the local level before they can fight their case at an inquiry. The system, though cumbersome, attempts to give a fair hearing to national and local interests. The various forces are delicately balanced and the limitations on the power of decision-makers is considerable.

The process invites a number of criticisms. The protagonists have differential access to decision-makers. The local interests may not be party to all the information available to the local authority. This was a major complaint of the local interests in this case and led to their suspicions of the role of the planning department. Whether or not there is an

[83]L. Allison (1975) *Environmental Planning*, London, Allen & Unwin, p. 84.

intention to withhold information, a more avowedly open approach might increase the confidence of all participants. The applicants did not have direct access to the members of the planning committee (though they did in the case of the chemical company outlined above). The applicants' case had to be interpreted by the planning officers. Again there seems to be no reason why they should not in every case be afforded the opportunity to put their case directly.

The role of the planning officers is crucial, for they have access to information and are in direct communication both with the applicants and with local interests. They are thus in the position to make a judgement based on assessment of all the information available to them. Much therefore depends on their ability to obtain the evidence rather than rely on single (and sometimes questionable) sources. It is to be expected that they will present the evidence in a way which substantiates their decision.

On many issues an officer's recommendation represents his political assessment of the case, and yet many planners insist that their decisions are based on professional judgement. 'This assertion — that politics can be avoided, and that we are better off without them — is the most truly political of all political ideologies, and the most frightening, for it transfers power to those who assert it, while simultaneously concealing the fact that this has occurred,'[84] This may be true if members blindly accept their officers' judgement, but that was not the case here. Since members are likely to assert their power to take decisions it can be argued that a recommendation from officers is at best superfluous and at worst confusing. If public confidence is to be secured then members should be seen to take decisions on the basis of their own careful examination and assessment of the evidence. This suggests a more active role for members and one which might require more time and training. It lends support to the view that local government should not depend on the services of part-time, largely unpaid members. However, even if members and officers had access to the same information, there is no reason to suppose that their views would coincide. Their judgement depends on how they evaluate the evidence, in other words on which influences seem most significant to them.

Where issues involve questions of national need, it might be possible to devise alternative methods of decision-making to the present system. There are precedents for this, notably the Committee of Inquiry on London's Third Airport. But such a system may leave local interests underrepresented and leave strategic decisions largely in the hands of appointed officials, though the Secretary of State would still have the final say. What is needed is a clearer national strategy providing a framework for discussions at the local level. In the case of rare minerals of potential strategic value there is a case for a national inventory of resources, and statistics of production, consumption, trade, and market trends which would reduce the dependence of decision-makers on the assertions of interested parties.

A national strategy on minerals might also remove the anomaly that permissions once granted, and provided they are renewed, can be implemented at the discretion of the applicant without any change in the conditions whatever the changes in local circumstances. The Clophill site on another part of the Greensand Ridge in

[84]E. J. Reade (1977) 'Some educational consequences of the incorporation of the planning profession into the state bureaucracy', paper for the Annual Conference of the Sociologists in Polytechnics Section of the British Sociological Association, Oxford, April.

Bedfordshire illustrates this point. Here a permission, with only one general condition,[85] was granted in 1952. Since then, environmental values, agricultural interests, and population have all changed, and there is little doubt that if permission were being sought in 1978 it would only be granted, as at Aspley Heath, after an exhaustive inquiry and with tight conditions. As things stood, the local interests had to depend on the county council's ability to negotiate a comprehensive scheme of extraction which would protect the local environment. But the council obviously possessed less muscle by virtue of the principle already being accepted. The answer here is for permissions only to be renewed subject to conditions appropriate to changing circumstances.

If a clearer national policy, and statistics and the ability to alter conditions were to be established, it might be possible to reach decisions on the basis of commonly agreed criteria. It should also prove possible to devise a system of decision-making on such issues which incorporates both local and national interests, that is both representative and accountable. All parties interested in the decision should have equal access to information and to the decision-makers. It might involve integrating the currently separate process of local decision followed by public inquiry. It might also require a wider perspective than that of the present counties, perhaps at a regional scale. It would not preclude the issue being finally determined by the Secretary of State if he felt he should intervene. But it would ensure that the issue is debated by all parties on the same basis, rather than, as at present, being debated at different levels, with different interpretations of the evidence and with little prospect of resolution between implacably opposed interests.

As against this it is possible that by increasing the flow of information, uncertainty and indecision would be encouraged. It would become apparent to all parties how complex the issue really was. They would each possess the same evidence but would make their own interpretation of 'the facts'. The partisans would become entrenched and unwilling to accept the kind of compromise formula that the Inspector was able to construct in this case. Any change in the system might make decision-making more difficult, but that is the price of a more open system than exists at present.

[85]See footnote 21.

CHAPTER 5

Councils in Conflict — Transport Planning in Bedford

FROM CONSENSUS TO CONFLICT

The shift from a pattern of policy-making that is consensual and provides continuity, towards one that expresses conflict and uncertainty, can be illustrated from the recent history of transportation planning in Bedford. A long period characterised by broad agreement over objectives among decision-makers who experienced little external interference and relatively few constraints, was succeeded by one of conflict between ideologies and between organisations responsible for policy, and of severe constraints imposed by declining resources. The outcome of this change was a new direction in transportation policy for Bedford but uncertainty over its future implementation.

Ideological conflict was introduced by the increasing influence of the Labour Party both as a strong opposition to the ruling Conservative group on Bedford Borough Council and, after 1974, as the leading party on the new county council. Labour intended to change the emphasis of transportation planning and received sympathetic support from the officials in the county planning department. Labour was further helped by the concentration of substantial policy-making powers in the hands of the county council as a result of reorganisation. Further support came from the changing emphasis at national level introduced by the Labour government, suggested in its Green Paper on Transport Policy,[1] and eventually endorsed in a White Paper.[2] Public opinion was becoming increasingly aroused over the implications of transportation planning and, to an extent, this too supported change. Declining resources also assisted any move to reduce expenditure on road schemes and car parking, which were major aspects of Labour's policy. These changes at the ideological, organisational, and resource levels all contributed to the new direction in policy-making.

On the other hand, the borough council, which was dominated by members and officials who supported the previous policies, retained significant power and influence. It had already achieved many of its objectives, and road and car parking schemes already implemented or begun were important constraints upon future policy. The long-standing decline of bus services, which accelerated during the early 1970s, and the weakness of local control over public transport, hindered attempts to shift the emphasis away from private to public transport. The possibility (indeed probability) that Labour's tenure of power at county level would be short, and that the resource position might improve and national priorities alter, suggested there was little certainty that the change in policy-making would be reflected in policy implementation. Instead of a shift from one direction to another there was a shift from one direction to uncertainty.

[1] *Transport Policy: A Consultation Document* (1976) 2 vols., London, HMSO, April.
[2] *Transport Policy* (1977), Cmnd. 6836, London, HMSO.

THE PERIOD OF CONSENSUS

Until the 1970s transport planning in Bedford, as in most small and medium-sized towns, was basically concerned with road building and car parking to overcome traffic congestion. The allocation of highway functions to the former Bedford Borough Council, the system of specific government grants for highway projects, and the general absence of political conflict or any apparent public antipathy to road-building policies encouraged an incremental but consistent effort to establish a road network that would accommodate anticipated growth in car ownership without any need for policies of car restraint.

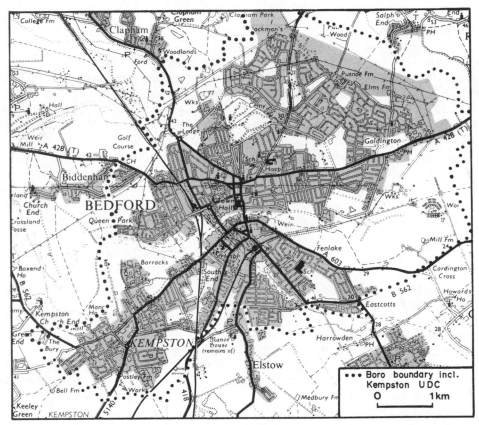

Fig. 5.1. Bedford — the shape of the urban area.

Bedford, with the contiguous area of Kempston, had a population of 89,000 in 1975. It has retained its several roles as county, market, and industrial town, though in employment terms the role of service industries has become, in common with national trends, increasingly important. The town spreads on either side of the River Ouse, and has an elongated shape stretching towards the north-east and south-west (Fig. 5.1). Employment is concentrated in the central area, with major industrial areas in the south-west of the town, in Queens Park to the west, and more recent developments on the northern and eastern fringes. Journeys to work and school have generated complex traffic flows during peak periods and a tendency for congestion to build up on the main radial roads. The river, which is crossed in three places, remains a significant barrier to traffic movement especially on the western side of the town. In addition to locally generated traffic problems, the town suffers from east–west flows of heavy goods vehicles, since it is on one of the major routes from the Midlands to the east coast ports. The problems of crossing the river, of congestion, and of east–west traffic movement have been the consistent themes of Bedford's transport planning since the war, and have been the major issues in various transport studies of the town.

1. The Max Lock Report, 1952

Although various road proposals have pre-war origins, the first explicit and comprehensive statement on Bedford's transport needs was presented in the Max Lock report of 1952.[3] It called for a 'bold policy' to overcome 'the present confusion and traffic congestion which have become a direct threat to the prosperity of the town'.[4] Among the proposals in the plan were a 'western relief road' which would pass through the working-class suburb of Queens Park, cross the river by a new bridge, and so provide a direct link between the main routes on the western and southern sides of the town. Although the Ministry of Transport had previously suggested a route to the west of Queens Park (fig. 5.2), Max Lock thought it would be too far out to take north–south traffic coming in from the south–west. A route further out still would be too long (20 miles), too expensive, and would interfere with the extensive brick industry of the Marston vale. The western relief road was conceived before the M1 was built, to form a bypass for through traffic then passing through the town centre, and would form a cross-town link for local traffic. The chosen route would require little demolition and 'would pass through no land suitable for housing',[5] although it would cross 'excellent housing sites in Kempston and Honey Hill, preventing their economical development as unified neighbourhoods, and itself using valuable housing land'.[6] In fact, 'The only serious disadvantage of the proposed line for the Western Relief Road is that it passes through the middle of the existing Queens Park neighbourhood'.[7] The significance of this statement was to become apparent twenty years later.

On the eastern side of the town the report adopted a proposal for another river-crossing which had been suggested by the Borough Surveyor in 1944. This would provide a link between the growing northern suburbs and the industrial areas to the south. The environmental issues later raised by the proposed bridge were not anticipated at all in the report. This scheme would be part of an inner relief road requiring new links immediately to the north west of the town centre and also on what was at that time the north-eastern boundary of the built-up area. Again the future conflicts associated with some of these proposals could not be foreseen. There still remained the problem of heavy traffic flows across the central bridges. 'The only solution lies in the bold step of building a third bridge in the heart of the town to carry a Central Relief

[3]The Max Lock Group (1952) *Bedford by the River*, London, John Murray.
[4]Ibid., p. 17.
[5]Ibid., p. 57.
[6]Ibid., p. 57.
[7]Ibid., p. 58.

Road to run as close as possible to the existing route'.[8] This would be reached by major road improvements to north and south. The central relief road with its proposed Batts Ford Bridge was to become yet another controversial scheme years later. Finally, the report suggested that a road be constructed to the east of High Street to provide further relief in the central area.

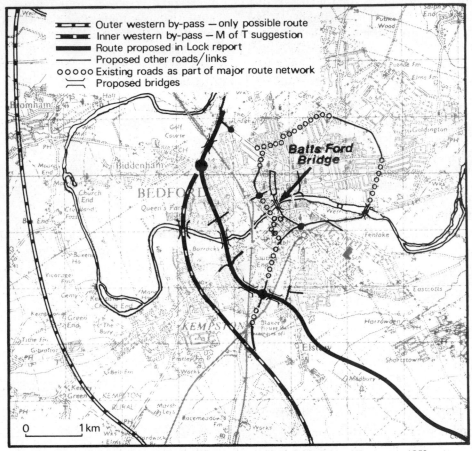

Fig. 5.2. Proposed routes for the western relief road, Ministry of Transport, 1952.

2. The Urban Transport Plan, 1970

The Max Lock report is significant in that it formed the basis of a transport planning philosophy that was pursued by the Bedford Borough Council in the following two decades. In 1970 the council published an 'Urban Transport Plan'[9] which, broadly, reaffirmed the principles of developing an inner relief road system and a western relief road. By this time parts of the Max Lock scheme had been implemented. A new road had been constructed as the north-eastern link of the inner relief road and the two approach roads to the proposed Batts Ford Bridge had been completed. The scheme for this bridge had been abandoned for the time being, owing to county council objection

[8]The Max Lock Group (1952) *Bedford by the River*, London, John Murray, p. 61.
[9]Borough of Bedford (1970) *Bedford: Urban Transport Plan 1968-1977,* October.

on amenity and traffic grounds. A traffic management system in the central area had been introduced to achieve a higher capacity on the existing road network. The western relief road and the eastern crossing for the inner relief road remained firm proposals. Opposition to the latter proposal was beginning to develop and the plan conceded 'that a small but essential part of the Borough Council's highway proposals would remain controversial'.[10]

At the time of publication of the Urban Transport Plan both the borough council and the county council, which shared highway functions at that time,[11] were in broad agreement on the philosophy of transport planning in Bedford. They differed over the question of accessibility to the town centre. The borough favoured an east–west link road across the central area in addition to the inner relief road to achieve maximum accessibility. The county council suggested a horseshoe-shaped road network left open on the southern side leaving the market square as a pedestrianised area to secure a good environment in the town centre. The conflicts over the central area were the beginning of what later became a more generalised conflict between the councils over transportation policy for the urban area as a whole. The breakdown of consensus began, however, with opposition from outside.

CONFLICT

External opposition to the plans

External opposition to the plans was directed at specific schemes, notably the proposal to link the northern and southern parts of the town by a bridge about a mile to the east of the town centre. The bridge would cross the eastern part of Bedford's most well-known amenity, the Embankment. The 'Bedford Society', an amenity pressure group whose chairman lived close to the area threatened by the proposed bridge, fought a successful delaying action. By 1972 the Bedford Society had been joined by another pressure group, 'Crisis', formed specifically to oppose the completion of the inner relief road which, in addition to spoiling the amenity of the riverside, would convey traffic through northern and predominantly middle-class suburbs. Their aim was to demonstrate an alternative strategic plan which could avoid 'the need to sacrifice those vital areas of residential and amenity life which are currently endangered'.[12] Essentially, their plan was to move the location of the controversial bridge further to the east and to link it up with the western relief road, so that east–west through traffic could pass round the south of the town, thus avoiding the northern part of the inner relief road (fig. 5.3). Although Crisis claimed that their scheme would save amenity and keep residential areas intact, its consequence would be the diversion of heavy traffic flows through Queens Park and through the residential districts of the south of the town, all of which were working class. Whether consciously or not, the outcome of the Crisis proposals would redistribute the environmental costs of highway improvements from the more middle-class to the working-class parts of the town. The opposition of the Bedford

[10]Ibid., Foreword.

[11]Until local government reorganisation in 1974, responsibility for highway planning was vested in highway authorities which included county, borough, and district councils. In 1974 the new county councils became transportation authorities covering road improvement, maintenance, traffic management, and public transport co-ordination. They could form agreements whereby district councils acted as their agents for the implementation of projects (see footnote 18 below).

[12]'Crisis' (1972) *Alternative Proposals*.

Society and Crisis was, however, unable to prevent the bridge to the east being constructed. But the campaign against heavy vehicles using the northern part of the inner relief road was successful, since the borough council imposed a 5-ton weight limit on part of it. This decision effectively maintained the route for heavy vehicles across the town centre.

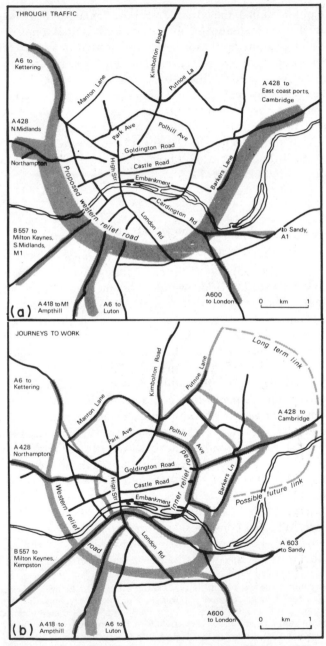

Figs. 5.3. (a) and (b) 'Crisis' transport proposals for Bedford, 1973.

Political opposition to the plans

The political effect of the borough's proposals on poorer districts such as Queens Park caused the breakdown of the existing political consensus. Bedford Borough Council was Conservative-controlled throughout the period from when the transport plans were first put forward until local government reorganisation in 1974. The broad objective of the council, in so far as it can be explicitly stated, was to secure the growth and prosperity of the town and maintain its attractiveness as a centre for the surrounding region. This was to be achieved by promoting industrial, commercial, and residential development, and in particular to develop the retailing and commercial functions of the town centre. In transportation terms this involved allowing 'the free movement of vehicular traffic around and on the approaches of the town centre'.[13] In the centre itself, pedestrianisation of the main shopping streets would be encouraged with sufficient off-street car parking capacity to keep ahead of demand. The emphasis of policy was to relieve congestion and accommodate future increases in vehicle movement. Although the Urban Transport Plan included as an objective 'to assist public transport', it did not foresee any new or improved services. 'It is not the Borough Council's intention to impose any undue restrictions on the use of cars for travel to work or to the shopping centre which would compel employees to use public service vehicles more than at the present time.'[14]

Until the early 1970s this approach had met with little political opposition. The small Labour group on the council had endorsed the transport plans, including the moribund proposal for a central relief road. In 1971 Labour won 5 of the town's 7 wards and in 1972 (the last council elections before reorganisation) 4, giving them a majority of councillors (11 Labour and 10 Conservative) but with only 1 out of 7 aldermen they could not command an overall majority. The new members of the Labour group had become identified with the opposition to the council's transport policies and succeeded in presenting an alternative ideological viewpoint. Like the pressure groups, their immediate concern was the environmental damage that was likely to result from the completion of the inner relief road, but it was the destruction of housing that would be necessary if the western relief road were constructed on the route envisaged by the borough council that led to the most sustained Labour attack on the road proposals. Labour's attempts to change policies were soon to succeed as a result of political and organisational changes combined with a declining level of resources.

THE CHANGING CIRCUMSTANCES

1. Organisational

As a result of local government reorganisation, Bedfordshire County Council became the transportation authority in 1974. A new system of annual transport policies and programmes (TPPs) was initiated, through which the county council submitted its policy and priorities to the Department of the Environment (after 1976 to the Department of Transport). The department then allocated a transport supplementary grant

[13]Borough of Bedford (1970) op. cit., p. 39.
[14]Ibid., p. 37.

(TSG) on the basis of these proposals.[15] The County Structure Plan submitted to the Minister for the Environment in 1977 included statements of transport priorities for the period up to 1991. In terms of the geographical areas of the county, Bedford was ranked third in priority out of four in the county,[16] and in terms of policy areas, road improvements and car-parking projects ranked below road maintenance and public transport.[17] Thus Bedford Borough's cherished road projects and car-parking proposals were low in the county council's scale of priorities.

The county council's control over the implementation of its policies was, however, limited. Central government controlled the allocation of resources, and public transport was in the hands of the National Bus Company and British Rail. The district councils had power to provide car parking and, as the local planning authorities and agents for the county council, they had considerable influence over transport policy for their areas.[18] They possessed considerable influence over implementation.

2. Resources

A second factor influencing a change in policy was the deteriorating financial climate. Even if the political will had favoured continuation of Bedford's transport policies, it became increasingly clear that there would be insufficient finance to complete them within the time-scale (1977) identified in the Urban Transport Plan. With about £2 million per year available for all road improvement schemes in the county, the western relief road, estimated to cost about £5 million, could absorb the total road budget for the equivalent of two and a half years. In sum, it became clear that financial support would only be forthcoming in the immediate future for those projects accorded highest priority, schemes which could demonstrate a range of environmental and public transport benefits as well as improving traffic flows generally. For the county council it became a question of weighing up the relative merits of investment in a range of schemes over the county as a whole, including roads to relieve congestion in the towns and bypasses to take heavy traffic away from villages. It was clear that certain schemes would have to be deferred for a long time or abandoned altogether.

3. Political

The third factor in changing the emphasis of policy was a changing political climate. Labour became, in 1973, the largest party on the new county council, which remained a

[15]Transport supplementary grant is explained in Chapter 3, footnote 11, p. 44.
[16]Bedfordshire County Council (1976) *Transport Policies and Programme 1977-8*, p. 44.
[17]Ibid., p. 39. Also Bedfordshire County Council (1977) *County Structure Plan*, pp. 27-28.
[18]As Chapter 3 footnote 16 explains, district councils may act as agents for county councils in certain transportation matters. Under the arrangements made in Bedfordshire, the North Bedfordshire Borough Council acted as agents for the county council for road maintenance, highway improvements up to £200,000, and traffic management. The arrangements could be renewed, amended, or terminated after a five-year period. Attempts to withdraw agency functions were made in 1977 by the outgoing and incoming administrations. In both cases district council pressure on county members was sufficient to ensure the arrangements were maintained.

'shadow' authority[19] until April 1974. The Labour opposition on the borough council had provided some of the leadership on the new county council. Four of the borough Labour councillors and one from Kempston had been elected to the new county council in April 1973. Two of them became members of the county's Environmental Services Committee, one as chairman and the other was the member for Queens Park ward through which the proposed western relief road would pass. During the transitional period 1973—4, with the county council preparing to take over from the borough council, Labour members were able to challenge borough policies both in opposition on the borough council and from a position of relative strength (though not overall control) on the new county council.

The western relief road was the source of the greatest antagonism between the two councils. The construction of the road required the demolition of 118 dwellings in the Queens Park area. The borough council, having secured planning permission for the route, had been purchasing the dwellings as they came on the market. To speed up the process they obtained a compulsory purchase order and applied to the Ministry for a financial allocation to construct the road. Meanwhile, the new county council had adopted Labour's resolution to review all aspects of transportation policy and accordingly 'all projects, including the Bedford Western Relief Road . . . [were] . . . subject to reappraisal'.[20] By the time the borough council lost its highway powers to the new county council, all but a few properties had been demolished, and the line of the road was ready for construction to begin. Thus while the supporters of the road had succeeded in having the houses demolished, its opponents were able to delay its implementation. It is arguable whether money would have been allocated to the scheme in the absence of political conflict. Paradoxically, the opposition to it may have encouraged the demolition of houses by the borough council who could thus hope to pre-empt any future attempt to prevent the road being constructed.

The conflict over the western relief road was the climax of a gradually intensifying conflict over Bedford's transport policies. It proved also a watershed. Transport planning had now become a major issue of political and public debate. The western relief road issue became subsumed in a more generalised and comprehensive confrontation between two councils. Although party-political differences were the catalyst of conflict, after reorganisation the conflict transformed itself into a power struggle between two councils which resulted in deadlock.

DIVERGING POLICIES

The conflict between councils had both a party political and a bureaucratic dimension. Although conflict had not been entirely absent between the councils before the emergence of public concern and political opposition in the 1970s, it had been confined to specific points of disagreement. Moreover, since both former councils had been predominantly Conservative the conflict lacked any party-political overtones. After 1974, the new county council's Environmental Services Committee, led by the Labour

---

[19]Elections for the new local authorities took place in 1973, a year before reorganisation occurred in April 1974. This gave the new councils time to establish their administration and appoint officers. It also led to conflict between the 'shadow' councils and the old councils due to retire in 1974.

[20]Bedfordshire County Council, 20 December 1973, Minute 73/196.

group and generally supported by the Liberals, provided a distinctive approach to transportation planning. The emphasis was on improvements to public transport, resistance to further car-parking projects in town centres, and careful reappraisal of all road projects. This broad programme was given general support by the officials in the county council.

In 1974 Bedford Borough became administratively part of a wider area including Kempston and the surrounding rural area. Although the Labour Party with 22 seats was the largest single party, the Conservative with 20 seats and the tacit support of the independent members effectively maintained their control over certain areas of policy, notably local planning and transportation. The chairman of the Public Works Committee (and later leader of the council) had been chairman of the Highways Committee of Bedford Borough Council during the period of growing political conflict before reorganisation. Continuity was also maintained in the person of the Director of Planning and Development who had held a similar post on the former borough council. The approach these men followed differed but little from that expressed in the Max Lock report and later reaffirmed in the Urban Transport Plan. Local government reorganisation changed the context of the conflict. In order to achieve consistency in policymaking, or to resolve differences, consultation machinery was established between the two councils. This included an exchange of observers at appropriate committee meetings, regular joint advisory committee meetings, a series of *ad hoc* meetings to resolve specific issues, technical meetings between officials, and the meetings of the Bedford Urban Transportation Study Steering Group and Technical Panel. During the space of a single year, 1975–6, forty-six meetings were held at various levels between the two authorities although the borough council claimed that the arrangements for consultation were 'completely inadequate'.[21] The frequency of meetings was a symptom of underlying and fundamental policy differences. Consultation provided a forum for procrastination rather than a vehicle for resolving conflict.

CONFLICT OVER CAR PARKS

North Bedfordshire Borough Council maintained the strategy towards car parking of its predecessor. This issued from its belief that 'the private car is an essential component of provincial life and one which no reasonable form of legislation can exclude from the social and commercial life of the community'.[22] Consequently 'unreasonable restrictions on car parking in the present climate of public opinion would deter the large shopkeeper from either coming to Bedford or expanding existing shops to the detriment of the centre as a whole'.[23] Car-parking policy was permissive, designed to ensure that the 'optimum amount of parking space was provided in the right place and subject to controls on its use that were appropriate to local circumstances'.[24] Certain minimum standards of parking were required of developers as a condition for planning permissions. In Bedford, however, this requirement could be commuted to a payment towards the cost of multi-storey car parks. This possibility minimised the demand for

[21]Views of North Bedfordshire Borough Council on Transport Policies and Programme 1977–8, p. 1.
[22]'Car parking and road proposals in Bedford central area', report for joint meeting of members of Bedfordshire County Council and North Bedfordshire Borough Council, 2 December 1975, para. 3.23.
[23]Ibid., para. 3.32.
[24]Bedfordshire County Council (1968) *Parking Standards*, November, p.i.

central-area land for parking and potentially brought more parking under public control. Multi-storey car parks were regarded as the best solution to the parking problem, as they could remove cars from the streets and from extensive surface car parks. Although they were costly to build, the borough council considered that land savings and the rateable value from ground-floor lettings should also be taken into account. In addition, multi-storey car parks brought unquantifiable environmental benefits and attracted central area investment.

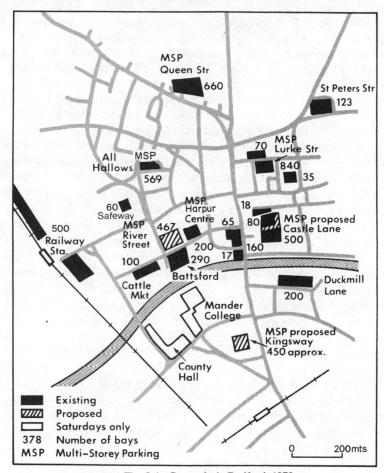

Fig. 5.4. Car parks in Bedford, 1978.

By 1975 Bedford had three multi story car parks which amounted to 58% of the total public off-street car-parking provision (Fig. 5.4). But public off-street accounted for only 42% of the total parking spaces in the town centre.[25] The borough council intended to build three more multi-storey car parks designed to replace some of the surface and on-street parking and to cater for increasing demand. The former county council had agreed in principle to two of these, and in 1973 granted an outline planning permission

[25] Of 8392 parking bays, 4074 (48.5%) were private non-residential, 3548 public off-street (42%), and 770 (9%) on-street parking spaces. Bedford Urban Transportation Study (1975), 'The car-parking situation,' p. 2.

for the third car park which was an integral part of a £10 million redevelopment site consequent upon the relocation of the Bedford Modern School (direct grant) from the centre of the town.[26]

The new county council adopted a fundamentally different attitude to car parking from that of the borough council. Their eventual aim was to achieve some balance in transportation strategy, and they contended that an excess of parking supply over demand could undermine this aim. By encouraging work journeys by car it could increase problems of peak-hour congestion. This would cause delays in public transport and loss of passengers. The borough council argued on this point that any transfer of passengers from cars to buses would accentuate the peak-hour problems of bus operation, that public transport could not cope with the transport needs of the rural areas, and that any encouragement of the off-peak use of the private car might result in a decline in public transport patronage.

The county council also argued against further car parking provision, on grounds of cost, including the three proposed multi-storey car parks formerly accepted in principle. At a time of declining public expenditure, especially in the field of transportation, it was irresponsible to build further car parks (however financed) which would inevitably mean that other (and by implication more desirable) programmes would have to be cut. If parking supply began to outstrip demand, the chances of securing higher revenues from car parking would be reduced. Apart from the cost of the car parks themselves, adequate road capacity would need to be created to service them and to contain the increased traffic flows that could result. The county council viewed car-parking restraint as an essential ingredient of an overall transportation strategy. By influencing the supply and use of car parking through planning policies and tariff structures, they hoped to achieve a balance between the various elements of transport and to make car parking financially viable.

In Bedford the possibility of using parking controls as a means of traffic restraint was found to be remote. A parking utilisation survey in 1972 had revealed that, on a typical weekday, average utilisation was 60.9%, and a follow-up survey completed in May 1975 showed a similar position of 60.5%. But the average utilisation of multi-storey car parks in 1975 was only 46.4% on a typical weekday.[27] Since multi-storey car parks were the most costly and least used, the chances of attaining financial viability would be difficult. A future projection to 1991, assuming no further car parks were built beyond those committed (i.e. excluding the three multi-storey car parks proposed by the borough council), forecast that demand would then amount to 84% of supply. On this basis it was possible to conclude that 'even if one allows a 4% p.a. growth in parking demand, and totally ignores any other influences then even at peak periods on market day, Central Area demand will not exceed supply until the late 1980s'.[28]

Between 1974 and 1977, the dispute focused around two of the proposed multi-storey car parks. The new county council, under the influence of the Labour group, anxious to bring car parking under its control, adopted an interim parking policy for the area south of the river in central Bedford, an area of predominantly commercial development

[26]Some of the land-use and financial implications of this relocation are dealt with in Chapter 6.

[27]Statistics of this kind are highly contentious. Nonetheless the lack of use of multi-storey car parks was clearly identified. The newest of the three had only an 8% utilisation when surveyed on a typical weekday shortly after it had been opened.

[28]Bedford Urban Transportation Study (1975) *Survey and Immediate Action Report*, A. M. Voorhees and Bedfordshire County Council, September, p. 65.

including County Hall and the Higher Education College. It was here that the borough council wished to site the Kingsway car park which would both redistribute existing parking provision in the area and yield about 500 additional spaces to account for the demand generated by new commercial development in the area. The county council stated that it 'will not permit the creation of further car parking areas in the town beyond those which are currently under construction, or which are required for operational purposes in connection with new development proposals'.[29] At the same time it had embarked on a major transportation study for the Bedford area whose outcome could be prejudiced by further car-parking development. The Kingsway car park would attract mainly journeys to work which would overload the road network with little prospect of road improvements being undertaken to cope with increased congestion.

Although the parking policy was an interim one pending the results of the transportation study, it marked a radical departure from previous policies. The Kingsway dispute was soon overshadowed by the county council's efforts to prevent the development of the car park on the Modern School site at River Street in the main shopping area north of the river. In the Kingsway case no planning permission had been granted, and both the county planners and the Labour members were anxious to forestall its development. River Street was a more sensitive and complex issue.[30] Planning permission had been granted by the previous authority, and the officials at County Hall were not enthusiastic about attempts to revoke or modify it. The Labour group regarded it as a central issue if their new parking policy was to succeed. The TPP suggested parking restraints, all transport projects were under review, a policy for restricting parking south of the river had already been adopted[31] and its principles could be extended to the central area north of the river. The Bedford transportation study had not included River Street car park in its committed projects, which would require an access road to be provided by the county council, and would introduce heavy traffic flows into the heart of the town on a trunk road. It was also possible that finance for the car park would have to be found out of the county council's transportation budget, thus absorbing funds that could be spent on projects of higher priority elsewhere in the county. To avoid this the county council refused to endorse the car park. Their next move was to attempt to stop the car park altogether, but the resolution of the Environmental Services Committee to discuss 'the possibility of modifying the extant planning permissions . . . so as to exclude the proposed multi-storey car park and to provide for some suitable alternative use of the site . . .'[32] met with formidable financial, procedural, legal, moral, and political obstacles.

[29]Bedfordshire County Council (1975) *Transport Policies and Programmes 1976–7*, p. 48.

[30]The car park (about 500 spaces) was in addition to one (200 spaces) already built on the site. They were integral parts of a multi-million-pound shopping development occupying a large island site in the town centre (see Fig. 5.4). The development of this site involved the two councils in disputes over road proposals in addition to the parking issue. The borough wanted a two-way road on the southern and western sides of the site to enable traffic to be removed from the other two sides. The county council preferred a one-way system allowing only buses to penetrate the main shopping street along the north of the site. The borough council's attempts to delay the county's scheme led to a vote of 'no confidence in the North Bedfordshire Borough Council's willingness to discharge certain highway functions on behalf of the County Council' being passed (Labour and Liberals for, Conservatives against) in April 1976. The new county council in 1978 were proving sympathetic to the borough's views on pedestrianisation of the central area.

[31]'An iterim policy for car parking south of the river, Bedford', Environmental Services Committee, Agenda Item 10 (23), 28 February 1975.

[32]Environmental Services Committee, Minute 75/k/87, 21 March 1975.

CAR PARKING — THE COMPROMISE

If the county council wished to prevent the River Street car park being developed, it had several hazardous courses open to it. The most dramatic would be a revocation of the planning permission. Such a step could involve the council in large claims for compensation from the various interests involved in the commercial development of which the car park was an integral part. All attempts to elicit the necessary financial information on the likely consequences of revocation failed, since the borough council, understandably, refused to co-operate. Nonetheless, in March 1976 the Environmental Services Committee resolved to revoke the planning permission (Labour for, Conservative against, Liberal abstained). This was done in the absence of financial information or any recommendation from the officers. It provoked a flood of letters from the interested parties in the development, all vigorously opposed to any change in the plans for the site. These spoke of a 'binding legal agreement', the rarity of opposed revocations being confirmed by the Minister, 'complete shock' at such a sudden change of plan, and long-standing agreement entered into 'in good faith'.[33]

Revocation would have been difficult to justify unless the county council had committed itself first to a new parking policy on the lines of the interim policy outlined in the TPP and which would replace the more permissive policy under which permission for the River Street car park had originally been granted. Accordingly, the Labour group, with some Liberal support, succeeded in establishing in July 1976 that in the major urban areas 'no new parking spaces for motor vehicles shall be provided, permitted or required beyond those which are currently under construction . . . or which are required for operational parking space . . . or which are required to accommodate disabled drivers'.[34] This represented a fundamental change from a permissive to a restrictive policy on car parking. By this time, however, a decision had already been taken not to persist with the revocation order but to open up direct member-level negotiations with the borough council.

The Labour group on the Environmental Services Committee had recognised the weakness of their position. They were not certain of carrying the support of the whole Labour group when the issue was put to the full council, let alone the other political groups which together outnumbered them. They lacked any firm support from their officers. Even if a revocation order had been passed, the chances of it being confirmed by the Minister after the inevitable public inquiry were, it was felt, slim. In the unlikely event of the order being confirmed, the council would still face an unknown bill for compensation. While this might have been reduced by the granting of an alternative permission on the site (e.g. offices), the gamble was too great to take, although the threat could be made in the event of a failure to achieve a compromise.

The negotiations revealed that the borough council were not prepared to reduce the size of the car park but would finance it themselves. If the car park became a charge against the county's allocation of transport supplementary grant, the borough would agree to a corresponding reduction in transportation expenditure on other projects in the Bedford area. Such a sacrifice indicated the importance they attached to a car park which completed a multi-million-pound shopping development in the town centre. At the same time the car park would largely replace existing surface parking in the area.

[33]Environmental Services Committee, various letters objecting to proposed revocation, Agenda Item 10, 4 June 1976.
[34]County Council, Minute 76/113, 8 July 1976.

Although the county councillors were anxious to secure a copper-bottomed agreement, the negotiations amounted to no more than a declaration of intent on the borough's part.[35]

This long bureaucratic and political struggle had, in the event, hardly changed the situation. Although the county council could claim the possibility that existing car parks would be soaked up when the new car park was built, this was a pyrrhic victory. The borough council had maintained their policy, any loss of surface parking was consistent with it, and they had left the way open for changes in the future should the political or financial climate change. However, so long as the county maintained its firm stand on further parking, future proposals could be resisted more easily. Despite posturing on both sides, a vigorous exchange of uncomplimentary correspondence, a resolution of no confidence in the borough passed by the county council, and attempts at revocation, little had been achieved and an enormous amount of energy, expertise, and resources had been absorbed in the conflict. The change in political and organisational power had been sufficient to alter the direction of policy but unable, on this issue, to reverse it.

The conflicts over the western relief road and the River Street car park produced the most rancour over transport policies in Bedford, but there were several other detailed disputes which were also symptoms of fundamental disagreement.[36] The balance of power was precarious and deadlock had resulted. But the environment of the debate could be altered by external factors, among them the availability of resources and changing political and public attitudes. Such a change was introduced through a transportation study of the area undertaken by consultants. The study had been set up by the county council in an attempt to gain a disinterested appraisal of Bedford's transport problems and in particular to try to break the deadlock over the western relief road and parking policy.

THE BEDFORD URBAN TRANSPORTATION STUDY

Criticisms of transportation studies

The Bedford Urban Transportation Study (BUTS) had been established at a cost of £113,000 in 1974 on the grounds that the Department of the Environment required comprehensive studies by an approved list of consultants to support TPP submissions; that such a study was essential in the preparation of the structure plan; and that the council had resolved to reappraise all transport projects and had no survey basis for such reappraisal in the Bedford area. It was decided to employ the same consultants (A. M. Voorhees) who had undertaken the Luton, Dunstable, and Houghton Regis study and the rural public transport study,[37] both of which had reported in 1974. As a further justification it was suggested 'that the study could well result in large savings elsewhere,

[35]This was evident from differences in wording of the recommendations of the two councils. The county council recorded that: 'the joint intention of the two councils is . . . that the following issues are agreed' whereas the borough's interpretation was 'the joint intentions of the two councils on the basis of which the multi-storey car park proceeds.' Environmental Services Committee, Agenda Item 4, 28 January 1977.
[36]These included the question of whether buses should be allowed in pedestrianised streets as proposed by the county council. A modest scheme closing one street to all traffic except buses took two years of negotiations before it was implemented.
[37]A. M. Voorhees (1974) *Luton, Dunstable and Houghton Regis Transportation Study, Phase 2,* 2 vols., June; A. M. Voorhees (1974) *Public Transport in Bedfordshire,* July.

e.g. if a result of the Study was that the Western Relief Road was deleted, this would mean an immediate saving of £5 million'.[38]

Transportation studies have become an accepted technique of planning and have been criticised on various counts.[39] Such studies tend to adopt a 'traffic functional' approach, that is, they start from the premise that there is a 'problem' of movement and accessibility, acute at peak periods when congestion is greatest, which requires solution through some combination of traffic management or restraint, and public transport and highway investment. The relative significance of the problems between different study areas has been largely ignored. Thus Bedford, which has a miniscule traffic problem compared to a large conurbation or even Luton, became nonetheless a worthy target for the panoply of sophisticated techniques at the disposal of the transportation planner. Among the technical criticisms are that transportation studies have tended to 'utilise the relationships established between the present-day land-use and movement and rest on the assumption that this relationship will not alter materially in future'.[40] They 'have been criticised as having a built-in bias in favour of the private car'.[41] They have concentrated on the quantifiable elements of cost and benefit. Attempts have been made to overcome some of these problems, and transportation studies have improved in their technical performance introducing alternative land-use forecasts, budgetary constraints,[42] flexibility to allow for uncertainty and changes in the relative attractiveness of different modes, continuous monitoring, and some assessment of the social costs and benefits of alternatives. A more fundamental criticism, perhaps, is the imputation that such studies have been 'conditioned to the use of those objectives implicit in the data collection and forecasting state'[43] and 'there is no doubt that too little attention has been given to the implicit assumptions of values within transportation studies'.[44] This raises the point that transportation is a political issue and that technical procedures have begun to outstrip political comprehension. It suggests that politicians need to be involved more closely in the policy- and decision-making functions.[45] Without political involvement, planners have fewer means to test the political credibility of their plans. Politicians may choose only those parts of the plan which attract them, which are least contentious, or easiest to grasp or implement. If full and public debate (including some involvement of the public) is not undertaken, a plan may well be exposed to subsequent attack from interests who feel they have been inadequately represented.

[38]Letter from the Deputy County Planning Officer to the chairman, Environmental Services Committee.
[39]See, for example, M. J. Bruton, (1970) *Introduction to Transportation Planning*, London, Hutchinson, 2nd ed., 1975; M. J. Bruton (1974) Transport planning, in M. J. Bruton (ed.) (1974) *The Spirit and Purpose of Planning*, London, Hutchinson; P. J. Hills (1974) Transport and communications, in G. E. Cherry (ed.) *Urban Planning Problems*, London, Leonard Hill.
[40]M. J. Bruton (1974) loc. cit., p. 183.
[41]M. Roberts (1974) *An Introduction to Town Planning Techniques*, London, Hutchinson, p. 382.
[42]The Transport Expenditure Planning Assumption (TEPA) was introduced by the Department of the Environment in 1970 to enable transport plans to be produced within the limit of resources likely to be available. It includes all transport projects, capital, and revenue, whether publicly or privately financed, except trunk roads, loan charges, and road maintenance.
[43]D. N. M. Starkie (1973) *Transportation Planning and Public Policy*, Progress in Planning Series, vol. 1, Part 4, Oxford, Pergamon Press, p. 346.
[44]M. Roberts, (1974) op. cit., p. 384.
[45]See T. M. Ridley and J. O. Tressider (1970) Replies to comments on 'the London Study and Beyond', *Regional Studies*, **4** (1) 81–83; A. T. Blowers (1977) Transport planning: a new direction? *Town and Country Planning Summer School, Report of Proceedings, Nottingham, 1976*, pp. 16–20.

Political and public involvement

Obviously greater political and public involvement does not of itself ensure that conflicts will be overcome and that a plan will gain general and continuing endorsement. But such an approach can lead to a full expression of conflict during the plan-making stage and a more informed basis on which political judgements can be based. The transportation study of the Luton area was undertaken by council officials and consultants, and elected members were not involved until a preferred plan was recommended. Given the controversies surrounding transport planning in Bedford, such an approach would have been politically unrealistic, and so a Steering Committee consisting of 5 county councillors (3 Labour, 2 Conservative) and 1 borough councillor (Conservative) was established. The committee included the chief protagonists in the dispute between the two councils. The committee was able to influence the terms of reference, the objectives, and the development of the study.

The Luton study had not been exposed to any public participation during its formulation. By the time of local government reorganisation, public involvement had become almost obligatory in planning, and it was felt that the relevance and acceptability of the Bedford study could be better assured if interested organisations and individual opinions on transport issues were canvassed. Accordingly, a Community Involvement Programme (CIP) was evolved, and this represented 'a change of emphasis from consultation to involvement and participation'.[46] The programme had three components. Firstly, there was a registration of the views of organisations. They were each presented with a booklet[47] inviting them to identify transport problems, set policy objectives, and, by means of a planning 'game', to design a transport plan for the area within a budget of £7.5 million. Altogether, 56 out of 130 organisations approached attended meetings, 30 submitted detailed plans, and 23 were still actively interested when consulted at a later stage on the transport alternatives for the area. Secondly, a series of household reviews was undertaken, stratified according to social class and socio-economic group, and controlled for various parts of the study area. 'The aim of the research is to provide a detailed understanding of the culture, life style, needs, desires, and transport problems of the people for whom one is planning.'[48] Finally, group discussions were held and developed around particular topics or problem areas.

The CIP performed two functions. One was as an integral component of the overall study. This is difficult to assess, but certain findings did have a material effect on the direction the study took. In general, people appeared to find journeys within the Bedford area easy to make (80% found them 'fairly' or 'very easy'). 'The main reason for difficulties in making journeys which were perceived as "fairly" or "very difficult" was seen to be inadequacy or inefficiency in the public transport and these reasons were followed by other traffic. . . . Parking did not feature very significantly as a disadvantage in the fairly or very difficult journeys.'[49]

This view reinforced the parking survey findings quoted earlier and led to the conclusion that car parking was adequate in the area. There was general support for

[46]Bedford Urban Transportation Steering Committee, report of meeting with local organisations, April 1975.

[47]Bedford Urban Transportation Study, Community Involvement Programme, *Views of Local Organisations.*

[48]Bedford Urban Transportation Study Steering Committee, Minutes, 9 April 1975.

[49]Bedford Urban Transportation Study (1975) *Survey and Immediate Action Report*, September, p. 45.

some traffic relief to the town centre using a western relief road. There were detailed suggestions for improving the bus service (better co-ordination, innovations such as minibuses, dial-a-bus, park and ride, etc.), and most people favoured encouraging cyclists. As a result of this latter point and the findings of the survey that almost as many trips (13.3%) were made by cycle as by bus (14.5%), it was agreed to propose the development of a cycle network as part of the final plan whatever other alternatives were adopted. In terms of objectives, relief from heavy through traffic, improved public transport, and pedestrianisation of the town centre were most important. There was little support for more car parks.

The second function of the CIP was to legitimise the planning process. It could be regarded as a means of informing the public and of providing support and justification for the plan eventually selected. Indeed, the study team openly admitted this was part of its function. 'Organised Groups and Associations often experience a desire to be consulted. Indeed *in extremis* they are the focus for protest and opposition. It is desirable, therefore, to consult and involve them at a very early stage in the planning process.'[50] As a means of resolving conflict, however, it was unhelpful since it was possible to find support for both sides from the CIP.

Constraints

Transportation studies are constrained by future land use, resource availability, and the time-scale adopted. In common with similar types of transportation study it was decided to test the Bedford plan against alternative land uses 'to assess the sensitivity of significant differences in distribution of population, employment and other land use developments in terms of broad travel movement in the Study Area'.[51] This would have indicated which land-use pattern might be appropriate to particular transportation strategies and vice versa. A budget had to be identified to forecast the level of expenditure on transportation projects that would be available during the period of the plan above the base system which included the existing and committed transport network and facilities. The committed projects did not originally include the multi-storey car park at River Street, but once the agreement with the borough council on this project had been agreed in principle, this, too, was included. The budget was fixed at £7½ million. The time-scale for the plan was the period 1976–86.

All these constraints were altered during the preparation of the plan. The alternative land uses were dropped on the grounds that commitments of land left little scope for significant change. The target date, too, was changed to 1991 as a result of a revision of the expenditure forecast. The original transport expenditure planning assumption of £7.5 million was based upon an annual expenditure of £12.2 per head of a population of 130,000 up to 1986. As expenditure cuts began to take effect, it was recognised that this level was optimistic and should either be reduced or the study period extended in order to be 'consistent with the traffic problems of Bedford in relation to other parts of the County'.[52]

[50]Bedford urban Transportation (1974) *Project Report Part I*, June, p. 20.
[51]Bedford Urban Transportation Study, *Notes on Review of the Work Study Programme*.
[52]Bedford Urban Transportation Study, *Progress Report* No. 7, 26 May 1976.

Once the purpose and methodology of the study had been established, much of the work followed technical routines. During the course of the study there were three critical points at which political judgements had to be made which conditioned its final outcome. These were (i) the definition of transport concepts for the area, (ii) the presentation of alternative plans, and (iii) the decision on the final recommended plan.

THE EVALUATION OF THE PLAN

1. Development of transport concepts

The study team had begun with 20 'concept packages' which were refined to 7 presented to the Steering Committee. 'This allowed "sensible" ideas to continue further onto the next stage but at the same time indicated those schemes which were considered to have little merit.'[53] The packages were intended to demonstrate 'the range of options and level of transport provision' that could be provided within the budget. They varied from extremes of highway provision to public transport with a mixture in between. They took into account land-use changes, growth in travel, environmental aims, various transportation proposals, and the community involvement responses. They incorporated two basic highway concepts, the improvement of the existing radial road system, or the construction of an orbital road system. For public transport a range of possibilities consistent with the size of the area and the budget was put forward. The possibility of a fixed track system was eliminated on grounds of cost and feasibility. The options included the existing radial bus network together with an orbital or flexible route system (such as dial-a-bus) to cater for journeys between and within suburbs. A secondary public transport system using such concepts as 'park and ride' and minitrams and various bus priority schemes was also suggested. Finally, there was general acceptance of the need to incorporate provision for cyclists.

Some of the concepts were rejected outright by the Steering Committee as being unrealistic. These included a scheme for six park-and-ride car parks on the main approaches to the town, rejected because they were too close to the town centre to encourage motorists and would not be used unless there was severe restraint on cars in the town centre; impossible, given the amount of car parking already existing there. It was agreed, however, to test a less extreme option with park-and-ride car parks on the southern and western approaches to the town, which would require restraint on vehicles entering from those directions. A proposal to introduce a relief road alongside the main railway line was also discarded on the grounds that it would be impossible to secure the land acquired. The minitram idea was also dropped since it would absorb £5.6 millions of the budget and could only serve the town centre for journeys which were within walking distance. The 'Le Mans' solution of an outer orbital dual carriageway road encircling all but the north of the town was disposed of since it would offer only marginal relief to internal congestion and provide no improvement to public transport. This left a range of possibilities. These included a western and eastern relief road, a central relief road at Batts Ford, park-and-ride, dial-a-bus, and various levels of bus frequency and bus routes, together with different concepts of pedestrianisation in the town centre.

[53]Bedford Urban Transportation Study (1975) *Development of Transportation Alternatives*, December, p. 29.

The next stage was the preparation of three alternative plans using mixtures of the remaining concepts which could be evaluated. The chairman of the Steering Committee insisted that the western relief road option was excluded from at least one of the alternatives. This was to ensure that the central political conflict would be exposed to evaluation.

2. The three alternatives

Three alternatives were presented to the Steering Committee at the end of 1975. The first (Fig. 5.5) was biased towards 'high mobility for private vehicles'[54] including three

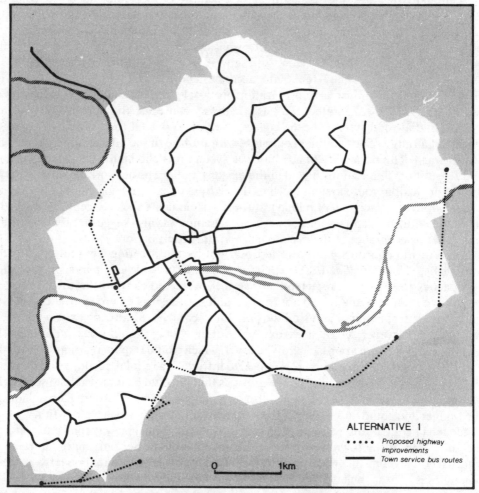

Fig. 5.5. Bedford Urban Transportation Study, Alternative 1.

[54]Bedford Urban Transportation Study (1975) *Development of Transportation Alternatives,* December, p. 53.

new river crossings — to the east, to the west, and in the centre at Batts Ford. In the town centre there would be complete pedestrianisation of the main shopping streets. No improvement to existing bus services was proposed and buses would have to circulate around the town centre. The second alternative (Fig. 5.6) suggested schemes which could complement both public and private transport. It included a western relief road, improved bus frequencies and an orbital service, a limited park-and-ride scheme, and the pedestrianisation of some of the central streets. Alternative three (Fig. 5.7) had a public transport emphasis with minimal road investment but the introduction of dial-a-bus covering the northern and southern suburbs, new bus services and higher frequencies, and the diversion of the Bedford–Bletchley railway line to the main station, together with the building of two railway halts to serve the southern part of the town centre and Kempston. In the town centre the main shopping streets would be reserved to buses.

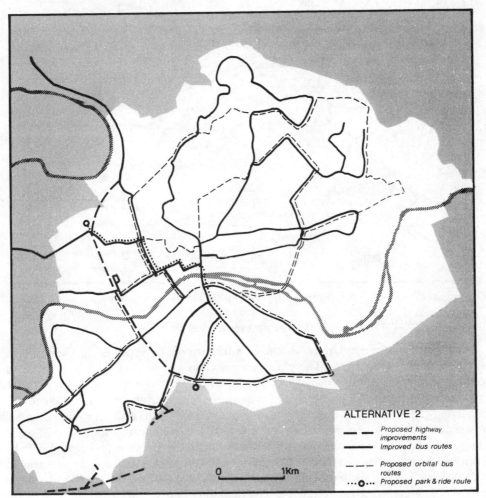

Fig. 5.6. Bedford Urban Transportation Study, Alternative 2.

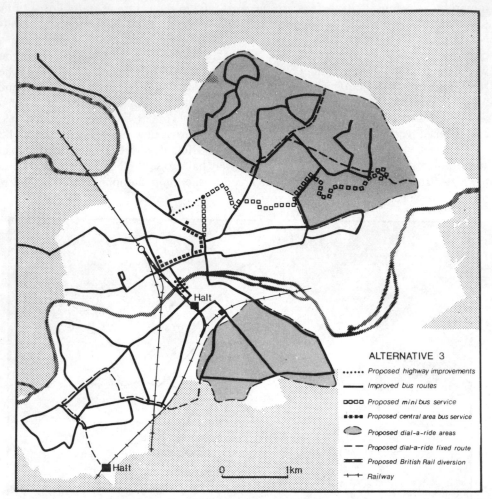

Fig. 5.7. Bedford Urban Transportation Study, Alternative 3.

3. The recommended plan

The final recommendations of the consultants took the Steering Committee by surprise (Fig. 5.8 and 5.9). The plan was based on assumptions of a 22% increase in population by 1991, and a rise of 53% in car ownership to a state where there would be one car for every three people, though a quarter of the households would have no car at all. The plan forecast a growth of 29% in journeys, with half of all journeys going to the town centre. It also concluded that even by 1991 car-parking supply would balance demand and that without any further investment or parking restraint 'peak hour conditions on the highway network will not be intolerable, although local congestion will occur'.[55] Analysis had demonstrated that significant lowering of public transport fares or an increase in the frequency of services did not result in any substantial increase

[55]Bedford Urban Transportation Study (1976) *Evaluation of Alternatives and Transportation Recommendations*, p. 26.

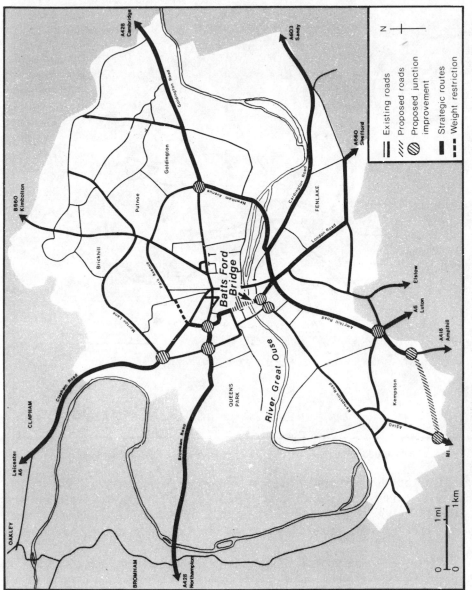

Fig. 8. Bedford Auth. Transport: Study, recommended 1991 highway network

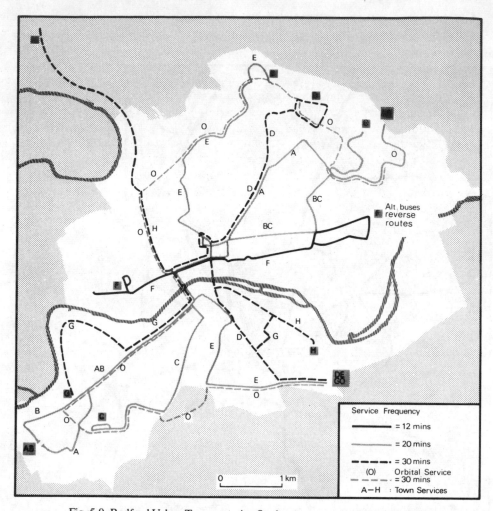

Fig. 5.9. Bedford Urban Transportation Study, recommended bus network.

in passengers but that any rapid increase in fares would lose passengers. An economic evaluation had indicated that the benefits from a high level of highway investment were not justified by the cost.[56] 'The economic evaluation of the Alternatives strongly suggested that heavy investment in either highways or public transport is not justified.'[57]

This led to the conclusion that: 'If the economic benefits from such a high level of

[56]Economic evaluation attempts to express in monetary values, the benefits of greater accessibility and ease of movement as against the costs incurred in providing improved facilities. The benefits to users are expressed as consumer surplus and there are also savings that may be made to transport operators. Each alternative strategy was evaluated against the base network (i.e. the network existing or committed in 1976) to derive the relative economic performance of each. Certain costs and benefits could not be expressed in monetary terms and were included under a separate environmental evaluation.

[57]Bedford Urban Transportation Study (1976) *Evaluation of Alternatives and Transportation Recommendations*, p. 71.

investment are low, then a more realistic expenditure should be sought.'[58] By abandoning the original investment figure of £7.5 million, the plan had effectively removed the western relief road as an option on economic grounds, a decision that was supported by operational and, to an extent, environmental evaluations.

Instead, the plan reinstated the river crossing at Batts Ford which had been rejected some years previously by the former county council. This was regarded as the least-cost solution to the traffic problems of the future which were only likely to be acute during the peak hours in the town centre. By contrast, the western relief road would only provide relief on the radial routes for short sections, would divide Queens Park, and open up the road through that area as a further main route into the town centre. The western relief road would not overcome the main problem which was the distribution of traffic wishing to go to the town centre. The benefits of the western relief road were on a localised scale and had to be weighed against its high cost and the severance and loss of land it would involve. The overall plan, which included various junction improvements, cycleways, some changes in the public transport system (including an orbital route), and pedestrianisation measures in the town centre allowing buses access, would cost a total of £3¼ million (1974 prices) with the road schemes totalling less than £2 million.

Undoubtedly the recommendations added technical and apparently disinterested support to the opponents of the western relief road on the county council, supplying them with the initiative in the debate. However, the decision to recommend firmly in favour of Batts Ford had only been taken by the study team a day before the Steering Committee met, suggesting a degree of subjectivity in the technical process. Immediate reactions were divided along familiar lines with the Labour members claiming vindication for their long-standing campaign. The hostility of the borough council was evident in the sardonic comment of their leading spokesman: 'The old County Council's mistake over Batts Ford was not being admitted and another mistake was being made in not building the Western Relief Road. A fourth river crossing is urgently needed but the difficulty is that a Batts Ford bridge would do nothing to relieve the big traffic queues entering the town.'[59] The leading officials of both councils had been committed to the western relief road. The borough's Director of Planning and Development and architect of their transportation strategy described the plan as a 'non-event' and prepared to continue his opposition to the county's approach to transport policy. The County Planning Officer was unhappy about a plan which opposed his previous commitments and he intimated to the chairman of the Steering Committee that he could not be expected to give the plan public support. The lines were now drawn between political parties and between the two councils. In these circumstances the plan was presented for consultation and public participation.

REACTIONS TO THE PLAN

The Environmental Services Committee's Labour group immediately capitalised on the recommendations of the consultants by drawing up an eight-point resolution calling for the adoption of the 'broad philosophy' of the plan and specifically proposing the

[58]Ibid., p. 61.
[59]*Bedford Record*, 19 October 1976.

abandonment of the western relief road as 'too expensive and unnecessary'.[60] They opposed further car parks and favoured bus penetration of the central area. Their main reservations concerned the need for any further river crossing, suggesting that, should one become necessary, then 'alternatives offering maximum relief at lowest cost near the central area be investigated and programmed accordingly'.[61] Such a veiled commitment to the possibility of Batts Ford was intended to head off opposition from Labour supporters in that area of the town which would suffer environmental problems as a result of the bridge.

The resolution was carried and subsequently endorsed by the council as the basis for consultation with the borough council and the public. The Conservatives opposed, and suggested that only those parts of the plan which were mutually agreed by both councils should be adopted. The consultation with the borough confirmed that there was little prospect of agreement over the main principles of the plan, and the familiar arguments in favour of the western relief road, full pedestrianisation, and car parking were rehearsed. The borough council put forward alternative proposals which included a link road to the town centre from the western relief road to avoid overloading the east-west route through Queens Park. The total cost of their scheme (excluding car parks) was estimated to be approaching £10 million, about three times the cost of the recommended plan. The borough held an exhibition designed to promote their alternative.

The county council also held an exhibition and consulted with the various organisations involved in the CIP. Public reaction, so far as it could be gauged from the small response to a questionnaire,[62] seemed evenly divided on the question of highway investment and bus-only streets, a majority favoured bus subsidies, and four-fifths felt there was sufficient car parking. The consultations spawned two further 'plans', one from the former Mayor of Bedford who, in attempting a compromise solution, suggested using railway land for roads. The other, from the resurrected Crisis organisation, favoured a different approach to pedestrianisation in the town centre, pointing out that the plan would have buses along every street except the one which 'perversely is the only part of the centre without significant shopping frontage'.[63]

The consultations produced little change in the recommendation of the Environmental Services Committee. The county council's transportation planners, from being luke-warm, had begun to show positive enthusiasm for the proposals. Further analysis by the planning department had indicated that within the central area the only feasible site for a bridge was at Batts Ford. Improvement to the existing Prebend Street bridge was both more costly, involved considerable demolition of property, and had inadequate approach roads. They had concluded that, apart from its high cost, the western relief road would not overcome the necessity for a crossing to be provided in the central area to accommodate the traffic wishing to go there. The previous resolution was refined to six points, but still contained clauses opposing the western relief road and further car parks. The committee amended its view on the central crossing saying that although 'no additional river crossing is necessary in the short term . . . should a further river

[60]Environmental Services Committee, Minute 76/K/304,1 viii, 1 December 1976.
[61]Ibid., 1 iii.
[62]A questionnaire was distributed at a public exhibition held by the county council. 1600 questionnaries were distributed and 176 were returned.
[63]'Crisis', Comments on the Bedford Urban Transportation Study, 2 December 1976, p. 2.

crossing eventually become necessary the bridge should be constructed at Batts Ford'.[64] The only concessions made to the borough's views were that the question of pedestrianisation and bus access to the town centre should be considered in terms of individual schemes treated on their merits.

The debate reached a dramatic climax in early 1977 near the end of the term of the 1974 county council. The recommendations of the Environmental Services Committee on the transporation study were part of a composite resolution on the structure plan presented to the county council for final approval. The Conservatives sought an amendment whereby the options on a further river crossing would be left open. The amendment came at the end of a long meeting by which time the Labour group had a slight majority of votes. The Liberals decided to support the Conservative amendment, and the vote was a tie at 30 each with 1 Labour member abstaining.[65] The chairman of the council cast his vote in favour of the recommendation and the Labour group had secured a victory by a hair's breadth.

At this point the Labour group had achieved its major policy objectives for transport-ation in the Bedford area. In some respects this was a remarkable change from the policy emphasis that had existed previously. But it represented not so much a triumph of political will as a combination of fortuitous circumstances. Among these were the constantly declining transport budget which resulted in the deferment or cancellation of road schemes; the geographical balance of the county council whereby there was considerable support for priority to be given to road schemes in the Luton area and to relieve villages and towns on the main east-west route across the county; and the bureaucratic support for Labour's initiatives. But it is the outcomes rather than the decisions themselves which matter. Decisions represent the balance of forces prevailing at a point in time, and this balance can shift. There was the possibility that the resources available could improve over the longer term. There was the probability that Labour would be out of office long enough for alternative policies to be implemented. So long as the site of the western relief road remained undeveloped that road was not dead. Indeed, events were soon to show the scheme was very alive. The events of 1974–7 had destroyed the pre-existing consensus over transportation policy. It had been replaced by conflict and the result in terms of policy-making was uncertainty that seemed likely-to prevail for a long time.

THE SOURCES OF UNCERTAINTY

The history of transport policy in Bedford during the 1970s is one of conflict and change. Until that time the ideological commitment to a particular philosophy of an organisation with effective control had achieved a broad consensus on policy and had

[64]County Council, Agenda Item 77/k/1, 24 February 1977.

[65]This was the penultimate meeting of the council before the elections the following May. It had been decided to take the item last on the agenda, by which time Labour had an overall majority for the first time that day. Even so a recount was necessary, owing to the uncertainty of a second Labour member whose vote was unclear on the first occasion. The Labour abstention was by a member representing the area which would be adversely affected if the Batts Ford bridge was built. Liberals who had previously supported the Environmental Services Committee resolution had already left the meeting. The narrow vote and the probability of a change in political control in the future underlined the uncertainty about the meaningfulness of the decision.

achieved progressive implementation of schemes essential to its strategy. The consensus achieved was among the decision-makers. This need not imply that policies were supported by those not participating in the decisions. This consensus was broken by ideological and organisational conflicts which, together with increasing external influence, altered the context within which policy was determined. The changing direction of Bedford's policy was a microcosm of changes taking place at national level. The change from consensus to uncertainty can be explained in terms of the model outlined in Chapter 1.

1. Ideological differences

During the 1960s and into the 1970s there was a palpable shift in national thinking on transport policy. Beginning with the Buchanan report[66] there developed greater concern about environmental values and later a growing concern about the distributional implications of transport policy, a central theme of the government's transport policy. Different attitudes became politically focused. In Bedfordshire the county council's Labour group represented the desire for new objectives and policies, while the Conservatives in North Bedfordshire maintained their allegiance to the existing policies.

Political conflict was echoed by professional rivalries between the officials of both councils. In the case of North Bedfordshire, influence and control over policy was substantially vested in the experienced and long-serving Director of Planning and Development. His willingness to use the complex financial and organisational arrangements of local government reorganisation, his grasp of detail and perception of opportunity, and his ability to sustain a consistent transport policy in the face of changing circumstances, were instrumental in the resistance that was offered to the new initiatives from the county council. The county officials found such single-mindedness difficult to combat. They were uncertain of political support given the minority government of the county council and certainly any longer-term strategy could be threatened by a change in political control that was far more likely at county than at district level.

The precarious balance of power enabled the county council to prevent schemes which it found undesirable, like the western relief road, but made it difficult to implement its own proposals. In the case of the River Street car park the Labour group found itself isolated and unable to risk the extreme solution of revocation, despite the accumulating evidence in favour of such a step provided by the transportation study. In different political circumstances, and with less intense professional rivalry, relationships may have been different and a more coherent policy may have been expounded.

The short period of Labour influence over transport policy-making (1974–7) had interrupted the slow development of a long-standing strategy. By the middle of 1977 both the borough and county councils were once again securely in Conservative hands. Although the principal architect of the borough's plans retired in that year, the borough council remained firmly committed to its road, car-parking, and town centre schemes. Political sympathies between the two councils suggested a reversion to the former policies. Certainly, the new county council was anxious to be in accord with the

[66]C. D. Buchanan, (1963) *Traffic in Towns*, London, HMSO.

borough. In its rejoinder to the detailed objections of the borough council to the transportation proposals in the structure plan, the county council went some way towards modifying the more provocative policies of its predecessor. On car parking it stated that it would adopt 'a pragmatic approach' and a 'flexible attitude'.[67] On the question of a further river crossing it reinstated the Conservative proposal that had so narrowly failed at the council meeting which adopted the plan. It reaffirmed the view that no new crossing was necessary in the short term. But the rejoinder added: 'the County Council will however, keep the matter under review, and will determine *the location* of any such river crossing that might eventually be required as part of this review.'[68] The unreality of this position was exposed by the chairman of the examination in public of the structure plan, who could not understand what new information had come to light since the BUTS study that enabled the county council to drop the Batts Ford bridge proposal. This was an essential element in the package, and without it all the other components must be in doubt. It appeared to him that the county council had no positive views of their own.

The council's view became clear by the middle of 1978 when it reviewed the question of the fourth river crossing for Bedford. A paper setting out the arguments went over the ground established in the BUTS report. A western relief road would disperse traffic and provide peak-hour relief from congestion. But to make efficient use of this bridge 'would require quite severe restrictions within the centre to force traffic out',[69] unlikely given the car parking available in the town. The bridge would be less attractive in terms of the economic criteria employed by the Department of Transport for evaluating road schemes. The problems of the large amount of traffic attracted to the town centre would remain, and the road would not correspond to the north-east/south-west orientation of traffic flows over the town as a whole. Above all the scheme was expensive — £5.7 million in total — of which the county council, on the most optimistic assessment, would have to find well over £1 million[70] The report pointed out that the cheaper scheme, Batts Ford, was 'more heavily associated with town centre plans and would give considerable flexibility and scope for longer-term traffic movement and environmental plans in the town centre'.[71] Neither bridge, however, offered adequate relief from the east-west movement of heavy vehicles across the town.

The report was hardly an unequivocal affirmation of the case for the western relief road, yet the Environmental Services Committee, under strong pressure from the North Bedfordshire Borough Council, decided to adopt it as a priority to the construction of a bridge at Batts Ford. This would involve a change in the structure plan and extensive public consultation, although earlier consultation had not revealed great public support for the scheme. The problem of timing and resources for the scheme remained. In this the council were helped by an invitation from the Department of Transport to suggest schemes that could be accelerated in the event of resources being transferred from trunk to local road schemes. The committee reacted by proposing that

[67]Bedfordshire County Council, *County Structure Plan, Response to Objections,* Report of the Planning Advisory Group, 26 August 1977.
[68]Ibid.
[69]Bedfordshire County Council Transport Advisory Group, 11 September 1978.
[70]Ibid. Assuming 70% TSG and possibly a further 10% grant from trunk road funds the county council would need to find £1.14 million of the £5.7 million total cost. For Batts Ford, a 70% grant would leave the council to pay £0.3 million of the total of £1 million.
[71]Ibid.

all existing major road schemes in the county should be advanced and that the western relief road should be incorporated in the programme and be constructed in two phases, in 1982/3 and 1985/6. As a consequence the capital programme for highways in the county would be increased up to 1988 by nearly £8 million to a total approaching £26 million, and an increase in staff to prepare the schemes would be necessary. Even the existing programme was well above the capital expenditure approved by the council. A decision to maintain the level of capital spending made it extremely unlikely that all these schemes could go ahead in the time planned. Furthermore, it became clear that not all members of the county council would accept the priorities established by the Environmental Services Committee and would advocate a different ordering or the inclusion of other schemes which reflected their own local interests.

Although the policy put forward by the previous county council had now been altered, the uncertainty was by no means relieved. Before the road could be built a number of important hurdles had to be overcome — the structure plan, the ordering of priorities, and the need for resources. Given political continuity there was the prospect that the road would be constructed in the foreseeable future. But the mere appearance of the road in a forward capital programme was no guarantee that it would be built. The political conflicts of the 1970s had at the very least deferred the scheme for a long period and made its future uncertain.

2. Organisational conflict

The introduction of the two-tier system had widened the opportunity for conflict between county and district and between different areas within the county. Although the county council had responsibility for transportation policy, its authority was weakened by the dispersal of powers of implementation among several organisations. We have seen how one district was able, partly by use of its local planning, car parking, and agency functions, to block the initiatives of the county. At the same time the borough was experiencing a disagreeable loss of power over policy-making. Resentment at having to contest its objectives with the county was evident in the increasingly strident language of its bulky output of documents. Over the years detailed responses were provided on every transport issue culminating in the borough's attack on the county structure plan. On no issue was there any sign of deviation from the course that had been pursued since the Max Lock plan. In its submission to the examination in public the borough recapitulated its goal to maintain the prosperity and competitiveness of the county town against the growing competition in the subregion. It found the county's proposals 'totally inadequate'. A sense of grievance at having to compete for resources and priority with other areas for its road schemes is evident.

> The Council does not accept, however, that a 15 year Structure Plan should be based on a temporarily depressed economy, that such resources as are likely to be available should be allocated in the main to transportation improvements in the southern half of the County, or that there should be the payment of substantial subsidies to public transport at the expense of other road users'.[72]

[72]North Bedfordshire Borough Council, Statement on the Matters to be Examined in Public for the Bedfordshire County Structure Plan, September 1977, para. H.8.1.

Reorganisation had reduced the powers of the borough but had not transferred full responsibility to the county. During 1973–7 two bureaucracies were engaged in counter-acting each other's policies. After the election of the new county council and the transfer of all transportation matters from the County Planner to the County Surveyor, relations became easier. But the technical basis for policy remained the BUTS study whose conclusions had to be ignored in order to revert to the proposals of the borough council.

3. Constraints

Throughout the period of consensus in transport policy, the main impact of financial restraint was to defer schemes that were generally agreed upon. In the years following reorganisation, the political and organisational conflicts were played out against a background of long-term decline in available resources for transport. It could be argued that finance was the determinant of policy and that, quite aside from other conflicts, central government — through its control of resources and its endorsement of the TPP would effectively control local transport policy. Certainly the worsening financial situation proved a useful ally for the county council's efforts to change the direction of Bedford's transport policy. Resources were a crucial factor in the argument in favour of Batts Ford. But the borough still managed to secure the finance from internal sources for its car park and could retire with its policies intact, awaiting the day when financial and political circumstances would be more propitious. The financial position contributed to the general stalemate but did not of itself bring about any fundamental change of attitudes.

Any change in the direction of policy would have to take account of the constraints imposed by the existing transport network. In particular, the extent of car-parking provision in Bedford precluded any attempt to restrict traffic flows into the town based on control over parking supply. The approaches to Batts Ford had been completed and so could more easily be connected by the bridge in the future. Part of the costs of the western relief road had already been paid for by the demolition of housing, and the site remained cleared ready for construction. Indeed, the borough, having ordered the demolition, subsequently argued that it would be most regrettable after 'the emotional disturbance of re-housing and displacement of other interests'[73] if the road scheme were to prove abortive. Thus step by step in a process of inexorable incrementalism, options were precluded as projects were implemented.

4. The role of public opinion

Public opinion had been instrumental in opening up the debate about transport policy in Bedford in the early 1970s. But it was restricted to middle-class pressure groups anxious to protect the amenity of certain parts of the town. They failed to prevent the bridge crossing the riverside area but managed to keep heavy traffic off the northern section of the embryonic inner relief road. There was little public resistance to the

[73]North Bedfordshire Borough Council, Further Statement on the Matters to be Examined in Public for the Bedfordshire County Structure Plan, November 1977, para. H (s) 7 (e).

demolition of housing in the disadvantaged area of Queens Park. The BUTS study involved the public on a greater scale than had previously been attempted, and considerable effort was made to use this involvement in the production of the plan. But once the plan emerged the debate was dominated by the two councils. At the examination in public most of the time devoted to the issue of Bedford's transportation was occupied by spokesmen for the two councils. The other participants were mainly representative of privileged groups in the town or national transport lobbies.[74] The prevailing pattern of power was ultimately institutionalised through the participation process. However, the introduction of the transport study had encouraged public debate outside the council chamber. It offered a new dimension to the planning process and provided a factual and analytical background against which certain assumptions could be tested. Although the study could not remove the sources of conflict, it had established certain parameters within which future debate could be conducted. In this sense a technical process could inform though not displace the political process. But it had performed two other roles which, in terms of policy-making, were more significant. Involvement of the public provided the appearance if not the substance of public participation in decision-making. Also, the setting up of the study had helped the politicians to avoid difficult decisions and to invoke a supposedly disinterested evaluation. The Labour group had bought time and had seen their views endorsed in large measure in the plan. But, just as they had established their policy, they were defeated in the election of 1977.

THE CHANGING PERSPECTIVE

Much of the debate over Bedford's transport policy has been internal among the members and officials of two councils. External influences, notably the availability of finance and increasing public involvement through the transportation study, became more important once consensus broke down after local government reorganisation. The protagonists were more concerned about the assertion of their power than about vague notions such as the public interest. Although distributional issues were central to the conflict they were rarely made explicit, and attention focused on the ability of one authority to impose its policy or to prevent the success of its opponent's. The politicans and officials involved tended to demonstrate loyalty to each other and to their own organisation. Their working relationships were close, whereas they were more remote from exposure to public opinion. In any case such opinion was rarely united. Politicians were able to advocate dissimilar policies secure in the knowledge that they would find some support from a section of the electorate. In any case transport policy was unlikely to feature as a decisive issue in the test of public opinion at election time.

From the citizen's point of view the intensity and tenacity of the conflict must have seemed inconsistent with the amount of action that resulted. The human cost of the western relief road had been paid for in the destruction of housing but no benefits had been derived for the motorist. Elsewhere, projects were at a standstill. Those people

[74]Apart from the councils the participants on the issue of transport in Bedford at the Examination in Public were the Bedfordshire Association of Architects, The Harpur Trust (a charity responsible for the four independent and direct grant schools in the town and the developers of the town centre site and the River Street car park); the United Kingdom Federation of Business and Professional Women; the Automobile Association; and the National Bus Company.

dependent on public transport saw only marginal improvements and increasing fares despite policies to improve 'levels of personal mobility especially for those sections of the community who do not have access, or who only have irregular access, to a car'.[75] There seemed to be an inverse relationship between the volume of proposals and the degree of implementation.

It is, perhaps, inevitable that any change in a previously consistent transport policy will take time to become generally acceptable. Where it is vigorously opposed, where the final responsibility is unclear, where there is political instability, and where the financial outlook is poor there is likely to be continuing uncertainty.

Some of this uncertainty might be removed by changes in the organisational framework, particularly if the two-tier system were abandoned. But transportation planning is, as the events in Bedford in the early 1970s show, a political issue. Technical information may be used to support a case, and in the BUTS instance was used to effect a change in the direction of policy. But, as the study recognised, 'in some instances authorities may not fully accept a basic philosophy embodied in the recommendations or may weigh up the benefits differently.'[76] The study confirmed Labour's view of the situation, but did nothing to alter the entrenched views of the Conservatives. Indeed, the succeeding county council ignored the study altogether and reverted to pre-existing policies. Enormous effort had been devoted to developing a technical basis for policy-making, and extensive consultation had been undertaken, but the conflict remained and the gap between policy-making and implementation remained wide. Labour had managed, with the help of a changing resource pattern and sympathetic national policies, to introduce new values and priorities but had achieved little by way of implementation. The new council promised to bring back the western relief road but still had to find the resources to achieve it. Continuity in transportation policy had been interrupted; it remained to be seen whether it had been broken. In purely practical terms, road projects deemed essential in 1952 had not been completed twenty-five years later and were by no means certain to be implemented by the fully motorised age of 1991.

[75]Bedfordshire County Council (1977) *County Structure Plan Written Statement*, p. 26.
[76]Bedford Urban Transportation Study (1975) *Survey and Immediate Action Report*, p. 69.

CHAPTER 6

The Politics of Land Development

PLANNING AND THE MARKET

Land allocation and development in the United Kingdom is a product of the interaction between the market and the planning process. Some commentators would argue that the market is the dominant element and that planners should be seen as in competition or collusion with market forces. Such a viewpoint corresponds, to some extent, with the contention (see Chapter 2) that planning, the arm of the state ostensibly responsible for the orderly development of the environment, is, in practice, weak. Planners merely respond to initiatives from private developers and financial institutions. The state — and its local component, the local authorities — is seen, in a Marxist analysis, as the agent of capital.[1] 'The key decisions are not made in County Hall. They are made in the City by the financial institutions which fund the developers.'[2] Planning decisions merely provide the imprimatur for patterns of land use that would have occurred anyway through market mechanisms. Simmie, for instance, concludes that 'In the most significant aspects of allocation, town planners achieve little in the way of really altering what would have happened without their mediation'.[3]

Such arguments tend to neglect certain significant facts. The planning process is responsive both to the market and to the state. There is a distinction between the state as investor and the role of the planning process as a state activity to arbitrate the spatial allocation of investment. In practice the planning system may be weak but the investment represented by the state may be very compelling in its influence upon the built environment and the pattern of land development. It has been estimated that about half the land development in the United Kingdom emanates from the public sector.[4] This fact might be countered by the proposition that the public sector is little different in its behaviour from the private sector and is capable of manipulation by powerful vested interests in favour of certain classes. This is not the place to explore such arguments, unsupported as they frequently are by detailed empirical evidence. This chapter examines the relationship between the planning system and those interests, whether public or private, which initiate proposals for land development.

Although the planning system may be weak in the sense that it is passive, the existence of planning controls can have outcomes in land development that are not easy to define or predict. By restricting the supply of land through development control, planning may contribute to the increase in land prices. The evidence on this is equivocal. Some studies have discovered that land supply responds to demand and that

[1]See, for example, C. Cockburn (1977), *The Local State: Management of Cities and People,* London, Pluto Press.
[2]P. Ambrose (1976) *Who Plans Brighton's Housing Crisis?* Shelter Local Report, 1 March.
[3]J. M. Simmie (1974) *Citizens in Conflict,* London, Hutchinson Educational, p. 154.
[4]School for Advanced Urban Studies (1976) *Positive Planning and Public Profit,* Community Land Training Programme, Background Paper 2, March, p. 2.1.

there is sufficient land committed in planning terms to accommodate the demands made upon it.[5] Planning policies also influence the distribution of land values and land use. The contradictions of derelict land in highly accessible locations, or of sporadic and poorly serviced development on the peripheries of cities, can only be explained by the problems of securing the right land at the right price and for the right use, which are, ostensibly, the objectives of the planning process. Some of the factors which determine the value and use of land are the subject of the case-studies in this chapter. The aspect that is focused on is the role of competing interests for land and the outcome of competition in terms of land use and value.

The use and value of land are political questions of national and local significance. National legislation on land, planning, and local government provides the context and constraints within which local decisions are taken, and is examined in the first part of the chapter. Conflict over land development arises at the local level, and it is here that the pattern of land development is ultimately determined. Yet little research has been done on the political process of land development at the local level. The second part of the chapter draws on examples of land planning within one area in the United Kingdom in an attempt to reveal the impact of planning policy, financial considerations, and ideological and organisational conflict on urban fringe land development. In the United Kingdom, 'Land use and urban development problems are in fact generally regarded as subjects as much for national as for local decision making.'[6] Any interpretation of the pattern of development must investigate the relationship between national policy and local decision-making.

1. NATIONAL LAND POLICY

Land policy has two distinct components. One is financial — the attempt to redistribute some of the private wealth in land to the public sector, usually through taxation policies. The other is a spatial or land-use component — the attempt to allocate land through planning controls.

(i) *The distribution of wealth in land*

Land ownership or, more specifically, the control of property rights in land, confers wealth upon those who hold the rights. In certain respects land is a unique form of wealth in that it is fixed in supply (though not in use), is immobile, indestructible, and essential for all forms of activity and life. Land requires no production or supply costs, and hence those with rights over land receive 'economic rent', a fortuitous and unearned income over and above that necessary to keep land in its existing use. This surplus or unearned increment 'has provided the main economic platform for attacks by

[5]Department of the Environment (1975) *Housing Land Availability in the South East, Consultants' Study*, concludes: 'the most remarkable single finding of this study is the extent to which the demand for housing is met by granting permissions on land *not previously identified* as available in planning terms' (p. 5). It is often argued that development control restricts the supply of land and thus forces up prices; that attempts to restrict industrial and commercial development through planning controls may starve certain areas of investment without necessarily creating it elsewhere. Evidence on these points tends to be conflicting and inconclusive.

[6]R. Thomas, *Planning, Housing and Land Values*, London, Land and Liberty Press, pp. 2–3. Undated.

land reformers upon private ownership of land'.[7] But the value of land in exchange rather than its value in use has been the major target for taxation policies in Britain since the war. The value of a piece of land depends in part on its physical characteristics but also on its geographical accessibility. We are familiar with the land value surface with very high values on premium sites, for which there is great competition among potential users in the centre of major cities, and declining values as distance from points of maximum accessibility increases. The difference in value between land in agricultural use and its exchange value as residential land can be very marked indeed. The process of urban development has a major influence on land values, creating what is known as *betterment* — the increases in value which accrue to owners from public expenditure and planning control.[8] It has been consistently argued that part, at least, of this betterment should be collected from the owner of the land for the community which has created it. The justification for such collection has grown as the difference between existing and development value has widened, as planning intervention has distributed betterment unevenly, as a check on land speculation, and as a means of securing resources for public sector development.

By granting or withholding permission to develop land and by specifying the type of development to which land may be put, planning authorities distribute benefits to owners who make successful applications and withold such benefits from those whose applications are refused. There is considerable development land available both on the fringes of cities and in the inner city (much of it owned by public authorities), but it remains unused, through lack of demand, at the price asked. Planning policies locate a 'hope' value on land that may be zoned r development at some future date. Not all such land will be developed, which raises the question of compensation for those refused permission to develop. In the United Kingdom compensation has been paid where land is compulsorily acquired but not on land which is refused permission.[9]

(ii) *The allocation of land uses*

A second aspect of post-war land policy has been the introduction of a planning system to control the use of land. This is the principle of development control which has been accepted by all governments. Such control is largely negative, applied in reaction to demands for development. The planning authorities lack direct control over investment in land and therefore, it is argued, their ability to ensure the implementation of planning policies is weak. This has led to various attempts to increase the initiative resting with the planning authorities. The White Paper on *Land*, published by the Labour government in 1974, stated as one of its major objectives the promotion of 'positive planning', 'to enable the community to control the development of land in accordance with its needs and priorities'.[10] For various reasons the notion of positive planning may be difficult to achieve. There are problems of ownership and value which make the assembly of land costly and time consuming. There may be legal and physical

[7]J. Barratt (1976) *Land and Inequality,* Unit 10 of Patterns of Inequality. The Open University, Milton Keynes, p. 29.

[8]Department of the Environment (1974) *Land,* Cmnd. 5730, London, HMSO, p. 1.

[9]Where planning controls prevent an owner any beneficial use he may have a right to claim compensation, or he can serve a purchase notice on the planning authority.

[10]Department of the Environment (1974) op cit.

restraints on development. The necessary infrastructure may be lacking. There may be conflicts between the organisations responsible for land development. During the last thirty or so years legislation to secure betterment for the community and to introduce the concept of positive planning has, from time to time, been enacted at national level. The influence and effectiveness of such legislation on the pattern of land use and ownership can only be established by detailed case-studies at the local level. National legislation provides the context within which land ownership and use is distributed at the local level. The relationship between the market and the state has undoubtedly been influenced by changes in land policy, local government, and the planning system. Whether the relationship has been altered fundamentally or only at the margin must be a matter for debate.

The Legislative Framework

(i) *Land*

Several attempts have been made to secure betterment from land for the community. During the war the Uthwatt Committee[11] proposed that all undeveloped land should be nationalised, but that the owner should still be able to use his land, losing only his right to develop it. Land for development would be purchased at existing use value, but developed land required for redevelopment or which had plans prepared for it would be acquired at its 1939 value (thus avoiding speculation). A 75% betterment levy would be charged on all increases in land value. This radical solution was only partially implemented in 1947 when all rights to develop land were nationalized by the Labour government. This is the fundamental principle of development control which is the backbone of the British planning system. But private ownership of land was not affected although an attempt was made to collect the betterment arising from changes of use by a 100% levy. This failed to work since it provided no incentive to the market and resulted either in inflated prices (through buyers paying both the development charge and a market price to the seller) or the need for compulsory purchase. Compulsory purchase was at existing use value, and a fund of £300 million was established to compensate those owners who had lost anticipated development value as a result of the Act. The Conservatives abolished the levy, but this resulted in a dual pricing system (full market value for those who gained permission to develop but existing use value for those whose land was compulsorily purchased). This anomaly was removed in 1959 by a return to full market value for compensation. During the 1960s the Labour government made a second attempt at securing betterment and state control of land assembly through the Land Commission, but this was abandoned when the government fell in 1970. During the 1970s the Conservatives, faced with a rapid inflation in land prices, resorted to urging local authorities to release land and used the taxation system to secure betterment. By this time, therefore, the principle of obtaining some betterment for the community and the system of development control were firmly established.

[11]*Expert Committee on Compensation and Betterment,* The Uthwatt Committee, Cmnd. 6386, London, *HMSO, 1942.*

(ii) *Planning*

The planning system has also changed during the post-war period. The system of development plans was established in 1947. These were in the form of land-use maps with accompanying written statements drawn up by the local planning authorities[12] to be revised every five years. Development had to be in accordance with the plan. Although departures from the plan were admissible either through revisions or the appeals procedure, reviews of the plan took far longer than had been anticipated. Criticisms of the system led to the more indicative structure planning system proposed in the 1960s (see next chapter). Structure plans were to reflect the changing social and economic forces which help to shape the physical environment. They would provide the statutory planning framework for more detailed local plans. Structure plans are intended to look ahead for about fifteen years but must be monitored and reviewed in the light of changing assumptions or conditions. They were also designed to fit into the framework of local government reform which was proposed in the 1960s.

(iii) *Local government*

The Redcliffe–Maud Commission on Local Government Reform[13] in 1969 proposed the establishment of unitary local authorities, and was accepted by the then Labour government. Such authorities would be responsible for the preparation of structure plans. These could be fitted into the regional plans being prepared in the 1960s, especially if regional authorities with power to co-ordinate and control strategic development were introduced. However, the Conservative 1972 Local Government Act set its face against both unitary and regional authorities and instead redistributed local government functions among two tiers of authority, the county and district councils, which shared the planning function between them. The problems this has caused have already been discussed in terms of transportation in the previous chapter, and the next chapter illustrates the difficulties of implementation which arise in structure planning partly as a result of the two-tier system. At the detailed level of land development the existence of two responsible authorities can intensify conflicts, as we shall see later. The role of central government in approving structure plans and in the arbitration of land-use conflicts is also significant.

By 1974 the problem of betterment had been partially tackled and publicly accountable local authorities had secured some control over the allocation of land use. But it remained essentially a system of coexistence of the market side by side with government intervention, a typical expression of the British concept of the 'mixed economy'. At the local level there were widely differing approaches to land development. Some authorities took the initiative as developers by buying up land cheaply and developing it in conjunction with the private sector. In many cases local authorities, apart from their own developments, played a passive role, accepting or rejecting initiatives from the private sector. Their powers to ensure the implementation of the objectives of their plans were limited. As a result urban development was in the main a piecemeal and unco-ordinated process. Planning intervention continued to

[12] At that time there were the 145 county and county borough councils.
[13] *Royal Commission on Local Government in England, Report* (The Redcliffe–Maud Report), Cmnd. 4040, London, HMSO, 1969.

create development gains in certain locations for those fortunate enough to possess an interest in land and to deny it to others. 'By and large the impact of planning is to shift land values about to different sites in a fairly arbitrary way.'[14] The failure of legislative efforts to secure control over land development, coupled with the rapid inflation of land prices in the early 1970s[15] and the growth of speculative investment in commercial developments resulting in empty office blocks in city centres, provided the incoming Labour government in 1974 with the incentive to have a further try at securing betterment for the community and a system of positive planning through the Community Land Act 1975.

(iv) *The Community Land Act 1975*

If another attempt to produce a comprehensive rather than an *ad hoc* approach to land planning was to succeed where previous ones had failed, it had to be both workable and politically robust. The Community Land Act attempts to meet both criteria by seeking to effect gradual rather than dramatic change and by attempting to strike a balance between the needs of the market and those of the planning authorities.

The Act is concerned with land needed for relevant development within ten years. Such land will be defined by the local authorities and will include all land which is neither exempted nor excepted.[16] The local authorities will submit to the minister land-policy statements based on the planning objectives for the area. A close link between land planning and the objectives of structure and local plans is therefore expected to make the scheme 'planning led'.

The scheme will be implemented in two stages, partly to enable authorities to build up the expertise and resources necessary for full implementation of the Act and partly to enable an orderly transition from development based on the market to development controlled by the authorities. During the first phase authorities may choose whether or not to acquire land for which planning permission is sought. Eventually, when the Act is fully implemented, all land must pass through the local authority. In the transitional phase land may be identified by the local authority and purchased by agreement or compulsory purchase. Or it may be identified by landowners or developers who will be given prior negotiating rights if the land is not required by the local authority. Local authorities will also be able to designate 'disposal notification areas' requiring those disposing of an interest in land to inform them so that they can say whether or not they propose to acquire that interest. This safeguards the position of authorities who intend but are not ready to buy development land.

The Act has attempted to tread the tightrope between public ownership of land and the need to retain a viable and active development industry. Local authorities will be responsible for ensuring a sufficient supply of land to be disposed of in order to maintain a healthy construction industry and a continuing building programme. Much will,

[14]School for Advanced Urban Studies, *Positive Planning and Public Profit,* Community Land Training Programme, Background Paper 2, p. 2.2, March 1976.

[15]Between 1966 and 1975 average house prices and average earnings tripled, but whereas house prices rose more slowly than earnings in the early part of the period they doubled between 1970 and 1973, land prices were even more erratic, rising six to seven times 1963–73 and doubling in 1972.

[16]Exemptions or exceptions include agriculture, forestry, land with planning permission or owned by a builder or developer before White Paper day, owner occupiers, churches, and charities.

therefore, depend on the attitudes of individual authorities. Considerable uncertainty is likely where developers may be prepared to put less effort into site investigation if the prospects of obtaining the development are weakened. 'It is an open question whether the Community Land Act will increase the risks for the housebuilder. On the one hand, the obtaining of land may become more orderly and less hazardous than before, but on the other, the operations of the local authority may introduce a new element of uncertainty for the householder.'[17] Without sensitive and objective policies on disposal the local authorities could sacrifice the resources and expertise that currently reside in the construction industry.

An attempt has also been made to maintain incentives for the sale of land during the transitional period. Local authorities will be able to purchase net of development land tax,[18] thus acquiring land cheaply and securing the betterment for the community when the land is developed. Owners will pay the tax at an initial rate of up to 80% of the difference between the market value and a use value which, broadly speaking, will be just above current-use value or the price at which the land was last sold, whichever is the higher. This is regarded as providing sufficient incentive to encourage landowners to bring land forward and to give the authorities sufficient time to prepare for the second phase when all development land will be acquired at existing use value.

Implications for Land Development

In some ways the Act has merely made obligatory to all authorities what a few enterprising ones have already been doing. They have long held powers to acquire land for their own purposes, and some of them have assembled land banks at attractive prices in anticipation of later development, thus realising the betterment for the community. Some have entered into partnership schemes with private developers, obtaining planning gains (e.g. car parks, housing, infrastructure) in comprehensive developments. They have been able to influence the dwelling sizes, density, mix, and layout of private development when granting planning permissions.

In other respects, too, the Act is hardly dramatic. The principle of a betterment charge has long been generally accepted. The exemptions and exceptions to the Act put beyond its scope agriculture and forestry, and, within areas of urban development, there are considerable exemptions. The long transitional period and the various compromises inherent in the Act, together with a shortage of both financial and manpower resources to implement it, suggest a slow and cautious approach.

The flavour of compromise and gradualness, and the partial nature of the scheme, render it far less radical than the advocates of state control over land planning might have wished. But this has not lessened its political vulnerability. The Conservative opposition spokesman described the measure as the 'greatest threat we have seen to the concept of the private ownership of property and consequently to the freedom of the individual'.[19] Such polemic has been matched by more sober academic condemnation.

[17]T. Stapleton (1976) *The Land Development Process*, School for Advanced Urban Studies, Community Land Training Programme, Background Paper 7, p. 7.6

[18]Development land tax replaces all other forms of taxation formerly used to secure some of the betterment arising from land transactions.

[19]H. Rossi (1975) Community land — the Conservative viewpoint. *Estates Gazette,* 21 June, p. 889–95, p. 889.

'What remains in very serious doubt is whether this most recent enactment is the most appropriate vehicle for implementing a policy of land reform. While undeniably standing as a statement of radical political philosophy it still reflects a fundamentally superficial analysis of the problem.'[20] Opponents of the scheme argue that its desirable features could be achieved in other ways (e.g. through taxation) or by developing existing arrangements. It is the political provocation of the Act rather than its technical weaknesses that must threaten its survival.

Whether the Act survives or not, it has once again exposed the conflicts between planning and the market which are inherent in a mixed economy. Although the Act is supposedly planning led, there is the very real possibility that financial objectives will determine planning decisions. This is partly because the government, anxious for financial return in the hope of making the Act more durable, has urged authorities to ensure a quick turnover of land.[21] Also the scheme provides greater incentive to acquire 'greenfield' sites, where prices are likely to be low, at or near existing use value. On such sites the development land tax will be high, and since local authorities purchase net of such tax it will prove attractive. Conversely, on those sites where market prices are high, where existing permissions are held and where the tax is correspondingly low, the incentive for purchase will be low. The Act may, therefore, continue to encourage the sporadic development of the urban periphery and do very little to encourage authorities to acquire and develop central and inner urban sites which have often lain derelict for years. Although structure plans may stress the need for using up existing sites to redevelop decaying inner areas and to prevent further encroachment on agricultural land, the financial realities may point in the opposite direction. Recent concern over the plight of the inner cities has, however, led the government to promise preference to proposals to develop land in inner areas using the Act.[22].

It is becoming clear that the Community Land Act will, in the short run at least, have relatively little impact. The drop in land prices giving a low rate of return, the bank of outstanding unimplemented planning permissions, the cost of holding land and preparing for disposal, the low returns available to local authorities through the distribution of surpluses formula,[23] and the lack of capital to finance the scheme[24] will mean that many transactions will take place outside the scheme and those within it will yield little in the way of surplus. The almost total dominance of Conservative administrations following the local elections of 1976 (district councils) and 1977 (county councils) has further reduced enthusiasm for the scheme. Even in the longer term should the Act survive, the impact may not be very great. The pressures for growth and

[20]J. Ratcliffe (1976) *Land Policy*, London, Hutchinson Educational, p. 68.
[21]This becomes clear from a careful reading of the advice to local authorities given as a result of public expenditure cuts. Although each application for loan sanction will require 'strong planning backing', selection will also depend on timing of acquisition and disposal and the cash flow in land accounts. Housing land will have to be disposed of within two years and recoup its costs. This will 'minimise the burden of holding charges and provide a sound financial basis for the land scheme' (Department of the Environment, Community Land Notes, GNLA/12 16 December 1976, p. 3).
[22]*Policy for the Inner Cities*, Cmnd. 6845, Annex, para. 12, London, HMSO, 1977.
[23]The surpluses made through the Community Land Act are to be distributed in the proportions 40% to central government, 30% to the authority making the surplus, and 30% to a redistribution pool to spread the benefits among all authorities. This low return and the small surpluses likely to arise in the early years result in a modest financial incentive to the local authorities.
[24]The initial annual borrowing capacity under the scheme for Great Britain was £102 million. This was reduced by £35 million as part of the public expenditure costs in 1977/8 and 1978/9.

development have abated as a consequence of economic stagnation and a slowing down of population growth. Most structure plans appear to be adopting a low growth profile. Attention has increasingly been focused on the inner city where the effect of the scheme is likely to be small. Elsewhere, especially on the urban fringes, much of the development land has already been 'committed' in planning terms. While the Act may affect the terms of transactions on some of the peripheral sites, it is unlikely that large new areas of land will be identified beyond the commitments already described in structure plans.

Potentially the most fundamental change will be in the relationship between the planning and valuation processes. This will occur wherever land developments are carried out under the Act. Although there is clearly a reciprocal relationship between planning and land values, it has tended to be obscured by the administrative separation of planning and financial decision-making within public authorities. Planning committees are expected to make their decisions on 'planning grounds'. Although applications are initiated by developers in the hope of financial gain, and although the decision to accept or reject has direct financial consequences, these are not regarded as relevant to the planning decision. The artificial segregation of planning and financial issues will be more difficult under the land scheme. Planners will not be immune from spelling out the financial consequences of their recommendations.

'The planner therefore is presented with a tough challenge. If he opts out of the debate, the trade off between profit and the achievement of other objectives will be decided without considering the implementation of the planning strategy. If, however, he enters the debate he will be faced possibly for the first time with justifying restrictions on development or insisting on certain planning standards against the possible gain to the land account of following proposals not in accord with the planning framework'.[25]

The financial stewardship of planners will be evaluated in several ways — the surplus made on transactions, the rate of turnover needed to avoid interest charges and administrative costs in holding land, and the maintenance of a healthy and viable construction industry. Local authorities will have a greater responsibility for both identifying land and deciding on its use. The system of public control over private initiative will be replaced by one where local authorities have responsibility for the promotion as well as the control of land development. There are considerable misgivings about the ability of local authorities to provide the initiative, take the risks, and secure the benefits for the community in both financial and planning terms. Despite its imperfections some commentators consider the market a better means of satisfying the preferences of society. 'Without some way of acquiring knowledge of preferences positive planning can easily turn into decision-making by a small group of decision-makers whose objectives may be unclear or contrary to the public's wishes, and whose activities are usually imperfectly monitored.'[26] On the other hand, the market is less well equipped to evaluate the social costs and benefits of individual developments.

The operation of the Community Land Act gives considerable discretion to local authorities. There is thus scope for differing interpretations and for conflict between

[25]School for Advanced Urban Studies, *The Planning Framework*, Community Land Training Programme, Background Paper 4, p. 4.3.
[26]A. Maynard An economic analysis of the Land Act 1975', paper presented at seminar of Chartered Institute of Public Finance and Accountancy, p. 15, 1975. Also in Local Government Studies, July 1976.

authorities encouraged by political differences and by the two-tier system. Both tiers have responsibilities under the Act which are specified in land acquisition and management schemes, some of which 'read like an international treaty, based on mutual suspicion and mistrust'.[27] Whether authorities are active or passive in their attitudes to the acquisition of land and whether they are motivated by planning or financial considerations is fundamentally a political issue. An attempt to promulgate the notion of positive planning by a piece of national legislation presupposes that there is a clear understanding of its objectives and a ubiquitous willingness to achieve them. Despite changes in the planning system, the reform of local government, and efforts to achieve greater control over the land market, planning has remained largely subservient to financial and local political circumstances. The development of land at the local level has less to do with grandiose conceptions of long-term positive planning than with the local circumstances prevailing at any one time. The following empirical examples will suggest the validity of Catanese's contention that 'the local political process will overrule long range and comprehensive plans based solely upon rationality principles of planning'.[28]

2. LAND PLANNING AT THE LOCAL LEVEL

The importance of changes in the planning, governmental, and financial framework lies not so much in terms of long-term planning policies and the general distribution of wealth and real incomes as on their effect on the balance between various interests in land at the local level. Decisions on land tend to involve ideological, financial, and planning considerations. Decision-makers are susceptible to pressures from the various interests involved. Those interests which are most likely to be successful are those most able to articulate their case and to gain access to the decision-makers. Thus land policy is likely to represent the balance achieved at any one time between various sectional interests. It is an intensely political matter although planners profess to operate here as elsewhere as disinterested protectors of 'public interest'. 'The belief that planning is non-political seems pathologically well-entrenched even ironically among those planners who accept the validity of the suggestion that "planning is political".'[29] In other words, professional planners tend to equate 'political' with politicians, and fail to recognise the significance of their own values in presenting choices. That their values and hence their choices differ among themselves and between them and politicians has already been evident in the two previous case-studies.

As well as treating politics with circumspection, some planners may also be hostile to the private sector, regarding it as 'motivated by greed, steeped in speculation, staffed by furtive entrepreneurs and marshalled by a landed profession sunk in abject cynicism'.[30]

The distinction between interests, especially between private and public interests,

[27]School for Advanced Studies (1976) *Management Implications*, Community Land Training Programme, Background Paper 8, March. p. 8.20.
[28]A. J. Catanese (1974). *Planners and Local Politics: Impossible Dreams*, Beverley Hills. Saga Publications.
[29]E. J. Reade (1977) 'Some educational consequences of the incorporation of the planning profession into the state bureaucracy', paper presented to the Conference of Sociologists in Polytechnics Section of the British Sociological Association, April, p. 13.
[30]J. Ratcliffe (1976) op. cit., p. 100.

may be far from clear. The public interest is not a unitary unequivocal conception. Instead of one common public interest there are many sectional interests — public and private. These interests may be in conflict or in concert. The distinction becomes even more problematic when decision-makers acting on behalf of the public are themselves involved in or influenced by private interests.

Broad generalisations about the role of interests in land and their relationship to the organisation of the state and a capitalist economy are unlikely to provide insight into the process of urban development. Such insight must be sought by the use of detailed empirical evidence gathered at the local level. 'However, the use of case-studies raises the obvious question of how "representative" the cases chosen are.'[31] It would be impossible to claim representativeness for the case-studies which follow. They are concerned solely with urban fringe development and are taken from one area in the United Kingdom. These examples do illustrate different aspects of the politics of land development and indicate the nature of the interests involved, the types of conflict to which they give rise, and the relative importance of planning considerations in arriving at decisions. They also help us to interpret the effect of national legislation upon local land-planning policy. These examples cover the period 1973–7, a period of administrative and political changes in Bedfordshire. It was also the time during which the Community Land Act was introduced and the county structure plan developed. The major aims of the structure plan, which was submitted in 1977, were to meet the county's housing and employment needs in a context of low population growth. The countryside and agriculture would be conserved by concentrating future development around the major towns.

(a) Bedford

The first case concerns a land transaction that took place in 1973–4 just prior to local government reorganisation and before the Community Land Act. Post-war urban development in Bedford has been largely on the north and east and south-west fringes of the town. Much of this development was undertaken by the former borough council buying up land well in advance of need, granting planning permissions, preparing the sites, designing the layout, and allocating the land to private builders and developers or using it for the council's own developments. In this role of estate developer the council was able to secure betterment on its transactions and to control the nature of the developments, a process not unlike that envisaged by the Community Land Act. Purchases were made as opportunities arose, and therefore urban development tended to be influenced by land availability and financial considerations.

The issue concerns three plots of land to the north-west of the town[32] (see Fig. 6.1a). The developer was the Harpur Trust,[33] which, as we saw in the previous chapter, had sold off a prime town-centre site occupied by one of its direct grant schools for

[31]S. J. Elkin (1974) *Politics and Land Use Planning, The London Experience*, Cambridge, Cambridge University Press, p. 10.

[32]This issue is described in more detail in A. T. Blowers (1974) Land ownership and the public interest: the case of Operation Leapfrog, *Town and Country Planning*. November, pp. 499–503.

[33]The Harpur Trust was a charity administering 4 schools — 2 independent and 2 direct grant (i.e. with a mixture of private and state-assisted pupils).

redevelopment as a shopping centre with an associated car park. An integral part of this deal was the relocation of the school on a site on the periphery of the town. The trust proposed to purchase 32 acres of land adjoining its new school and owned by the council for playing fields (site A on Fig. 6.1b), enabling it to release its existing playing fields which occupied two sites (9 and 19 acres, sites B and C on Fig. 6.1b) separated from the new school by a road. Part of the smaller of these two sites (site B) would be dedicated to the council for open space (4 acres), an option for housing development would be granted to the council on the rest of that site (5 acres), while the developer would sell his larger site for private housing (site C).

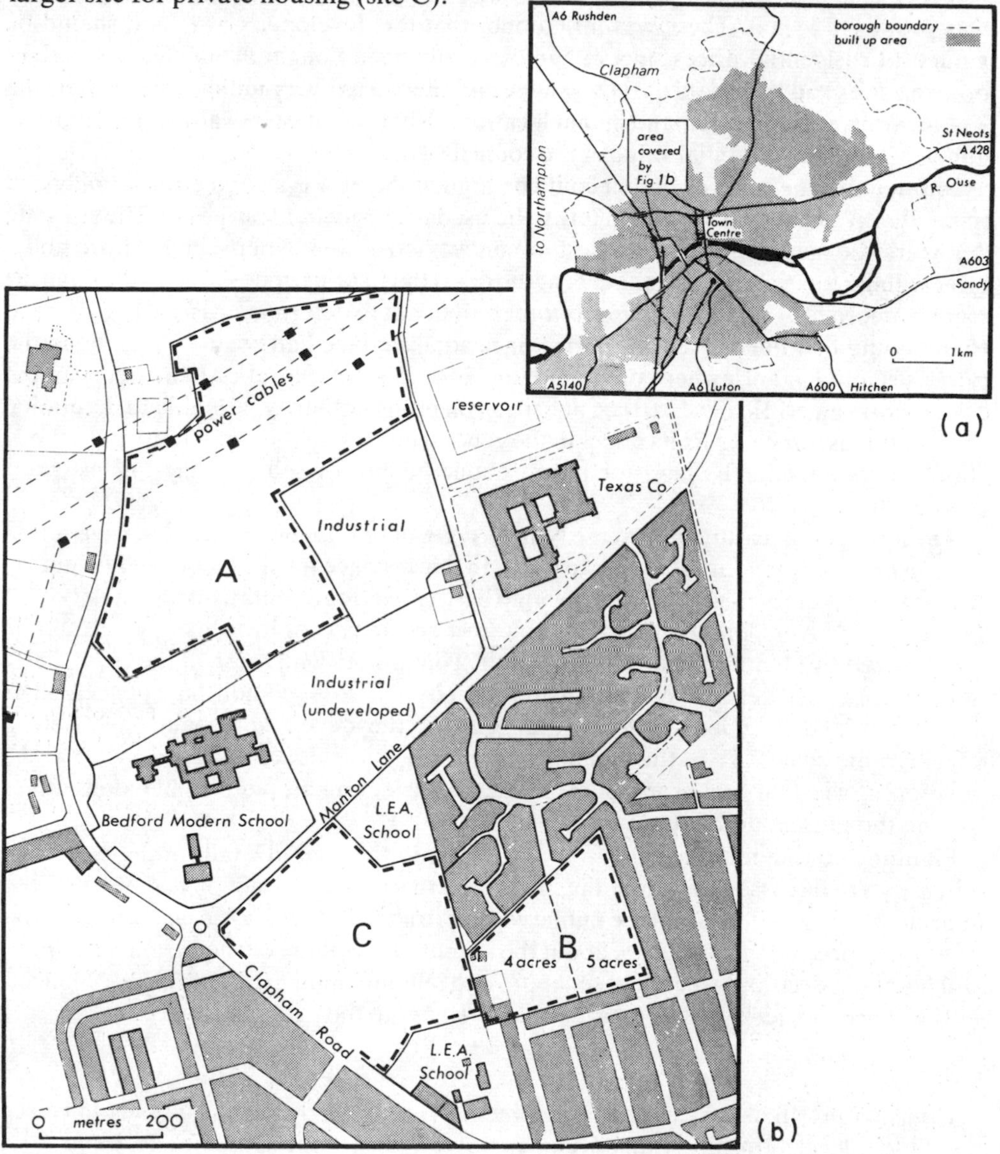

Fig. 6.1(a). Bedford — location of study area. (b) Bedford — location of individual sites.

In planning terms the trust would clearly benefit by having playing fields as an integral part of its new school campus. The council, too, would gain the immediate benefit of open space and a site for its housing but would forfeit the future potential use of its own large site. The transfer of the 19-acre site (C) from private playing fields to private housing development would mean the loss of open land but the gain of housing. The financial aspects of the deal proved controversial. The council's land would be sold at existing use (agricultural) value plus a premium at £2000 per acre, thus realising £64,000. But the developer's land would be sold at residential value (at that time possibly as high at £50,000 per acre) realising potentially £1.2 million for the 24 acres it was proposed to sell. There was little doubt that the developer's own land should be valued at residential prices since it had originally been bought at such values, neighbouring sites had been sold at such values, and there was every indication that housing was an appropriate use for land in that location. What was at issue was the potential use and therefore the potential value of the council's land.

In favour of the price offered it could be argued that it was a good offer for hilly and unproductive land which was unlikely to be used for residential purposes. The site (site A) would be landscaped and would form an attractive wedge between Bedford and a large village to the north. Opponents of the deal (the Labour opposition on the council) were concerned to establish its appropriate value, not to determine its use. They argued that it could be valued at a higher price since adjacent land had been sold for industrial purposes and land elsewhere on the urban fringe in similar locations had been sold at residential values. In any case the council, as planning authority, was able to determine its use and, as owner, to fix its price. In the general interest of the community the council should either retain the land for future public benefit or sell it at the highest price possible.

The interesting feature of this case is that a developer was able to initiate a transaction on conspicuously favourable terms to itself. In this instance the developer was helped by the fact that there was considerable overlap between its representatives and members of the council.[34] Any potential conflict of interest on the part of these members could be rationalized by identifying the interests of the community with those of the trust. Early negotiations were kept secret. Even in the absence of a close relationship between seller and buyer and in a less secretive atmosphere, the developer would have held a considerable advantage as the initiator of the transaction. The council was put into the position of reacting to a proposal rather than considering all the possible alternatives both in the present and future.

Planning considerations played very little part in the issue. Details of the particular scheme were discussed only after the financial terms of the transaction had been agreed in principle. Objections from the public were restricted to the specific planning application which precluded any debate about the potential use of the council's land. Financial and planning decisions were kept separate, and public comment on the financial aspects — the central issue — was disregarded as irrelevant to the planning issues.

Conclusions In its residential developments, Bedford Council had already nurtured the kind of relationship with developers envisaged by the Community Land Act.

[34]Eleven of the thirty governers of the trust were also members of the borough council, and four were members of the council's Estates Committee which dealt with land transactions.

Developments had proceeded according to opportunities rather than according to any master plan. In the case considered here the borough had not made its future intentions for the land clear. Under the Community Land Act the council would be expected to designate land for relevant development. If it did not do so, there is nothing to preclude a deal similar to that initiated by the developer. The power to determine the use of the land and its price would remain, as it did before the Act, with the council.

With the development of structure and local plans the public are afforded an opportunity to debate the alternative uses of land, which was not the case with the deal considered here. However, such plans are intended to be flexible and can be revised in the light of changing circumstances. Their implementation is likely to be incremental and the original objectives of a plan may well be subverted over time.

It is difficult to evaluate the public interest in land since this is composed of several interests both now and in the future. In the case considered here the present population could benefit by the acquisition of some open space (site B) in an older housing area but a future population could be denied a potential amenity (site A). The public could be said to benefit from the sale of land (site A) at above the existing use value but lose the opportunity of future sale at a possibly higher value. The benefit to the trust was not merely a private one since the acquisition of playing fields brought educational benefits to that part of the public who could afford or achieve access to its schools. The distribution of costs and benefits embraces all those opportunities, present and future, foregone or created both financially and in terms of planning as a consequence of the deal. Such a comprehensive evaluation of a transaction is neither practicable nor politically realistic. At any one time where one interest recognises an opportunity from land development it is likely to achieve its objectives so long as there is no clear and generally accepted alternative in sight. In the Bedford case the Harpur Trust, quite aside from its access to decision-makers, had a clear objective. Its opponents were forced into objecting to the scheme as proposed without presenting any clear alternative. Discussions of the financial aspects of the deal were precluded from public debate until the crucial features had been settled. Where alternative proposals for land development do exist and are marshalled by competing authorities each purporting to be acting for the public interest, the outcome is less certain, as the next case demonstrates.

(b) Luton

(i) *The 'Green Wedge'*

Luton, the largest town in Bedfordshire, is a product of growth in the car industry. The Chiltern Hills and Luton Hoo (areas of high amenity) to the south and east of the town have been largely responsible for its eccentric shape since outward growth has been confined to the north and west of the town centre (Fig. 6.2). Dunstable and Houghton Regis to the west have begun to coalesce with Luton. The remaining open space between these three settlements — the Green Wedge — has been the subject of pressure for residential development and other urban uses. The case studied here

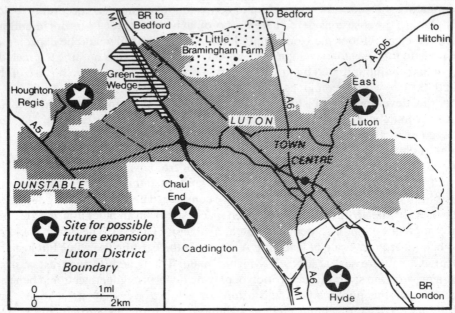

Fig. 6.2 Luton, Dunstable and Houghton Regis — location of sites.

reveals the problems which arose in attempting to define the use of this land. It occurred after local government reorganisation and during the preparation of the county structure plan.

The area consists of 97.5 acres just north of the built up area of Luton, bounded on the west and south by residential land, on the east by the London–Birmingham motorway M1, and to the north by the boundary of Luton with South Bedfordshire, beyond which is an area of open land. The whole area (475 acres) lying between the three settlements and stretching across the M1 is all that remains of the Green Wedge which the Greater London Plan (1944[35]) indicated should stretch over 2500 acres and maintain the separate identity of Luton and Dunstable. Since the war the Wedge has been progressively eroded as the suburbs of Luton and Dunstable have been developed and the village of Houghton Regis transformed by the introduction of London 'overspill' population. The issue was whether that part of the Wedge remaining within Luton and owned by the borough should be developed for council housing, thus further reducing the Green Wedge.

Earlier decisions had indicated the conflict between housing pressure and the need to preserve an open area (Figs. 6.3 and 6.4). After a public inquiry, which released 850 acres in 1956, the Minister commented: 'Although the existing Green Wedge between Luton and Dunstable cannot be fully preserved, some green space should be maintained between the communities, particularly in the area flanking the proposed motorway.'[36] Part of the eastern edge was released for warehousing, though part was later refused for similar purposes. On this occasion (1971) the Inspector reporting the public inquiry stated:

[35]P. Abercrombie (1945) *Greater London Plan*, London, HMSO.
[36]Bedfordshire County Council (1974) *Luton/Dunstable Green Wedge*, Joint Appraisal, 8 November, p. 3.

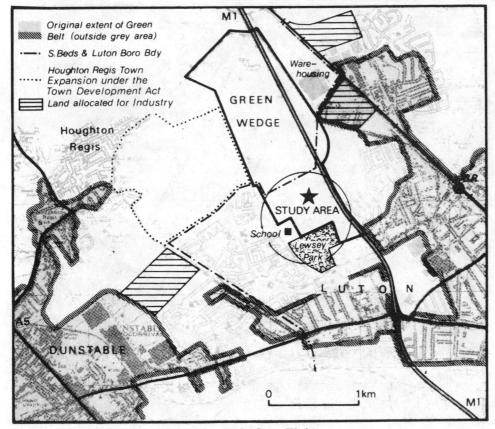

Fig. 6.3 Luton, the Green Wedge.

I accept that visually the Green Wedge is marred by Electricity power lines and also that the clamour of the Motorway is a predominant and ugly feature, nevertheless it is possible to find reminders that this was once pleasant country. I do not feel, however, that the loss of visual amenity can be regarded as a major issue in this case. What does matter is the retention of open land on the outskirts of a large town where there is obvious pressure.[37]

To the north of the Wedge the London overspill scheme was designed to retain a substantial area of green space, but there were pressures from a private developer for housing land. It appeared that resistance to further development was hardening when proposals to develop a hypermarket and housing in various parts of the Wedge were refused. By 1974 a large part of the Wedge had been absorbed for various kinds of development, but at each stage there had been reference to the desirability of maintaining some open land between the three converging settlements.

It was in these circumstances that Luton Borough Council proposed to develop the remaining land within their boundary, aptly named Pastures Way. They proposed that part should be retained as open space (32.5 acres), part for schools (41 acres), and the

[37]Ibid., p. 6.

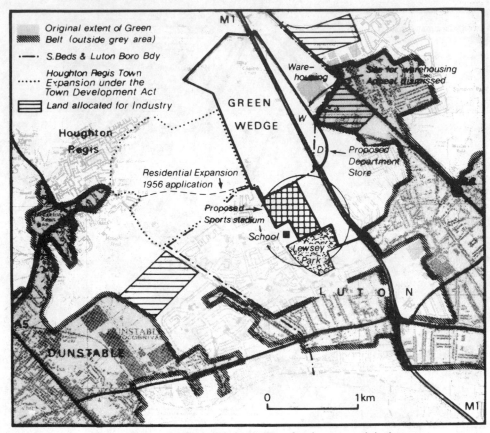

Fig. 6.4. Luton, the Green Wedge — Past-planning proposals in the area.

remainder (24 acres) should be developed for council housing (Fig. 6.5). It was the residential proposal that brought the borough into direct conflict with the county council. The county council argued that 'retention of the character of the area is of paramount importance'.[38] They were prepared to concede the use of the land for schools or recreation, which were not felt to be incompatible with the concept of the Green Wedge. But they feared that the release of land for housing would make it difficult to resist the pressure for development on the remaining part of the Wedge. In sum their position was: 'The residential proposal would be completely contrary to the established policy to retain the "green wedge", and if permitted, would create a serious precedent whereby it would be difficult to resist other similar proposals in this area.'[39] The borough council who owned the land argued that the land was essential to meet their housing needs. Luton was a housing stress area with a waiting list of 4000 families, and there was no immediately available land, apart from the site, to help meet their housing needs. They did not consider that residential development 'would represent

[38]Department of the Environment (1976) 'Proposed residential development on land off Pastures Way, Luton', Inspector's report, para. 86.
[39]Bedfordshire County Council, Environmental Services Committee, Agenda Item 23, 26 April 1974.

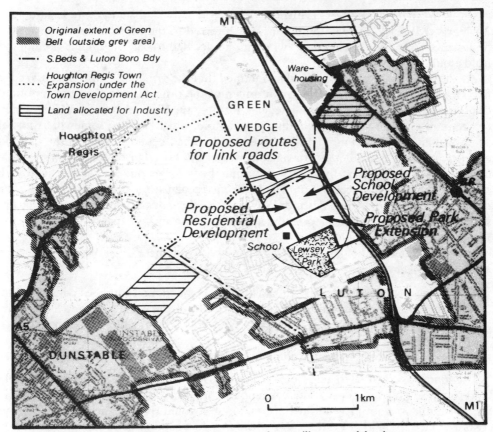

Fig. 6.5. Luton, the Green Wedge — borough council's proposed development.

more than marginal visual intrusion detracting from the character and quality of the area'.[40]

The conflict led to divisions on political, professional, and geographical lines. Consultations were held between the two councils. In June 1974, the county's Environmental Service Committee reaffirmed its view that the proposal was contrary to established policy which aimed to retain the open land on the outskirts of Luton and Dunstable and to prevent their coalescence. Luton's pressure on the county council was maintained, and it was eventually decided to arrange a joint meeting between the three councils involved (Luton, South Bedfordshire, and the county council). At this meeting the divisions between and within the councils became apparent. The officers of the county council and of Luton maintained opposing positions, whereas South Bedfordshire's officers were prepared to accept a small amount of residential development but not the whole 24 acres. However, the South Bedfordshire members at the joint meeting supported the county council's line. Luton's members were, as expected, fully in favour of the proposal. The county members were divided. At the subsequent meeting of the Environmental Services Committee to discuss the consultation, 7 members supported Luton (all Labour, 4 from Luton) while 11 opposed it (7 Conservatives and 4 Labour, 3

[40]Bedfordshire County Council (1974) op. cit., p. 20.

of whom were from South Bedfordshire). There were also 3 abstentions (1 Labour and 2 Liberals).[41] Early in 1975 the matter was referred to the Minister as a 'substantial departure' from the development plan, and he decided to call the application in and hold a public inquiry.

At the inquiry the county council maintained that the principle of the Green Wedge had been vindicated despite the loss of much of the original land. They also poured doubt on Luton's housing programme, claiming that the borough owned sufficient land to accommodate an increased building programme, which, though somewhat short of the borough's proposed rate, was much faster than had been achieved in the past. In addition there was further land available within the borough to accommodate 3500 dwellings within the next five years and a number of sites outside the borough with reasonable rail or road access. Luton had failed to recognise the need for overspill. 'The only merit in developing the Pastures Way site is its cheapness to the borough which has shown a parochial approach to land acquisition and a lack of foresight. There is no insuperable shortage of alternative land.'[42]

Luton countered this by suggesting that policy on the Green Wedge had been ambivalent over the years. They concluded that:

'the original Green Belt concept had long been abandoned with tacit consent from Ministers. Now any suggestion of keeping the built-up areas of Luton and Dunstable separate is irrelevant. What is left is the green wedge which, within the Borough, has little visual importance, its only possible function being the preservation of *some* open space between residential communities and the M1.'[43]

The land was essential to help Luton achieve its housing programme. The alternative land suggested by the county council was not immediately available, was not owned by the borough, was not provided with services, and would result in heavy construction costs. Failure to build at Pastures Way would leave a gap in the building programme. The county council's approach was 'the planning approach which ignores the delays and snags which a housing authority must first overcome'.[44] 'It is a theoretical approach to the problem but we have got to look wider than pure theory.'[45]

Not surprisingly the Inspector regarded Pastures Way as a 'finely balanced case in which two important issues are in direct conflict'.[46] He accepted the county council's arguments that the proposed housing programme could not be achieved and that other sites were available. He concluded: 'I think the time has come to call a halt to all further inappropriate developments within the green wedge unless there are overwhelming reasons for allowing them.'[47] He did not consider the housing needs to be overwhelming and therefore recommended that the permission be refused. However, the Minister disagreed with this conclusion. He felt the housing needs were the prime consideration and the immediate availability of the site had been largely ignored. Moreover, he

[41]At the following meeting when the committee received a formal application from Luton the voting was 5 for (all Labour) and 10 against (5 Conservative, 3 Liberal, 2 Labour). As a result the matter was referred to the Minister.
[42]'The grim battle to provide homes' *Luton Evening post.*
[43]Department of the Environment (1976), op. cit., p. 4.
[44]Ibid. p. 8.
[45]*Luton Evening Post*, op. cit.
[46]Department of the Environment (1976), op. cit., p. 1
[47]Ibid., p. 2.

emphasised the economic arguments in favour of the site which had been ignored by the county council and not given great prominence by the borough. He said: 'at a time when savings must be made in all fields of public expenditure the comparative cheapness of the application site must be counted an important consideration.'[48] He made the obligatory reference to the Green Wedge concept and his sentiments were not very different from those voiced when the Wedge had been breached on previous occasions. 'This decision is not to be taken however as indicating abandonment of the green wedge which is considered in general to be sound and valuable, nor is it meant to be significant in relation to any other development proposals within the green wedge.'[49]

Conclusions. In this case the debate was over the use of a piece of land — not over its value — since it was already in public ownership and there was no question of its sale. Both protagonists could claim to be serving the public interest, the county asserting the long-term desirability of maintaining an amenity and Luton stressing immediate housing need. The long-term strategic concept of a green belt had, by a process of incrementalism, been subverted and transformed into the more modest aim of protecting some open land as a green wedge. Planning policy in this area — and arguably in many similar areas — had responded to immediate pressures and reflected the political and economic situation existing at different points in time. The county council could maintain a strategic view regarding the development within the context of potential (and less environmentally damaging) development elsewhere whether in Luton or outside. Luton, embarking on an ambitious housing programme, were unimpressed by such arguments and concerned to occupy the site as the most readily available. The forces were evenly matched at local level, leaving the issue to be settled by means of a public inquiry.

The inquiry process is supposedly neutral, weighing up the different arguments to provide an informed judgement. In this case the Inspector was overruled by the Minister who was able to provide a different interpretation to the evidence presented. The introduction of new arguments by the Minister to support his disagreement with the Inspector's findings was unprecedented. But pressure had been applied on the Minister both by the MP for Luton West and by the chairman of the Luton Housing Committee, both of whom were Labour. It may well be that such informal approaches were decisive. Certainly the County Planning Officer described it as a 'political decision'.

Such a reaction misses the central point that such decisions are intensely political. Planners offer advice based on their own ideological predilections. 'There simply cannot be any objectively correct answer to the question of how resources should be allocated. It is a question for politicians, not experts.'[50] If it were possible to argue objectively, then we might assume that all planners would arrive at similar conclusions. This was manifestly not the case here. Evidence was selected, sifted, and interpreted in arriving at recommendations. It is also important to recognise the significance of the circumstances prevailing at the time the decision was taken. A little later the county planners might have been strengthened by a much greater resistance from the Ministry of Agriculture unwilling to lose valuable agricultural land. A little later, too, the downturn

[48]Ibid., p. 3.
[49]Ibid., p. 3.
[50]E. J. Reade (1975) 'An attempt to distinguish planning from other modes of decision making', seminar paper, University of Manchester, Department of Town and Country Planning, 24 November, p. 8.

in the economy, widespread public expenditure cuts, a new (Conservative) administration in Luton less concerned to build council houses, might have weakened or removed altogether the case for housing at Pastures Way. The conflict between short-range incremental planning against long-term strategic planning is always likely to be resolved in favour of the former. It is unlikely that the Community Land Act or the structure plan would have changed the situation. The land was, in any case, publicly owned, and the structure plan would only deal in broad land-use terms, leaving local land allocation to be resolved through local plans.

It is interesting to compare Luton Borough's arguments about their housing needs with actual performance once the permission was granted. The borough had stated that 129 houses would be built in 1976/7 and the remainder in 1977/8. By the middle of 1977 only 75 were under construction and altogether four phases were proposed, the second to be completed by 1980. The arguments advanced at the time may well have been very genuine but it does show how rapidly events (political and economic) can alter the circumstances of a case.

(ii) *Little Bramingham Farm*

The largest remaining undeveloped plot of land within Luton was Little Bramingham Farm (375 acres) to the north of the town (see Fig. 6.2). In this case the dispute was not over the use to which the land should be put, there being general agreement that it was suitable for housing, but whether it should be used for public or private housing. The issue arose in 1976 just at the time when the Community Land Act came into operation, when the draft structure plan for Bedfordshire was published, and when political control in Luton changed from Labour to Conservative.

The site, in private ownership, was capable of accommodating a population of about 7000, an industrial area, and the facilities necessary to create a residential neighbourhood. Both the county and borough councils were committed to the principle of housing development for this area. The Ministry of Agriculture were opposed to the loss of this grade 2 land, but despite this and the structure plan's emphasis on conservation of the best land, an outline planning permission was granted to the borough in 1976. It was accepted at that stage that the land would be purchased under the Community Land Act as a mixed public and private development but with substantial amount of council housing to meet the borough's housing needs. This would enable the development to corespond to the structure plan's aim to meet local housing needs by concentrating future development around the major urban areas.

After the change in political control from Labour to Conservative in May 1976, the new administration in Luton published an outline development plan which appeared to threaten the strategy of the structure plan. It envisaged that some of the development would be for private housing, although it favoured giving local people priority in the purchase of dwellings. Phased release of land 'to meet the needs of Luton's natural increase only is vitally important if the strategic aims outlined by the county structure plan are to be achieved'.[51] The county planners argued that there were practical difficulties in achieving this since there was evidence that half of the purchasers of

[51]Borough of Luton, 'Little Bramingham Farm, Outline Development Plan', September 1976, p. 1.

private houses came from outside the county. The level of public housing proposed was too low to meet the housing needs of those unable to purchase houses. If the development attracted people from outside the area then land would have to be released elsewhere to meet Luton's housing needs. This could result in a higher rate of development than was proposed in the structure plan. Despite efforts to discuss the issue, the borough as the housing authority were able to develop the area in any way they wished, arguing that a phased release of the land would enable them to meet local demand as it arose.

It is significant that the Labour administration had decided to purchase the land under the Community Land Act, which was designed largely to deal with private housing development rather than through the Housing Acts which gave loan sanctions for council housing projects. This seriously weakened attempts made by the Labour MP for Luton West to persuade the Minister to intervene in the issue. He argued that loan sanction had originally been given for the purchase of the site to enable Luton to tackle its housing problems.

'The officers of the County Council from the Chief Planning Officer down have asked if there is any way I can help to make the Council face up responsibly to its obligations . . . The new Conservative Council has added massive stupidity to ideological spite in their housing policies . . . It may not be possible to save the Council entirely from its follies but a quiet word now could avoid a future disaster.'[52]

The Minister replied that the loan sanction had been granted without conditions as to the mix of public and private housing and, in any event, the community Land Act was intended to ensure a sufficient supply of land for private development. He adopted the conventional ministerial stance of non-interference with local authorities, saying it was up to the council to determine its programme. The MP was not satisfied: 'it is difficult to think of anything more irresponsible for a housing authority to do than to wash its hands like Pontius Pilate as Luton is doing of the problems of thousands of families. I hope this hand washing does not become infectious.'[54] He regarded the policies of Luton as 'inspired by a pathological class hatred of council tenants'.[55] However, it was clear that the Minister was not prepared to intervene.

Conclusions. Little Bramingham Farm is of interest since it was debated at a time of considerable change in the national and local circumstances governing land transactions. It exposed a crucial weakness in the structure planning process, namely, that housing and growth policies left much to the interpretation and determination of local housing authorities. Both Labour and Conservative administrations in Luton, with vastly differing ideologies on housing, could claim they intended to meet the housing policy of the structure plan. Once the county council had accepted the principle of housing development in the area there was little more they could do to influence the type of development pursued. Likewise, whatever the postures struck by the local MP, the Minister forbore to intervene in such a sensitive local issue as housing or to risk a

[52]Letter from MP for Luton West to Parliamentary Under-Secretary of State, Department of the Environment, 8 November 1976.
[53]Ibid, 27 December 1976.
[54]Letter from MP for Luton West to Chief Executive, Borough of Luton, 3 January 1977.

clash with a local authority of a different political complexion. Indeed, the Community Land Act, with its emphasis on achieving quick returns on private housing development, lent support to the policy pursued by the borough council. At least it gave them potentially more control over the development than if it had been undertaken by the private sector. In any case, if the council had wished to develop predominantly council housing it had the necessary compulsory purchase powers and loan sanctions available to it. But such a large development could have implications for the future strategic development of Luton and the problem of finding land for future expansion.

(iii) *The expansion of Luton*

The question of land for the future expansion of Luton had been raised in the debates over the Green Wedge and Little Bramingham Farm. It became a major controversial issue in the preparation of the structure plan. The structure planning process is the subject of the next chapter — here I shall deal with one of the issues it was expected to resolve. The broad aim of the structure plan was to make the best use of existing resources and to conserve agriculture and the countryside by concentrating future growth around the existing urban centres. Projections of future population for the Luton area indicated that room for about 3600 dwellings would be needed beyond land already committed by 1991. It had been accepted that such land should be found within the county rather than outside it at Milton Keynes. Four potential sites had been identified (see Fig. 6.2). One, to the east of Luton, was generally acceptable as a natural extension of the existing built-up area, but another, to the south at Caddington, was ruled out on grounds of aircraft noise from the flight path associated with Luton Airport. The county planning officers preferred a third site to the north-west at Houghton Regis on grounds of good transportation links and because it would not interfere with high-grade agricultural land. They also argued: 'Development at Houghton Regis could have the added positive value of helping to improve the provision of social and commercial facilities.'[55] Certainly the GLC's housing development at Houghton Regis had given rise to social problems.[56] A fourth site, to the south-east of Luton, at Hyde on the Hertfordshire border, had been suggested during consultations with Luton Borough Council. 'A possibility not identified in the Strategy is development in the Hyde area which is largely free from constraint, is closer to the town centre facilities than any site to the north and which could utilize road and rail without adding immediate congestion to existing patterns of travel.'[57]

Houghton Regis had originally been selected by the Environmental Services Committee on the insistence of the County Planning Officer who managed to persuade a small majority to support it at the end of a long meeting with only a few members present. This was the idea put forward for public consultation leaving little scope for public debate about the merits of the Hyde site. After the period of public participation on the structure plan, the Luton Labour members succeeded by a narrow majority in deleting Houghton Regis and substituting Hyde. The plan was twice debated by the

[55]Bedfordshire County Council (1976) *County Structure Plan, Draft Written Statement*, September, p. 72.
[56]M. Price (1976) *Houghton Regis Town Development Scheme: A Study*, Cranfield Institute of Technology, Cranfield, Beds.,
[57]Bedfordshire County Council, *Public Participation Phase I, Report*, p. 20.

county council. On the first occasion the Labour group with the support of the Mayor of Luton and the Leader of Luton Council (both Conservatives who were also members of the county council) maintained the preference for Hyde.

The County Planning Officer described the move as 'a political decision steam-rollered through' but he was reminded that he had employed similar tactics to secure the adoption of Houghton Regis in the first instance. Certainly the Luton Labour members had applied their political muscle. Their motive ostensibly was that the natural area for growth was to the south of Luton, though the fact that Hyde adjoined the Luton Hoo Estate, part of which had long been coveted by Labour politicians, was not unconnected with their decision. The support of leading Conservatives had been decisive, indicating that it was still possible for political differences to be submerged when the interest of the former county borough was at stake. What had clearly emerged was the antipathy of some members to the idea of development at Houghton Regis. The local member claimed that the area should be left alone to recover from problems already experienced through rapid development in the past.

The council's decision released a barrage of criticism on the grounds that public debate on the merits of alternative sites had been avoided. There was a well-orchestrated protest from Hertfordshire led by the Harpenden Society. Local authorities, councillors, and organisations in Hertfordshire registered firm opposition to the proposal. Nearly a thousand individual protests were received before the council met to make its final decisions on the plan before it was submitted to the Minister.[58] the opponents were concerned that no opportunity had been given for objections to be made during the period of public participation. Their objections were based on the loss of amenity and agriculture, the transportation problem, and the high construction and sewerage costs that would result from any development at Hyde. Behind the protests also was the fear that Luton's overspill would adversely affect the environment of Harpenden, a salubrious commuter dormitory on the Bedfordshire border.

The scale of the protest caused the Labour group to reappraise its position and it modified its decision. At the county council meeting (February 1977) when the plan was finally approved, the group passed a motion that should any future land for Luton's needs be required then the county council would examine other sites close to the urban area, including Caddington and Hyde. Although Hyde had not been positively excluded (as a defeated Conservative amendment would have intended) it remained open to debate. Hertfordshire County Council found the proposal 'completely unacceptable' and resolved to carry its objections to the examination in public of the structure plan.

Meanwhile the county council elections produced a Conservative council that might be more sympathetic to the arguments against any expansion at Hyde. In the 'rejoin-der'[59]to the objections to the structure plan the new council maintained that it was probable 'that there will be a need for some additional land to be released to meet the housing needs of the urban area towards the end of the Plan period'. Such need, if it arose, would be accommodated in East Luton. 'Beyond this, the County Council would be prepared to accept an amendment to the submitted Structure Plan to reflect a greater degree of caution about whether additional sites would be required.' Thus all references

[58]The objections included 4 local authorities, 11 organisations, 134 individuals, and 790 signatures to a petition.

[59]Bedfordshire County Council, Planning Advisory Group, 'County Structure Plan: Response to objections', 4 August 1977.

to specific sites could be deleted. If, however, monitoring showed that additional land was required, then 'possible sites close to the urban area will be investigated in conjunction with the District Councils involved'.

The retreat was not enough to allay the fears of the Hertfordshire interests. This issue accounted for 136 out of a total of 241 objections to the structure plan. Of the 136 (127 from within Hertfordshire) 118 were from individuals, 12 from organisations, 5 from local authorities and 1 from an MP. The opposition was carried to the examination in public where the councils involved, two MPs, and the Harpenden Society represented by a QC, explained their opposition with only the Luton Trades Council speaking in favour of development at Hyde. The opponents argued that higher-density development on committed land could accommodate much of the increase and that some diversion of growth to Milton Keynes could be accepted. If further land was to be identified, then all the statutory processes would have to be gone through before any decision was made. The Harpenden Society reiterated the objections to Hyde and suggested that the best approach was to identify the constraints on development around Luton and determine how much could be accommodated within them. They pointed out also that the county council's volte-face in substituting Hyde for Houghton Regis brought about conflicts with other major policies in the structure plan. Thus a manoeuvre by a few Labour members late in a meeting when several members had left had been responsible for a *cause célèbre,* unleashing the passions and encouraging the organised resistance of people from beyond (though only just) the county's borders.

Conclusions. In this example the planners' original proposal had been overturned by the politicians who, in turn, had capitulated in the face of concerted public protest. It demonstrated that where the particular interest of an existing population is directly threatened it can, if properly focused, succeed in preventing development. The ability of well-organised and articulate pressure groups to prevent or modify undesirable development has already been demonstrated in earlier chapters. It is an incidental but ironic feature of this issue that it aroused more public participation — and that from beyond the borders of Bedfordshire — than any other aspect of the structure plan.

The question of the expansion of Luton illustrates once again that any attempt at long-term strategic planning is vulnerable to attack and change. Instead of presenting a clear indication of the location of future growth, the structure plan had been forced, by local political circumstances, to defer a decision and to keep the options open. It always proves easier to avoid conflict by not making a decision. But the existence of conflict leads to future uncertainty, as was the case here. As with the other examples described in this chapter it appears that the urban land development process is characterised by short-term incremental changes rather than responding to a grand design.

3. THE NATURE OF LAND DEVELOPMENT

In the United Kingdom the process of land development is a combination of the market and attempts to influence it on the part of the public planning authorities. At the national political level, land policy has for long been a controversial issue. Successive

Labour governments have tried to increase the control of the planning authorities over the market and to secure the profits in land development for the community. Conservative governments used planning controls and taxation as means to regulate the market while maintaining the profit motive. Conservatives reject direct intervention, as is evident in their distaste for the Community Land Act. But, as is often the case in British politics, the ideological differences suggest greater divergences than have occurred in practice. There has been a general acceptance of the principle of development control and of the desirability to secure at least some of the betterment in land for the community. Proponents of the unrestrained free market, or of complete state control through nationalisation of all land,[60] remain a relatively small minority and have failed to convert governments to their views. In broad terms the experience of national legislation so far on land has been to accept the balance of power in society rather than to attempt any radical redistribution of wealth in land.

The detailed pattern of land development remains largely a matter for local markets and local authorities. We have seen how the Community Land Act will take a long time, even if it survives, to have any marked impact on local land policy. The Bedford case-study suggests that private initiatives will continue to influence both the use and value of development land. Decisions affecting specific parcels of land will reflect the conditions prevailing at a particular point in time. Each of the case-studies has emphasised the tendency for land development to be an incremental rather than a long-term process. This is so despite the introduction of structure planning which assumes that land development will respond to long-term strategies based on participation to satisfy the preferences of the community. Such preferences, as we shall see in the next chapter, are often difficult to interpret in terms of land planning and assume a consensus of viewpoint which can only exist, if at all, in the vaguest terms. Participation is hardly representative of the community as a whole and public opinion is only aroused when, as in the case of the prospective development at Hyde, a particular group feels itself threatened by a planning proposal.

Land development policy is rarely the product of consensus but usually arouses conflict and controversy. In the case studied here conflicts occurred between different interests which were reflected in competing political and professional attitudes. There are other cases where conflict is latent or suppressed. As we shall see, the structure plan assumed a widespread consensus over many issues, but such consensus was the product of agreement over general principles which satisfied the existing power structure rather than agreement over the details of development. The appearance of consensus over the principle of the Green Wedge or over the use of Bramingham Farm for residential development was transformed into conflict when each issue reached the agenda for political choices to be made. The apparent long-term continuity of policy becomes, when examined, the uncertainty of implementation. Land development, like other aspects of planning, is the aggregate of many different decisions taken at different times in changing local circumstances.

[60]See J. Brocklebank *et al.*, *The Case for Nationalising Land,* Campaign for Nationalising Land, 139 Old Church Street, London. Not dated.

CHAPTER 7

The Politics of Consensus — The Bedfordshire Structure Plan

THE POLITICS OF STRUCTURE PLANNING

So far we have focused on the relationships between politicians and planners and the constraints on their power in taking decisions on specific issues or specific areas of policy such as transportation. In each case some power to take and implement planning decisions was enjoyed by the decision-makers though, in the cases examined, the balance of power was often so delicate that conflicts occurred and the resulting outcome was a degree of uncertainty. Such uncertainty could be resolved by appeal to a higher authority as in the case of the fuller's earth issue or remained with little prospect of reconciliation of divergent viewpoints as in the case of Bedford's transportation policy. This chapter examines a style of planning rather than a single issue, a form of comprehensive, strategic planning known as structure planning.

Structure planning, the subject of this chapter, purports to be all-embracing, a definitive statement of policies covering every aspect of environmental planning for a defined area. Thus it embraces policies for specific issues, such as an application to exploit minerals, and for specific policy fields, such as transportation. The concept of structure plans was introduced by the Planning Advisory Group (PAG)[1] in 1965, and was the basis of the new planning system introduced by the Town and County Planning Act in 1968. It sought to overcome the basic criticisms of the land-use map system of development plans which had been in operation since 1947. Among these criticisms were that the system was too detailed, too centralised, too slow, too inflexible, that it could only influence the location and not the quality of development, and, above all, that it was concerned with the control of land use rather than (as was originally intended) indicating the general principles upon which development would be promoted and controlled.[2] The development maps were attempts at 'projections twenty years forward of land use survey maps',[3] and were quite unable to keep pace with events or to deal with the complex problems facing many authorities. The new system introduced statutory structure plans to be submitted by the county planning authorities, after consultation and public participation, to the Minister for the Environment. He would then decide on the key issues which would be examined in public. On the basis of the advice received from the examination he would decide whether to accept or modify the plan.

These plans would 'present the policies and proposals designed to achieve the stated

[1]Planning Advisory Group (1965) *The Future of Development Plans*, London, HMSO.
[2]J. R. James (1965) The future of development plans, *Town and Country Planning Summer School, Report of Proceedings*, University of St. Andrews, pp. 16–30.
[3]Ibid., p. 19.

planning aims for the area',[4] and would 'set out the main problems, alternative solutions and reasoned arguments for the proposals adopted'.[5] The process would be continuous, with monitoring systems, and would incorporate the need for public participation identified by the Skeffington report.[6] Structure plans would relate to national and regional policies and provide the framework for new-style local plans which were introduced at the same time. With this new policy-based approach it was hoped to overcome the criticism of planning as a negative, reative process. The move towards a more 'positive' approach to planning was further underlined by the later introduction of the Community Land Act,[7] described in the previous chapter.

Experience of the new system has raised various criticisms, some of which, like the problems of delay, were familiar criticisms of the former system. But, whereas the land-use maps were criticised for being too precise, structure plans are attacked for being too vague, and incapable of implementation.[8] To an extent the criticisms arise through local government reorganisation with the problem of a two-tier planning structure. The criticisms could be applied to any system of planning in a market economy, and especially to one which, during the 1970s, faced quite different economic, demographic, and administrative circumstances from those in which the system was conceived.

Structure plans revolve around certain assumptions about population and employment levels which are used as the basis for policy guidelines for a period of about fifteen years ahead. Such an approach raises questions about the precision of forecasting and the ability of planning to guide the future in a particular direction for a long period. Consciousness of the problems of implementation has led planners to rely on gestures of competence. For instance, the Bedfordshire planners stated: 'The need to coax private investment into satisfactory channels, or, conversely, to circumvent the exigencies of the "free market" will be important considerations in producing a rational and practical plan.'[9]

Emphasis on rationality is deeply embedded in the ideology of professional planners as was demonstrated in Chapter 2.[10] Bedfordshire's planners stated, 'The Structure Plan must be a rational plan.'[11] The emphasis on rationality and related concepts like optimality and comprehensiveness tends to neglect the problem of changing economic and political circumstances. This is theoretically handled by recurrent stress on flexibility, monitoring, evaluation, and review. But structure planning is also a political

[4]Ministry of Housing and Local Government, The Welsh Office (1970) *Development Plans: A Manual on Form and Content,* London, HMSO, p. 5.

[5]J. R. James (1965) op. cit., p. 25.

[6]Ministry of Housing and Local Government (1969) *People and Planning* (report of the Committee on Public Participation in Planning; Chairman, Arthur Skeffington), London, HMSO.

[7]Department of the Environment (1974) *Land,* Cmnd. 5730, London, HMSO.

[8]G. Smart (1977) Structure plans, *County Councils Gazette,* **69** (11) (February) 286–8.

[9]'Introduction to the Structure Plan', report circulated to members of Bedfordshire's Structure Plan Advisory Group, p. 17.

[10]There has been considerable discussion of the concept of rationality in planning in the literature, and the subject was introduced in Chapter 2. The discussion has its origins in M. Weber (1964) *The Theory of Social and Economic Organizations,* edited with an Introduction by Talcott Parsons, New York, The Free Press (first published 1947). For its application in planning see E. C. Banfield (1959) Ends and means in planning, *International Social Sciences Journal* **XI** (3): M. Meyerson and E. C. Banfield (1955) *Politics, Planning and the Public Interest,* New York, The Free Press; J. M. Simmie (1971) *Citizens in Conflict,* London, Hutchinson Educational; and J. Friedmann (1966) Planning as a vocation. *Plan* 6 (3) 99–124.

[11]'Introduction to the Structure Plan', report circulated . . . , p. 6.

process incorporating the values of those who secure access to the decision-making process. In practice the area of political controversy may be narrow, either because the plan is substantially predetermined by existing constraints or because so much is beyond the control of the planning authority, or because the decision-makers have excluded those issues which do not fall within their ideological predilections. Party political debate over structure plans tends to centre upon relatively small-scale localised issues or upon those which are perennially in dispute between the parties. Political passion is absent precisely because the decision-makers perceive the limits of their power or recognise the weakness of the planning process.

Structure plans appear to be an elaborate expression of political consensus. But they contain policies which may be revised and even reversed when the balance of power changes. Consensus over policy-making is achieved through recognition that local planners have little control over the plan's implementation, acceptance of the continuous revision of the plan in the light of changing circumstances, and expression of policies in terms likely to prove acceptable to the majority of the population. Structure plans contain policies over which there is broad agreement, which are likely to be maintained, and which will provide continuity in policy-making. This is true of many policies affecting the physical environment. They also contain policies whose implementation becomes increasingly uncertain through changes in political or external circumstances. The development of the Bedfordshire Structure Plan illustrated the means by which political consensus and continuity of policy can be achieved. It also demonstrates the influence of external factors and existing constraints which limit the choice available to decision-makers and lead to uncertainty over the implementation of the plan.

THE POLITICIAN'S ROLE

The significance of the political dimension is widely recognised, but the precise role and influence of politicians in the planning process is rarely evaluated. Commentators have stressed the need for politicians to be involved throughout the planning process. Yet many authorities work on the principle that the generation of the plan and its objectives should, initially at least, be achieved by officials. Some even go so far as to present ideas to the general public before the plan is debated by the members of the authority. While such an approach may suit those areas where there is stability of political control, elsewhere it can emasculate the plan's political content and transfer power from the politicians to the officials. Grauhan argues that 'the preparation phase within the administrative machine must become more accessible to members of political bodies, because it is *their* choices which it has to prepare'.[12] Unless there is such involvement the breakdown of representative democracy at the local level will become even more apparent than it is now. Unless there is member involvement there is the danger that the status quo will be unchallenged. Various radical changes may be discussed within the department but will be suppressed before policy proposals are put to the members. Relatively few alternatives will be presented, and the eventual plan will attempt to accommodate as many viewpoints as possible, while reflecting the

[12]R. R. Grauhan (1973) Notes on the structure of planning administration, in A. Faludi (1973) (ed.) *A Reader in Planning Theory,* Urban and Regional Planning Series, Vol. 5, Oxford, Pergamon Press, p. 315.

presumed consensus. Unless members are involved it will be the officer and not the member who is legislating on the community's behalf. David Lock has analysed the implications of such a trend:

'This new relationship between the officers and electors means that the common experience of local government for the ordinary elector is not that of the altruistic member giving his spare time to community concerns, but that of the professional administrators: this may be increasing the fear that local government is not open to democratic checks and balances. Political and financial constraints tend to be presented as inevitable by the officers, whereas a member's starting point is that both can be altered significantly'.[13]

Conversely, it can be argued that political domination produces plans which 'read like a party manifesto and which have the weakness of those documents as a long-term guide to action'.[14] Given a free hand, members might endorse a plan which satisfies their own view but not those of their opponents. High political content might encourage resistance to implementation when political circumstances change. In Bedfordshire an attempt was made to avoid problems of officer or member domination by encouraging close interaction between politicians and officials in the preparation of the structure plan. This, it was felt, would help to overcome the barriers between members and the planning department, a situation described by Friend and Jessop as:

Mistrust of members by officers, arising from the fear that their judgements might be distorted by their political motivations or by an unbalanced appreciation of the practical implications of major policy decisions, and also mistrust of officers by members, arising from a suspicion that officers had the ability to manipulate the flow of information in such a way as to reduce the members' effective power of strategic choice.'[15]

By increasing the flow of information between the politicians and the planners it was hoped to overcome reticence, caution, and ignorance, and to expose issues to full debate.

From the officers' viewpoint it was important to secure political commitment to the objectives of the structure plan, especially as there was no overall control in Bedfordshire during the period of its preparation. A political consensus could not be assumed — it had to be created. For the members, greater involvement during the early stages of the plan provided the opportunity for the exercise of political influence. But the development of the structure plan involved complex, detailed, and often abstract issues which simply could not be debated by a full committee dealing with a formidable range of business much of it requiring summary resolution. Strategic issues are rarely susceptible to specific decisions but develop gradually as constraints are recognised and the feasibility of different alternatives is tested. They need to be tackled in depth by informal processes which 'serve to make good the shortcomings of the formal system as a practical instrument of control'.[16]

Member and officer participation in the development of the Bedfordshire Structure

[13]D. Lock (1965) 'Structure plans: a review of public participation methods and current ideas', paper at Town and Country Planning Association Conference, Shepperton, 25–27 April, p. 6.

[14]A. Thorburn (1975) Structure plans and local government, paper at Town and Country Planning Association Conference, Shepperton, 25–27 April, p. 5.

[15]J. K. Friend and W. N. Jessop (1969) *Local Government and Strategic Choice,* London, Tavistock, p. 66.

[16]Ibid., p. 54.

Plan was confined to a small, informal group known as the Structure Plan Advisory Group (SPAG). The group consisted of seven members and officers at various levels in the hierarchy.[17] The more junior officers were present to provide information and to present reports, not to participate in the political debate. This concept facilitated the decision-making process, but at the expense of wider participation by other members. It underlines the tendency towards oligarchy (see Chapter 1), a tendency likely to increase as the work of local authorities becomes more demanding and less comprehensible to many part-time back-bench members.[18] The principle of advisory groups for strategic policy became adopted elsewhere on the council,[19] thus underlining the tendency towards a concentration of information and power in the hands of a few leading members and senior officers. It must be said that there was little reaction by those members not on the groups but a general willingness, amounting in some cases to relief, that the few should carry the burdens of the many.

THE STRUCTURE PLAN ADVISORY GROUP

SPAG had no executive powers, but full committee approval was only required when the major documents of the plan[20] were presented for consultation. Ultimately the Policy and Resources Committee and the council were responsible for the structure plan, but were largely uninvolved until the final stages had been reached. Within SPAG there was little political disagreement. Some issues were agreed upon by all party groups as uncontroversial, which is not to say that controversy could not exist over them; others were controversial but did not arouse conflict since they were intangible, could be changed at any time, or were regarded as beyond the competence of the authority. There were also issues over which there was agreement despite different ideological attitudes. For instance, the broad statements on housing policy could satisfy both major parties, as we saw in the case of Bramingham Farm in the previous chapter. Meeting local housing needs under conditions of low population growth could be achieved by a vigorous local authority housing programme or by careful control over land allocation and development by the private sector. In any event the group recognised that the implementation of the housing proposals was largely in the hands of the district councils. Where conflicts over policy did occur, as, for example, over transportation, they were fought out elsewhere, not through the structure plan.

[17]Although individual membership varied during the preparation of the plan, the SPAG consisted of 7 members, 3 from the Labour and Conservative groups and 1 Liberal. It was chaired by the main committee's chairman and met informally with officers drawn predominantly from the policy group responsible for work on the structure plan. The SPAG examined background papers and drafts of policy documents, made recommendations to the main committee, and carried out consultations with other bodies on behalf of the council. As its name implies, the group had no formal powers and votes were rarely taken.

[18]The Bains Report (1972) *The New Local Authorities, Management and Structure,* London, HMSO, characterised several possible roles for members but warned, 'the present tendency to grade the various areas of work from "policy" as the most important to "constituency" as the least important inevitably leads to dissatisfaction and inefficient use of qualities which individual members bring to the work of the authority' (p. 9). See Chapter 2 of this book for discussion of the various roles adopted by members.

[19]Notably the Policy Review Group of leading members of the council who examined and reported on policy priorities and budgetary implications of services ranging right across the council. Later on, a Structures Review Group examined possible changes in the administrative organisation of the authority.

[20]These were the *Report of Survey,* the *Report on Alternative Strategies,* the draft *Written Statement,* and the two reports on *Public Participation,* which are discussed below.

Political commitment to the plan was thus secured through the SPAG. But while the officials were a party to political debate among members, members did not experience the conflicts and debate which had preceded the presentation by the officers of the 'department's view'. This accords well with the British governmental tradition where 'the great bulk of administrative operations continues in political obscurity',[21] and with the corporate solidarity enshrined in the departmental loyalty which is a feature of bureaucratic hierarchies. In conditions of minority control, as in Bedfordshire, it is clearly in the officers' interest to avoid too close an identification with one party. The chief officer will be anxious, in any case, to preserve his position, independence, and authority in the face of political change. The means open to him were described in Chapter 2. He will be unwilling to surrender the power that issues from his ability to control the flow of information and the timing of decisions. Departmental solidarity is also in the interests of junior officers anxious to maintain their career prospects. Such pressures upon the chief and his staff instinctively dispose them to caution and the suppression of 'extremist' views. The combination of politicians restricting the scope of debate and arriving at consensus over wide areas of policy, and bureaucrats anxious to express a departmental view which does not excite political conflict, is a recipe for pragmatic planning which will not disturb the status quo.

ALTERNATIVE STRATEGIES

One of the early decisions of the SPAG in 1974 was to set certain aims for the Bedfordshire Structure Plan, which any eventual strategy must be able to fulfil. This was explicitly recommended by the government:

'A statement on aims will be valuable as a broad indication of what the Plan is trying to do, and the direction which should be taken by the changes it proposes: it will secure the co-ordination of the policies and proposals in the Plan. Without this statement the authority, the public, and the Minister will have difficulty in judging the individual decisions which make up the strategy.'[22]

Four aims were formulated: (i) to ensure the county's housing needs were met; (ii) to maintain the viability and effectiveness of existing industry and commerce in the county; (iii) to improve the social and physical environment; (iv) to conserve the county's natural resources. The intention of establishing aims was to provide control over the direction of the plan. 'By selecting goals at an early stage, it will be possible to defend discarding proposals at a later stage which do not fit in with these goals.'[23] The goals were couched in vague and general language and, therefore, not surprisingly commanded widespread support. It was only when such terms as 'housing needs' were more closely defined that conflicts were likely to arise, and eventually lead to an inconclusive debate at the examination in public. Although the SPAG had attempted to assert its control by stating the aims of the plan, in reality this amounted to little more than enunciating bland and universally acceptable hopes for the future.

[21]P. Self (1972) *Administrative Theories and Politics*, London, Allen & Unwin, p. 151.
[22]Ministry of Housing and Local Government, The Welsh Office (1970) op. cit., p. 28.
[23]Notes on the SPAG meeting, 23 April 1975, pp. 5–6.

The second stage was to define alternative strategies for public debate. The idea was 'to state policies and proposals in an emphatic and positive manner, rather than "hedge" or "fudge" the situation. In this respect they have been written deliberately to provoke comment and discussion.' Although 'framed in a contentious manner it must be remembered that they do not represent independent and discreet plans from which one will eventually be chosen'.[24] Initially, the generation of alternative strategies was undertaken by a policy group of fourteen professional planners within the planning department. Common to all alternatives were assumptions on future population and employment trends, and existing housing trends and future commitments. Each alternative had to take into account the assumptions made, to interpret the four aims, and to express the relationship of the strategy to regional and national policies. Each strategy had a distinctive 'theme'. Within the department 21 part strategies were combined into 10 'second-stage' strategies. Some of these had a distinctly ideological ring. For example, one aimed 'to develop a future for the County based on the principles of redistribution, and discrimination in favour of the underprivileged'. Local housing authorities would be expected to apply the panoply of interventionist measures available to them — compulsory purchase orders, a high rate of council house building, liberal allocation policies, clearance measures, designation of housing action areas and general improvement areas, and improvement grants.[25] High-cost commuter housing would be resisted. Social services would be boosted in areas of deprivation, public transport improved, and manufacturing industry encouraged because of the higher incomes it promised to skilled and unskilled manual workers. Environmental policies would have a lower status and there was an almost vindicative attitude towards more privileged groups: 'The specialised demands (e.g. golf; sailing) of the more affluent sections of the population take second place in this strategy and the demands of these sections are to a large extent met ouside the county.'[26]

Conversely, more affluent groups would be well looked after in other strategies which represented the opposite end of the political spectrum. Such strategies emphasised private house building, increasing car ownership and a concomitant decline in public transport, the encouragement of commuters, and the diversification of employment to provide greater emphasis on service occupations. 'The more serious social problems can be expected to be "exported" to the growth areas.' Such strategies were, in sum, designed for 'an increase in affluent commuters, a need to emphasise and encourage private housing within the county, and a requirement to negotiate overspill arrangements with external areas to meet housing "need".'[27]

The other strategies discussed within the department gave varying emphasis to environmental improvement, industrial development, and housing needs, including, in one case, the proposal for a new town of 80,000 at Sandy in the north-east of the county.

[24]Bedfordshire County Council (1976) *County Structure Plan, Alternative Strategies, Consultation Report*, p. 3.
[25]In an attempt to accelerate the scale of improvement of older housing areas, local housing authorities may designate specific areas as general improvement areas (GIAs) where environmental improvements are combined with efforts to encourage owners to take up improvement grants. Housing action areas (HAAs) require immediate treatment including clearance of unfit housing. More recently the idea of comprehensive local housing strategies and housing investment programmes demonstrating the whole range of housing policies within each authority have been suggested as the basis for financial allocation from government. (*Housing Policy*, A Consultative Document, Cmnd. 6851, London, HMSO, 1977.)
[26]Second-stage Combined Strategies, Strategy A, drafts circulated within County Planning Dept.
[27]Ibid., Strategy D.

These approaches were intended to pose the alternatives and were couched in provocative language. The strategies as they stood were impracticable in many ways. It would not be possible given prevailing political, economic, and demographic circumstances to reserve the county either for a young, mobile, and affluent population, or to base its future development entirely on policies intended to aid the underprivileged. Such strategies were too discriminatory and too exclusive. Recognition of this, and apprehension about the reaction of members, led the chief officers in the planning department to subdue the more overt political messages of the strategies before they were presented to the politicians for discussion.

It could be argued that it was the members' responsibility to ensure that the structure plan embodied their political alternatives. Since the political balance within the county council was a fine one, and since there were clear differences between the county council and the four district councils, it was unlikely that a party political position could be adopted and, even if it were, it would be unlikely to survive in the implementation of the plan. That the chief planners recognised this basic political fact was evident from their wish to avoid a polarization of the debate between the political parties. Nonetheless, the seven alternatives which were presented to members embraced significantly different directions and provided the opportunity for political differences to be identified for public debate. The seven alternatives are summarised in Fig. 7.1a—g. Within these strategies variables were manipulated — the rate of in-migration and commuting, the ratio of service to manufacturing employment, the proportion of public to private housing, the emphasis on private or public transport, the amount of resources devoted to housing improvement, and so on. Four strategies projected a high growth rate with population rising from 484,000 (1974) to 650,000 at 1991. This high population forecast could be accommodated by growth around the two major urban areas or in a new town at Sandy, by modified dispersal to the smaller towns and selected rural areas, or by more general dispersal. Three strategies aimed at low growth, reaching 540,000 by 1991. There was more than enough land already 'committed for development to accommodate a low growth strategy'.[28] In these strategies different ideologies were expressed. For instance, one would seek 'to maximise economic growth' by attracting affluent commuters, allowing some housing needs to be satisfied outside the county, and emphasising service industry and private transport. Conversely, another strategy would concentrate resources on inner urban areas, public housing provision, manufacturing industry, and public transport to meet the needs of 'the relatively less advantaged sections of the County's population'.[29] The effort had been to achieve compatibility within each option, although between them there were conflicts of priorities and approaches. These conflicts would have to be resolved in the evolution of a final plan. The most fundamental political conflict arose over the differential emphasis given to the private and public sectors in housing and transportation. Labour members naturally favoured those strategies which concentrated on improving the inner urban areas, boosting public transport, and emphasising urban industrial development. Conserva-

[28]'Committed' land includes (i) land owned by the local authority for future housing provision, (ii) land in private ownership which enjoys a planning permission, and (iii) 'sites without permission but which are either allocated for residential purposes on existing development plans or have been otherwise identified as suitable for residential purposes' (*Written Statement*, p. 13). Estimates of 'commitments' varied as the plan developed, but in 1977 there was reckoned to be sufficient committed land for 29,000 dwellings.
[29]*Draft Report on Alternatives* (see Fig. 7.1 for summary).

tives did not give outright opposition to these views but adopted a more pragmatic line.

When the seven options were presented to the Environmental Services Committee in secret session, an attempt was made to combine some of the strategies to produce four. This was successfully resisted by the County Planning Officer, and the committee resorted to a vote which resulted in the Labour group outvoting their opponents to eliminate two strategies to which they were ideologically opposed.[30] These, they argued, could not satisfy the aims of the plan since they were directed towards the more affluent population, would require some housing needs to be met outside the county, and placed too much emphasis on service industries. They also rationalised their decision by suggesting that seven options were far too many to put out to the general public. Both the Conservatives and the planning officers argued that the removal of these options had restricted the area of debate and might well provoke a reaction from those who favoured some of the principles in the discarded options. The five remaining options approved for consultation and summarised in Fig. 7.1 were (new members in brackets) A(1), B(4), C(2), D(3), and G(5). Three aimed for high growth — one by concentration around the major towns, one by dispersal, and one by the development of Sandy new town. The remaining two were low growth options, one stressing environmental goals, the other (the so-called 'socialist' option, option 5) aimed at overcoming social deprivation. By their move the Labour members had managed to retain the option likely to prove most attractive to them while removing those which they suspected would more closely accord with the views of their opponents.

Alternative Strategy A(a) — Fig. 7.1a on P.145

Fig. 7.1. Bedfordshire Structure Plan, alternative strategies

Summary:

Theme: Concentration of resources and improved accessibility for all groups to a wide choice of jobs and facilities. A high growth strategy.
  Housing: Meets both local needs and demands from in-migration. New developments primarily around Bedford and Luton/Dunstable.
  Employment: Jobs increased in line with population growth, concentrated in Bedford and Luton/Dunstable. Chiefly manufacturing growth in former and service growth in latter.
  Transport: Public transport heavily emphasised. Changes to strategic highway network will mean some road building.
  Environment: Concentrate upon environmental improvements in urban areas. Improved access to countryside with major visitor facilities concentrated on urban–rural fringes.

Alternative Strategy B(4) — Fig. 7.16 on P. 146.

Summary:

Theme: Environmental conservation and urban containment in a low-growth context.
  Housing: Improvement of present stock based upon district plans with emphasis upon conservation and improving residential environments. Private housing meeting needs of in-migrant population, and some local needs met outside the county.
  Employment: Decline in manufacturing industries but increases in service employment. Increases in out-commuting. 'special case' treatment for Luton regarding office development permits.
  Transport: Public transport emphasised, road improvments limited to TPP strategic network.
  Environment: Subject plans for forestry, minerals, and conservation. Areas of significance for agriculture and wildlife.

[30]These were draft alternative strategies E and F (see Fig 7.1 for summary).

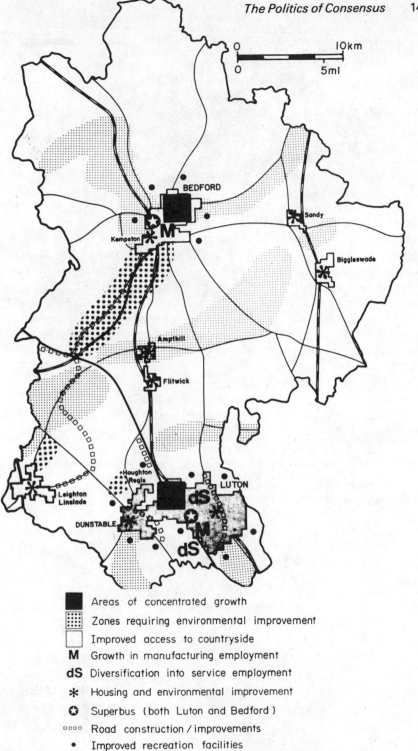

Fig. 7.1a (Summary on p. 144.) Bedfordshire Structure Plan. Alternative strategy A(1).

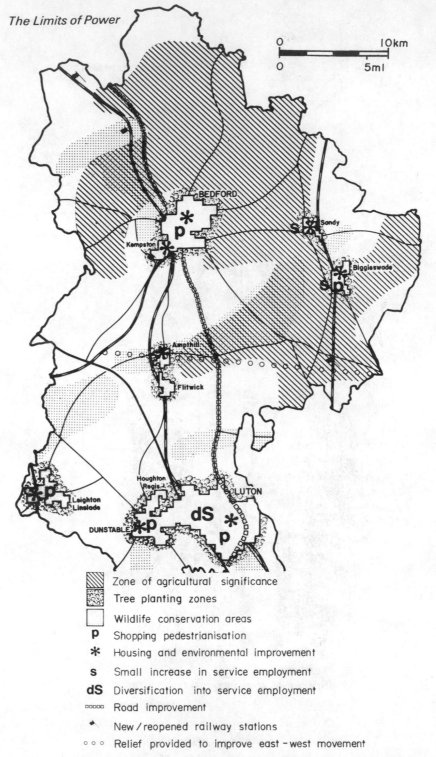

Fig. 7.1b. (Summary on p. 144.) Bedfordshire Structure Plan. Alternative Strategy B(4).

Alternative Strategy C(2), fig. 7.1c., p. 148
Fig. 7.1. Bedfordshire Structure Plan, alternative strategies.

Summary:

Theme: An extrapolation of recent trends. Growth located at smaller towns and larger villages in order to improve the general level of services and opportunities in rural areas. 1991 population of 650,000.
    Housing: Substantial in-migration supported by a high level of private house building. At the same time municipal house built to meet local needs. Past trends in public/private building (25/75) will be utilised.
    Employment: County retains present specialisation in manufacturing in order to decentralise employment to rural areas. Fairly rapid increase in jobs being created. Commuting will increase as a result of high levels of in-migration.
    Transport: Public transport system improved in urban areas and expanded rural areas. Increased internal commuting will necessitate road improvements to employment centres.
    Environment: Growth in this form will consume rural land of great value or high quality. Intrusion will be minimised by ensuring that high standards of design are maintained.

Alternative Strategy D(3), fig. 7.1d., p. 149

Summary:

Theme: Environmental protection and enhancement within a context of high growth.
    Housing: Improvements to present stock limited to current district proposals. Most new housing at Sandy with new-town style management by county council. Smaller development in south of county to meet local housing need.
    Employment: Diversification of industrial base at Luton/Dunstable. Largely manufacturing growth at Sandy. Reduction of net out-commuting flows.
    Transport: Although a balanced policy involving the encouragement of public transport, selective major road schemes needed.
    Environment: Adoption of positive environmental strategy producing area management schemes for restoration, enhancement, and protection. Closure of Luton Airport a long-term aim.

Alternative Strategy E, fig. 7.1e., p. 150 (not published for public consultation)

Summary:

Theme: A high growth strategy reflecting increasing economic affluence with most emphasis upon market forces to achieve the key aims.
    Housing: Improvement of present stock, partly dependent upon private initiative, and partly by a programme of housing and environmental improvement. Most new houses built for the private sector, and some local housing needs satisfied outside the county.
    Employment: Substantial increase in out-commuting. A policy of diversification into service employment. Luton Airport expanded to 10 million passenger throughput.
    Transport: Reliance upon private car for most trips, but some restraint in Luton/Dunstable. Public transport rationalised, but some major road schemes.
    Environment: Some adverse effects upon the physical environment accepted. Dispersed residential pattern and increased recreational pressures.

Alternative Strategy F, fig. 7.1f., p. 151 (not published for public consultation)

Summary:

Theme: A strategy which seeks to maximise economic growth within the constraints of low population growth.
    Housing: Improvement of present stock and residential environments aimed at meeting needs of in-migrants as well as local needs. New private house mainly middle and upper bracket homes, while an expansion of public sector housing over current programmes, partly to meet labour requirements.
    Employment: Rate of job increase matches population increase, with limited diversification of Luton's industrial base. High gross commuting flows, both in and out of the county, reflecting subregional employment specialisations.
    Transport: Reliance upon private car for most trips, but some restraint in Luton/Dunstable. Public transport rationalised, but some major road schemes.
    Environment: Rural objectives accorded priority, but emphasis upon stabilising present relationships. A mixture of phased developments and conservation in urban areas.

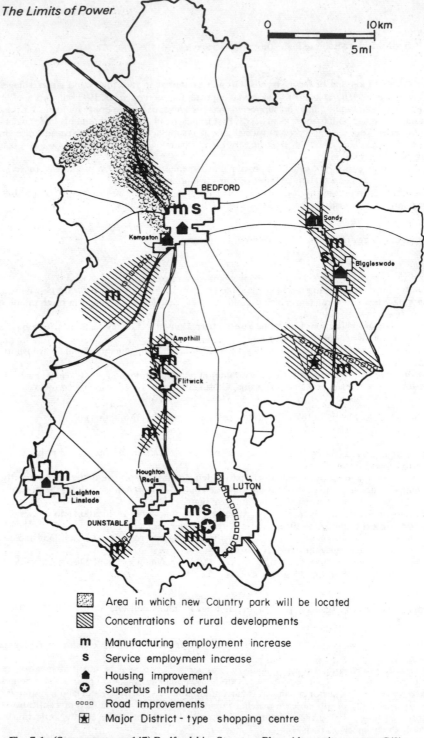

0 _____ 10km

5ml

Area in which new Country park will be located

Concentrations of rural developments

m   Manufacturing employment increase
s   Service employment increase
🏠   Housing improvement
✪   Superbus introduced
□□□□   Road improvements
✷   Major District - type shopping centre

Fig. 7.1c (Summary on p. 147) Bedfordshire Structure Plan. Alternative strategy C(2).

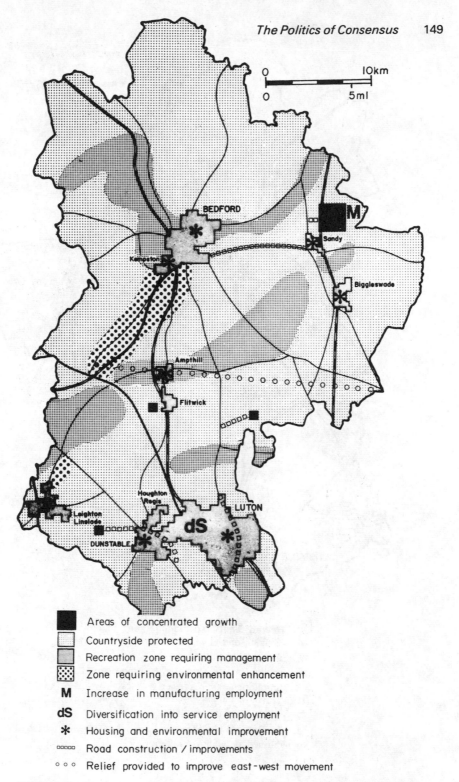

Fig. 7.1d (Summary on p. 147) Bedfordshire Structure Plan. Alternative strategy D(3).

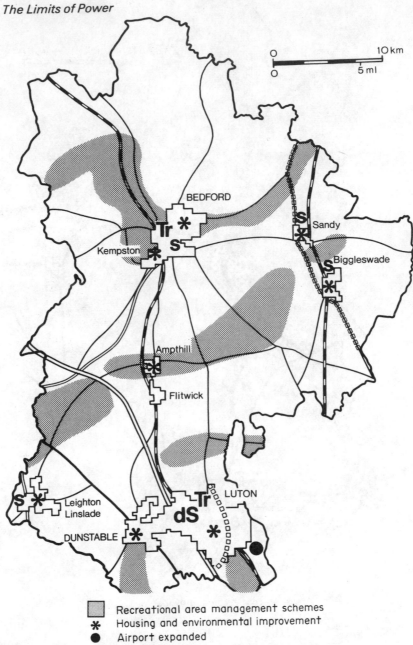

Fig. 7.1e Bedfordshire Structure Plan. Alternative strategy E.
Not published for public consultation

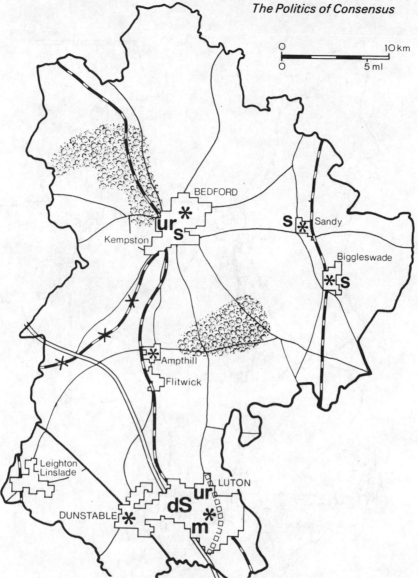

Fig. 7.1f (Summary on p. 147) Bedfordshire Structure Plan. Alternative strategy F.
Not published for public consultation

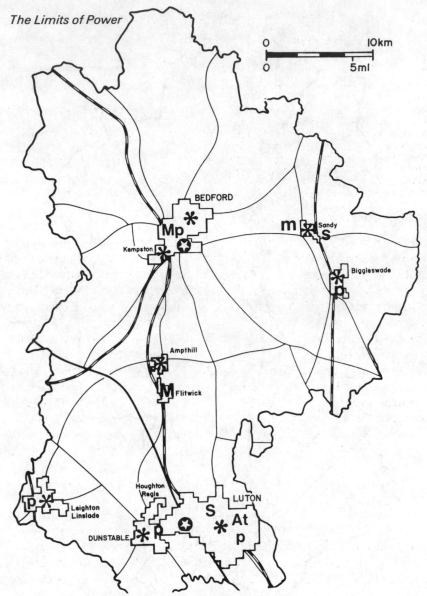

*   Housing and environmental improvement

M   Increase in manufacturing employment

m   Small increase in manufacturing employment

S   Increase in service employment

s   Small increase in service employment

At   Area Traffic Control

p   Pedestrianisation of shopping areas

✪   Superbus services

Fig. 7.1g (Summary on p. 153) Bedfordshire Structure Plan. Alternative strategy G(5).

Fig. 7.1 Bedfordshire Structure Plan, alternative strategies
Alternative strategy G(5), fig. 7.1g, p. 152

Summary:

Theme: Meeting the needs of the relatively less-advantaged sections of the county's population in a low-growth situation.
   Housing: Improvement of present stock, both now and in the long-term, an important priority. A concentration upon greater local authority control over new dwellings.
   Employment: Local employment needs met as far as possible within the county. A faster increase in manufacturing jobs than service jobs.
   Transport: Public transport a major priority in improving overall accessibility. Improved road schemes approved mainly to ease public transport flows.
   Environment: Protection to agriculture and landscape, chiefly by reducing developmental pressure arising from the low-growth situation. Otherwise no specific, large-scale environmental policies.

THE LIMITS OF CONTROL

Up to this point control over the direction of policy in the structure plan had been concentrated in the hands of the planning officers and committee members. In theory the possibilities were considerable. The evolution of the alternatives had demonstrated the variety of themes and ideologies that could be reflected in the plan. The planners and politicians had refined the options, defined the issues, set the goals, and selected the alternatives for public debate. Some of the debate had been confined to the planning department, and views expressed there were filtered before reaching the members. Members in their turn had narrowed the focus still further. By the time the structure plan made its first public appearance, several critical decisions had already been made by a relatively small group of members and officials.

But control over the aims and approach of the plan was only part of the story. Much of the content of the eventual plan was predicated on the assumptions made about the future. Many of the processes which would influence the plan (population, employment, housing trends, and so on) were substantially outside the contol of the county planners and politicians. Further limitations on the possibilities were imposed by existing commitments, environmental constraints, and resources. In any case control over the implementation of the plan was in the hands of many different public bodies. At least as important were decisions made in the private sector. 'It is no exaggeration to say that investment decisions taken in the private sector . . . influence, to a large degree, the individual welfare and quality of life of almost every one of the County's resident population.'[31] The performance of industry, commerce, and the construction industry was outside the control of the local authorities. Their role had been to react to development pressures without, except in such activities as public housing, education, and amenities, being able to influence them. The desire to influence the pace, nature, and location of development was one of the motivations for the new planning system. To achieve it at a time of economic depression and slow population growth posed new and unforeseen problems. Further limitation on the freedom of the county planners and politicians stemmed from the requirement for 'a statement of the public participation carried out by the authority'.[32] An environment for the expression of public opinion on the alternatives and proposals had to be created, and this would further modify the degree of control exercised by the decision-makers.

[31]'Introduction to the Structure Plan', report circulated. . . p. 13.
[32]Department of the Environment, Welsh Office (1974) *Structure Plans,* Joint Circular, 98/74, 168/74, July, para. 21.

A structure plan, therefore, embodies not merely the ideas and desires of the central decision-makers but is conditional on three other influences. These are: (1) existing constraints, processes, and policies which influence the content of the plan; (2) the role of external organisations which influence the implementation of the plan; and (3) the views expressed through consultation and participation which help to secure some legitimation for the plan. All these influences largely pre-empted the structure plan for Bedfordshire.

THE KEY ISSUES

In preparing structure plans, local authorities are advised to 'concentrate on those issues which are of key structural importance'.[33] These include the location and scale of employment and of housing, and the transportation system as key issues, together with some other issues such as conservation, recreation, reclamation, and shopping. Bedfordshire stuck closely to this advice, identifying housing, employment, transportation, and environment as the four key issues. Such key issues require 'a choice between two or more possible policies'.[34] The eventual choice would need to show that the policies adopted are 'practical in terms of available resources, and are consistent with, and related to, each other'.[35] The assumptions on which the policies were based would have to be explicitly stated and the plans should cover a period of about fifteen years. Bedfordshire's plan thus proffered choices of futures covering the period up to 1991.

Environmental policies aroused little debate. Employment policies, too, were generally agreed, but it was widely recognised that the local authorities possessed little power in this field. Housing and transportation aroused more debate since there were political divisions and organisational conflicts between the county and district councils. Lack of control in some areas, and political and organisational controversy in others, cast a shadow of uncertainty over the implementation of the plan. However, the uncertainty and the flexibility built into the plan helped to secure widespread support for its principles, though this could not guarantee its implementation.

1. Population and housing

Housing policies had to be related to the first aim of the plan 'to ensure the County's housing needs are met'. Housing need was interpreted as including the homeless, those in unsatisfactory accommodation, new households formed within the county, those sharing or in temporary accommodation, and the special needs of the old, disabled, and single-person households. In addition there would need to be sufficient housing to ensure an adequate labour supply in order to achieve the employment aims of the plans.[36] Housing policies relied for their achievement largely on land allocation, planning, and financial policies which were divided between the county and district councils, central government, and the private sector.

Housing policies depended intimately on forecasts of future population and analysis

[33]Department of the Environment, Welsh Office (1976) *Structure Plans,* Joint Circular, 98/74, 168/74, July, para. 5.
[34]Ibid., para. 9.
[35]Ibid., para. 10.
[36]Bedfordshire County Council (1977) *County Structure Plan, Written Statement.* 3.1.8.

of the existing housing stock and future commitments. Population projections were expressed as a range between a 'low growth' of 540,000 by 1991 (mid-1975, 489,000) which could arise through natural increase, and a 'high growth' of 649,000 if net in-migration continued at past levels. It was estimated that something in the region of 568,000 population would result from policies designed 'to solve existing housing problems and accommodate local need'.[37] Such a population would require about an extra 29,700 dwellings.

TABLE 7.1. Estimates of land 'committed' for housing development in Bedfordshire, 1976 in dwellings

District	Total committed dwellings	Privately owned with planning permission	Local authority owned	Private but no planning permission
North Beds.	7,250	2,550	2,800	1,900
Mid-Beds.	6,800	5,150	1,150	500
South Beds.	7,550	3,700	3,750	100
Luton	7,500	1,950	4,800*	750
County Total	29,100	13,350	12,500	3,250

*Includes Little Bramingham Farm.
Source: County Planning Department.

There was already sufficient land 'committed' for housing in the county to accommodate this forecast need, reflecting the boom in house building in the early 1970s and government pressure for housing land to be identified. But it was not merely a question of identifying sufficient land. If housing needs were to be met the location and type of housing would have to be carefully controlled.

A substantial part of the 'committed' land was in the private sector (Table 7.1). Surveys had demonstrated that about half the new housing constructed was sold to people moving into the county from elsewhere. The private sector was difficult to control, though councils could assist buyers through mortgage schemes and control the size and density of dwellings which would indirectly affect the price of housing. More interventionist policies such as the purchase of housing from the private sector, greater control of land through the Community Land Act, and arrangements with private developers to give preference to certain purchasers could be explored, but district councils might be reluctant to pursue them. Housing needs might be met outside the county or by the export of population to growing centres such as Milton Keynes, but there would be resistance to such policies. There remained the council housing sector as the most certain method of meeting housing need. About a quarter of the county's

[37]Note for the SPAG on population assumptions, 13 May 1976. The district council's collective estimate amounted to about 600,000 population but was revised downwards in the light of a lower forecast birth rate.

dwellings were in council ownership, but the proposed council building programme of 6900 fell short of the 14,000 estimated to be needed during the period of the plan. Council housing also had to deal with the problems of unfit dwellings and temporary and shared accommodation.[38] Insufficient land was held by the local authorities to achieve the predicted council building programme. Thus one analysis by the county planners demonstrated 'that the amount of land in public ownership scheduled for development is at present totally inadequate and would have to be at least trebled if needs were to be met'.[39]

Another problem was the mismatch between land supply and demand. Although nearly three-quarters of the committed land available was around the urban centres, Luton would be unable to meet its potential requirements within its own borders. There were also problems of finance. Government housing finance for the building or improvement of housing was vulnerable to national economic needs. Policies designed to achieve quick turnover of land in order to avoid heavy interest charges and to achieve profitability on land deals were also unhelpful — 'longer term strategies will not be assisted by the Government's present policy of achieving a quick turnover of land purchased under the Community Land Act'.[40] 'Other factors such as land ownership, the availability of services and material, labour shortages, difficulties in financing, the size of the builder's land bank, even personal preference, will influence the true rate at which land is taken up'.[41]

A low growth strategy seemed to offer the best hope of meeting local needs. Emphasis could be placed on improving the existing housing stock, concentrating around the urban centres where most of the committed land existed, placing greater emphasis on council housing, and influencing the private sector to provide for local needs. It was accepted that to ensure sufficient land was available to meet needs in the right place and at the right time, some new land would have to be earmarked around the major towns. The location of such land for Luton led to controversy during the later stages of the plan's preparation. Elsewhere, apart from some new land in east Bedfordshire, a restrictive policy on residential development would be adopted. In terms of policy, the consensus had achieved a notably progressive approach on housing. But the interpretation of the policy would be crucial and left room for different emphasis to be placed on the definition of need, as the Bramingham Farm case illustrated in the previous chapter.

2. Employment

Employment policies were mainly related to the plan's second aim — 'to maintain the

[38]The council housing programme had to deal with the 2800 dwellings identified as unfit for human habitation and about 1500 needed for those in temporary accommodation or sharing a dwelling, as well as existing and new households who would depend on the councils for housing. In addition the plan forecast that a further 12,000 dwellings would need improvements over the period of the plan, though these would be in both the public and private sectors.
[39]'The estimate of housing need', explanatory note for the SPAG, para. 9.
[40]'Housing — third discussion draft' for the SPAG, p. 3.
[41]Bedfordshire County Council (1976) *County Structure Plan, Report of Survey*, January, p. 142.

viability and effectiveness of existing industry and commerce in the County'. Such an aim would seek to maintain a balance between job opportunities and population growth, and would both contribute to the county's needs and, it was felt, the health of the national economy. The local authorities could affect the location of industry through zoning policies. But, as with housing, there existed substantial commitments of industrial land in planning permissions amounting potentially to a further 34,000 jobs. But there was no indication of how much of this floorspace would be used as replacements for existing jobs and how much of it would be taken up for new development.[42]

TABLE 7.2. Bedfordshire 1971 employment structures (%)

	% workforce employed	
	Manufacturing	Services
Great Britain	34.5	55.9
South-east (excluding London)	31.9	60.0
Outer South-east	28.1	62.9
Outer Metropolitan Area	35.0	57.7
Bedfordshire	50.0	41.4

The rate of job formation in the county was heavily dependent on the performance of a narrow range of activities. As Table 7.2 shows, Bedfordshire, compared to neighbouring counties and the nation as a whole, has a high degree of dependence on the manufacturing sector (see Chapter 3). Among major employers, the vehicle, engineering, and brick industries dominate, and the south of the county is particularly dependent on manufacturing. In recent years there has been rapid growth in the service industries, and the north of the county, especially Bedford, has a diversified occupational structure.

There has been a palpable shift in employment trends over recent years. During the 1950s and 1960s there was a rapid rate of employment growth leading to a situation, typical in the south-east, of 'job surplus' combined with a shortage of skilled workers. Since that time the county has become a net (though only slight) exporter of labour, unemployment rates have risen (though still, apart from Luton, below the national average), and manufacturing industry has ceased to grow. There has been anxiety about the future of car manufacturing. Future trends are exceedingly hard to predict but greater productivity and a depressed economy has shifted the emphasis of planning forecasts from fears of job surplus to fears of higher unemployment or greater commuting over the long term. But conflicts could appear 'between the short term demands of industry for labour and a possible return to a labour shortage situation and the longer term declining or static employment levels'.[43]

[42]In 1971 there were roughly the same number of jobs (210,000) as workers (215,000) in the county. While Luton and Bedford had more jobs than resident workers, outward commuting was particularly marked from East Bedfordshire and Leighton-Linslade. It was estimated that, to maintain a balance between resident population and employment opportunities and to cater for the needs of a growing population, about 288,000 jobs would be needed by 1991.

[43]Report on Employment to the SPAG, 1 April 1976, p. 1.

That the local authorities were powerless to control events was plainly admitted. 'Simply, there are too many unknowns and the degree of control a local authority has over the rate of job formation, whether exercising its planning functions or otherwise, is very limited.'[44] The regional plan did not consider Bedfordshire as an area for major growth and there was potential conflict here should an expansionist industrial strategy be put forward. Similarly, government policies seeking to encourage growth in the assisted areas were unlikely to look benignly at applications for industrial development certificates or office development permits (although there was considerable doubt as to how effective policies of restraint had been in the past). But, above all, Bedfordshire's economy was dependent mainly on decisions taken in the private sector. Its heavy dependence on a handful of foreign-owned companies meant that such decisions would be very sensitive to international economic conditions. The economic future of the county was not a matter for local or even national control, but was substantially in the hands of international corporations. The role of local government, even of the state itself, is weak in the vital economic decisions which affect a county like Bedfordshire.

Concern about future employment levels led to general support for the development of existing industries. Since capital investment was largely immobile and heavily concentrated in the major urban centres, such support would give added endorsement to a strategy of urban concentration. The desire to diversify and increase employment to match population growth might come into conflict with regional and national strategies, and locally the needs of rural areas would have to be considered. Within Bedfordshire there proved to be consensus based on an awareness that there was little, if anything, that the local authorities could do to ensure their employment strategies.

3. Transportation

The structure plan included the long-term strategic proposals and priorities for transportation in the county which had been identified in transport policies and programmes and a series of transportation studies. Transportation policy was an intensely political issue during the period of preparation of the structure plan. Labour's initiatives, giving priority to public transport and the major urban areas (notably Luton) and attempting to apply some restraint on car parking, had been vigorously challenged, and there was little certainty that these policies would be maintained if political control changed. The uncertainty over transportation policy was increased by the conflicts with district councils and the county council's lack of control over public transport operators. Central government exercised considerable influence through its control over finance, the nationalised transport undertakings, and its advice through various circulars.[45]

The transportation policies put forward in the structure plan were essentially those which had been painfully established by the Labour group with the support of the officials since 1974. They aroused little debate within the SPAG or between the parties on the council since the major debates on these issues had already been fought at other

[44]Bedfordshire County Council (1976) *County Structure Plan, Report of Survey*, p. 24.

[45]In order to encourage transportation authorities to abide by the government's policy to maintain bus services through subsidy, the government adopted, in its 1978 transport supplementary grant allocations, the sanction of withholding grant for roads from those who refused to give sufficient support to bus services.

times. It was a case of brittle consensus, concealing fundamental conflict over some policies and uncertainty over implementation. The exception to this was the conflict over transport in the Bedford area and proposals only crystallised during the last stages of the plan when the recommendations of the Bedford Urban Transportation Study were revealed (see Chapter 5).

4. Environment

'Environment' is a portmanteau term which, for planners, embraces both the natural and built landscape. Environmental policy involves land-use allocation and aesthetic objectives. Conservation and improvement of the environment is a major strand of planning ideology.[46] The Bedfordshire Structure Plan provided a very detailed treatment of environmental issues,[47] covering agriculture, landscape, wildlife, mineral extraction, recreation, pollution, and waste disposal. Environmental issues were predominant in the third and fourth aims of the plan ('to improve the social and physical environment, and to conserve the County's natural resources').

Many environmental policies were long term and generally acceptable. Some were so vacuous or general that they amounted to little more than wishful thinking (e.g. Policy 55: 'The local planning authorities will seek to conserve all that is good and attractive in the landscape and promote and secure improvements to its appearance.'[48]) Conflict is often implicit in the choice between alternative environmental policies. For instance, the plan accorded agriculture higher priority than landscape or recreational needs in the event of conflict between them. This was an issue that had to be faced immediately after the plan was adopted when a bypass for Ampthill was considered. One possible route ran north through an area of high landscape value and one ran to the south over high-grade agricultural land. The agricultural priority did not prevent the Environmental Services Committee adopting the southern route, thus indicating the doubtful utility of its long-term policies. The conflict between landscape and mineral extraction is a complex issue and generalisations are impossible, but the problem was at the heart of the fuller's earth dispute analysed in Chapter 4. The conflict between conservation and development is also at the nub of the planning control process.

> The preservationist view is to see the intrinsic value of the environment as paramount. Its consequence, by protecting the environment against other demands of society, is to restrict access to attractive elements of the environment. The developmental view is to see the attractive elements of the environment as resources to be positively used to provide places to live and to spend leisure time.'[49]

Distributional issues are also present when arranging environmental priorities. For instance: 'The improvement of areas of dereliction and under-use within the urban environment should arguably be rated of high priority, since these impinge directly on

[46]D. Foley (1960) British town planning: one ideology or three?, *British Journal of Sociology*, **11**, in A. Faludi (ed.) (1973) *A Reader in Planning Theory*, Oxford, Pergamon Press.
[47]The level of detail is indicated by the number of policies concerning the environment — 52 (38%) out of a total of 137 of policies.
[48]Bedfordshire County Council (1977) *County Structure Plan, Written Statement*, 3, p. 42.
[49]Bedfordshire County Council (1976) *County Structure Plan, Report of Survey*, January, pp. 166–7.

most people, and their utilisation may remove the need to develop land elsewhere in more sensitive situations.'[50]

To some extent the problem of choice was reduced by acceptance of certain major environmental constraints. There was a general consensus backed by a Government White Paper (*Food from our own Resources*)[51] that the best grades of agricultural land should be reserved for development. Since about 44% of Bedfordshire is covered by agricultural land grades 1 and 2 (England and Wales 17%), this presumption ostensibly removed almost half the county's land surface from land-use conflicts. In practice, matters were not so simple, as was quickly discovered when the issue of Luton's expansion had to be resolved. Apart from agriculture, areas of landscape value were also recognised as areas that should be protected from development as far as possible.[52] Finally, there were areas effectively sterilised by pollution. Among these were the brickfields of the Marston Vale in the centre of the county, and the area falling within the 'noise shadow' cast by Luton Airport. Figure 7.2 summarises the physical constraints on development.

In the sense that a 'general presumption' against development emerged, covering the best agricultural land and areas of great landscape value, a consensus over a large part of the land area was achieved. But it was a consensus which implicitly recognised that certain breaches were inevitable, especially where minerals exploitation and residential development were concerned. It was also a consensus among decision-makers who chose to ignore certain issues affecting the environment. There was an implicit recognition that little could be done by the county council to alter dramatically the appearance and pollution of the brickfields, and that the environmental management of the agricultural areas and access to the countryside was largely a matter that would be left to landowning and farming interests. The consensus over environmental policies implied acceptance of short-term environmental changes when development pressures could not be resisted. It was also clear that even in this traditional area of planning concern the power to implement policies was dispersed among several authorities and private interests.

The environmental issues, like the other major issues, led almost inevitably to a policy of urban concentration and low growth. In terms of settlement strategy, a policy of urban concentration had its corollary in the rural area where the local authorities would resist any development beyond commitments. The direction in which examination of the key issues seemed to point was further reinforced when the resource implications of alternative approaches were analysed.

RESOURCES

The structure plan was conceived at a time when financial retrenchment was following a long period of rapid growth in public expenditure. For the period from 1976/7 until 1979/80, the Public Expenditure White Paper outlined no overall growth and reduc-

[50]Bedfordshire County Council (1976) *County Structure Plan, Report of Survey, January, p. 169.*

[51]Ministry of Agriculture, Fisheries and Food (1975) *Food from our own Resources*, Cmnd. 6020, London, HMSO.

[52]As described in Chapter 3 these were the Chilterns area of outstanding natural beauty, and the areas of great landscape value designated by the council covering the Greensand Ridge and the Upper Ouse Valley (Fig.).

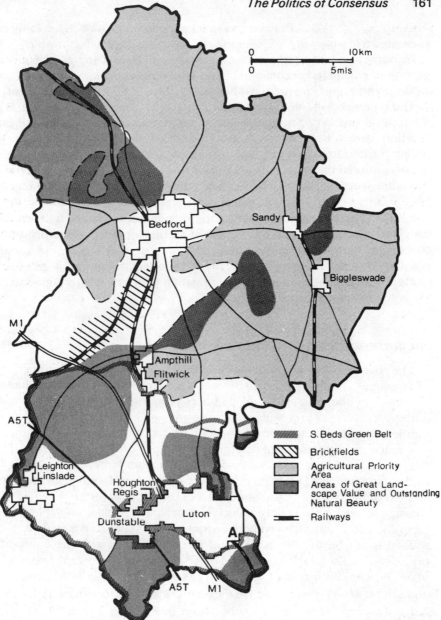

Fig. 7.2 Bedfordshire constraints on development.

tions in certain sectors, notably transportation.[53] It was argued that, in the short term at least, high levels of growth require investment levels from local resources which are not recouped in increased income until later. Certainly, additional population could not 'be relied upon to provide substantial resources for the improvement of services currently provided'.[54]

[53] *Public Expenditure to 1979–80*, Cmnd. 6393, London, HMSO, 1976.
[54] Bedfordshire County Council (1977) *County Structure Plan, Written Statement*, p. 63.

Coupled with the forecasts of reduced population growth the scarcity of resources suggested a low growth profile for the county. 'One general factor which perhaps needs to be borne in mind is that in relation to current national demographic forecasts, a high growth rate, with its concomitant higher level of investment, may only be able to apply by diversion of investment from other growth areas in national and regional policies.'[55]

The regional plan, on the basis of an admittedly generalised assessment of development costs and capacity, reached the tentative conclusion that the most economic location for new development in the South-East was likely to be in those parts of the region furthest from London, at locations which had spare infrastructure capacity, and in concentrated developments of at least 40–50 persons per hectare gross.[56] 'Costs of providing certain public services tends to suggest a minimum urban unit in the 50–100,000 population range, and there are potential economies of scale at different levels for different services up to a total population of around half a million.'[57] This conclusion lent support to the view that further growth in Bedfordshire should be concentrated around its existing major urban centres. Although the resource analysis pointed towards low growth concentrated around the towns, it also implied that a strategy based upon substantial commitment towards increased public investment was likely to prove unrealistic.

THE INFLUENCE OF EXTERNAL ORGANISATIONS

The power of other organisations who themselves take decisions affecting the choices of strategies and the implementation of a structure plan is a further limitation on the influence of the politicians and planners preparing the plan. The county planning authority is obliged to consult with the various government departments and agencies, public authorities, neighbouring councils, and statutory undertakers, and their collective reactions are a powerful determinant of much of the content of the plan. Consultation with the district councils is essential in that a substantial part of the implementation of the structure plan falls to them and the preparation of local plans must be seen in the context of the structure plan. Since most of the public investment required to fulfil any strategy is outside the county council's control, and since it is unable to secure implementation of its objectives without district council support, it is evident that the county council is at a severe disadvantage in its consultations with these powerful external organistions. The county council can try to persuade other organisations to endorse the plan. Where conflicts arise the county council may have little power to secure its objectives. Thus it is very much in the county's interest to gain commitment to the plan not only from its own members but from those other bodies whose power may be decisive.

1. Central government departments

The power of local over central government has already been discussed (Chapter 2). Through its control over all forms of public investments and its influence over the

55 'Resources — Interim Report', p. 6.
56 South East Joint Planning Team (1976) *Strategy for the South East: A Review, 1976*, pp. 10, 43, 66.
57 Ibid., p. 43.

private sector, central government clearly dominates strategic policy-making. The Department of the Environment sets out the procedures and format to be adopted in the formulation of structure plans. The procedures assert that the final arbiter of any plan is not the authority which produces it but the Minister (or more realistically his officials). Government departments or agencies which have an interest in the policies covered by the plan must be consulted. Since the departments had already conditioned the thinking behind the Bedfordshire plan, it was not surprising that most of them endorsed its principles and proposals.

Government also influences local planning policy through major strategic planning decisions. An obvious case is airport location. During the period of preparing the Bedfordshire Structure Plan there was intensive debate at national and regional level about airport strategy following the government's abandonment of the Maplin project.[58] Since Luton Airport was the country's third largest and since Thurleigh, north of Bedford, had been one of the original four sites studied by the Roskill Commission[59] which investigated the Third London Airport issue, the county had a major interest in any decision that was taken. Further development at Luton would have important implications for local employment, transportation, and housing policies.

2. Public corporations and statutory undertakings

The bodies responsible for the provision of much of the infrastructure — gas, electricity, water, public transport, sewerage — were also consulted, since the capacity and location of their investments would become an important constraint on the spatial strategy projected by the plan. In general there appeared to be little conflict over gas and electricity supply (although the possibility of a nuclear power station 2 miles south of Bedford would be likely to arouse antipathy if it ever materialised). The National Bus Company were heavily involved in the county's transportation strategy, which had incorporated their views. British Rail, however, had announced their intention to electrify the St. Pancras — Bedford line without consulting the county council on its planning implications. Similarly, the Anglian Water Authority in 1975 announced their investment programme for the county without any consultation. Among the sewerage schemes were several connecting up villages with mains drainage in order 'to remove development restraint' or to permit housing development'. Whatever the merits of such schemes, the proposed justification was entirely contrary to existing county policy for restricting rural growth, a policy which was to be even more strongly reaffirmed in the final plan. Of more significance was the proposal for the Bedford south orbital sewer, designed for a sixty-year life, and with a capacity sufficient to accommodate 158,000 population in the area of north and mid Bedfordshire, as compared with the 29,000 anticipated under existing commitments. The county council, while accepting the need for some improvements in the area, argued in favour of a lower level of investment. The

[58]Department of Trade (1974) *Maplin, Review of Airport Project,* London, HMSO: (1975) *Airport Strategy for Great Britain,* Part 1: *The London area,* A Consultation Document; (1976) Part 2: *The Regional Airports.* A Consolation Document, June, London, HMSO: (1978) *Airports Policy,* Cmnd, 7084, London, HMSO.
[59]*Report of the Commission on the Third London Airport,* London, HMSO, 1971.

Anglian Water Authority held that the cost differences between a large- and a small-scale project were marginal when compared to total investment costs. The issue once again illustrates the dependence of the structure plan on decisions taken outside the planning authority, a point made clearly by the county council:

> 'To embark now on the projects in the Authority's programme means that either the huge resources committed will be substantially wasted because the anticipated growth will not happen, or that the planning processes are negated because, regardless of other considerations, growth must take place in a particular area by virtue of the fact that the sewerage investment has been undertaken there.'[60]

3. Regional planning

Regional planning, in the absence of regional government, amounts to a co-ordinating and advisory function undertaken by central government on advice from regional economic planning councils and standing conferences.[61] Although regional strategies are not statutory documents, structure plans are expected to observe the principles of the regional plan. The *Strategic Plan for the South East* had been published in 1970.[62] In order to accommodate a forecast population of 20 million in the region by 1991 (1970 population about 17 million) it envisaged five 'major growth areas', six 'medium growth areas', and restraint on development over much of the rest of the region. One of the major growth areas, Milton Keynes/Northampton, is on the borders of Bedfordshire. Within Bedfordshire the regional plan anticipated that 'in the north agricultural and other countryside objectives should take precedence',[63] while in the Luton area the conflict between 'potential for employment growth' and 'environmental and transport constraints'[64] would have to be assessed by the county's structure plan.

At the time both the Luton and Bedford councils felt the regional strategy was too restrictive. In any case, within a few years the whole regional strategy was being questioned and a review was undertaken even before the original strategy had begun to bite. During the 1970s resources had declined, and population projections were suggesting a static population of around 17 million in the region by 1991 although movement outwards from London was likely to continue. Above all, the economic prospects looked much bleaker than they had in 1970. Despite these fundamental changes the review was an updating, not 'a completely new strategy',[65] although it might well have been asked whether any of the premises of the original plan remained relevant in the wholly different situation of the late 1970s.

The review put forward a 'contingent strategy' 'neutral and cautious'[66] for the early period, which would leave the way open for later changes depending on the economic conditions prevailing. 'The contingent strategy itself depends on taking an attitude about the next five to ten years and, during that period, formulating responses will

[60]Environmental Services Committee, Agenda Item No. 4. 29 August 1975.
[61]See Chapter 3, footnote 14.
[62]South East Joint Planning Team (1970) *Strategic Plan for the South East,* Report, London, HMSO.
[63]Ibid., p. 109.
[64]Ibid., p. 102.
[65]South East Joint Planning Team (1976) op. cit., p. 1.
[66]Ibid., p. 62.

depend on how the situation evolves.'[67] 'It is not in any sense a decision making document dealing in resource-allocation terms with specific development programmes.'[68] Although its methodology might be realistic its nebulous quality invited a variety of interpretations. The Bedfordshire Structure Plan had relatively little difficulty in adapting to the regional strategy. Whereas the original regional plan had implied restraint throughout the county, the review was more encouraging for the industrial needs of the Luton area. Although the principles of major growth areas and of areas of major restraint were reaffirmed, the review recognised that there would be areas which fell into neither category. The Bedfordshire Structure Plan endorsed the concept of major restraint by its restrictions on development in the best agricultural areas, in the areas of high landscape value, and in the Chilterns; and the proposed green belt was extended to cover a large part of the south of the county. A policy of restricting growth in the rural area generally was further support to the concept of restraint. Outside these areas were the two major urban areas where existing industry would be encouraged to expand in order to cater for the employment needs of the existing and future population. Such an approach was well within the eventual ideas in the regional plan, where it was recognised that severe restraint could suppress industrial development and result in labour shortages and high costs of housing. 'Areas not selected on regional grounds for restraint or positively identified for growth should accommodate housing and employment development associated with local needs.'[69] This echoed the Bedfordshire strategy and may be regarded as an expression of acceptance of possible outcomes rather than any attempt to influence them.

In many respects the regional strategy was profoundly unclear. It tended not to distinguish between population growth, employment growth, and economic growth. 'Areas such as Luton which have an important economic contribution to make in national terms and which have existing problems such as the need for urban renewal and transportation investment, could find it increasingly difficult to find the necessary public and private expenditure.'[70] There appeared to be an inherent contradiction between the idea of restraint to help London and the growth areas and the idea that such restraint could be breached in many local instances. Ironically, the Bedfordshire plan was berated by the South East Economic Planning Council for adopting a 'negative attitude towards growth',[71] when the plan was attempting to veil its expansionist strategy to conform with a regional strategy which maintained its adherence to the principle of major growth in a few selected areas. The Standing Conference, aware of the inherent contradiction in the review, proposed that the term 'growth area' should be dropped.

This contradiction was underlined by the discussion of the role of one of the major growth areas — Milton Keynes. There were fears that, with the need to revitalise inner cities established by the government,[72] coupled with the GLC's retrenchment on

[67]Ibid., p. 52.
[68]Ibid., p. 52.
[69]Ibid., p. 59.
[70]'Development of the Strategic Plan for the South-East — a critique', report to Environmental Services Committee, 3.3.
[71]South East Economic Planning Council, 'Bedfordshire Structure Plan — Council Response to the Consultation', November 1976.
[72]*Policy for the Inner Cities*, Cmnd. 6845, London, HMSO, 1977.

dispersal policies,[73] the development of Milton Keynes would be slowed down.[74] To counter this it was proposed to extend the catchment area of the new town together with those of Northampton and Peterborough 'to relieve pressure on areas where restraint is necessary but where overheating of the local economy is still prevalent'.[75] Bedfordshire was included in this area. It was not clear if the intention was that local housing needs and future employment growth should be siphoned off to Milton Keynes from Bedfordshire. If so, the regional strategy when applied would vitiate the structure plan for Bedfordshire which, with the approval of the South East Economic Planning Council, sought to meet local housing and employment needs within the county. The Standing Conference felt the catchment area proposed should be withdrawn.[76] Thus although the regional plan appeared open to many interpretations, when its details were scrutinised they appeared in some apparent conflict with its principles. Any decision taken to support the growth of Milton Keynes by diverting growth from Bedfordshire would further weaken the control of the local planning authority over the implementation of the structure plan. The regional strategy as a whole provides further evidence of the weaknesses inherent in attempts at long-term strategic planning in a mixed economy subject to unplanned change and a dispersal of control.

4. Neighbouring authorities

One of the functions of the regional plan and of the Minister in approving structure plans is to ensure compatibility between the proposals of neighbouring counties. Although structure plans can vary widely in philosophy, often reflecting the political culture of their territory, their proposals on such key issues as levels of growth, employment and housing policy, and transportation strategy must be seen to be achievable in conjunction with the policies of neighbouring areas. This requirement can further narrow the scope for differentiation and render differences of approach more apparent than real. Of the four counties surrounding Bedfordshire, Hertfordshire was a little ahead in the preparation of its plan, Buckinghamshire was broadly coincident, and Northamptonshire and Cambridgeshire were behind. The problem which all five plans faced was the possibility of development pressure being pushed from one county to another, and particularly from Hertfordshire into Bedfordshire and from Bedfordshire northwards towards the 'A1 corridor' in Cambridgeshire or the A6 towns in Northamptonshire.

The most sensitive border was that with Hertfordshire. East Bedfordshire is an area of high-grade agricultural land, and 30% of the working population commute to areas outside the county, mainly to the north Hertfordshire towns. The alternative strategies proposed for Hertfordshire caused some disquiet in Bedfordshire, especially as two of them assumed further residential development in Bedfordshire to meet that county's

[73]Greater London Council (1975) 'Planned Growth outside London', December.
[74]In April 1977 the Secretary of State for the Environment announced a reduction of 300,000 in the proposed population of the six third-generation new towns. Milton Keynes would grow to possibly 200,000 rather than the 250,000 originally envisaged. Northampton's target was revised downwards from 230,000 to 180,000 and Peterborough's from 180,000 to 160,000.
[75]South East Joint Planning Team (1976) op. cit., p. 60.
[76]Standing Conference on London and South East Regional Planning (1977) ' "Strategy for the South East: 1976 Review" — a Conference response to Government', Agenda Item 7b SC 700, 17 February, p. 13.

employment needs and to protect its environment. Hertfordshire's preferred plan envisaged a green belt covering the whole county, and was generally restrictive in its attitude towards industrial development. At various points it expressed opposition to growth at Luton Airport and would resist any development in Hertfordshire linked to expansion of employment in the Luton/Dunstable area. It went as far as to suggest that 'Housing development in South Bedfordshire might make a limited contribution to Hertfordshire's labour supply.'[77] Restrictions on development in Hertfordshire could intensify the development pressures on east Bedfordshire. This led to Bedfordshire pointing out that it was 'no valid solution to Hertfordshire's problems merely to shunt them northwards into Bedfordshire'.[78] Bedfordshire sustained its objection at the examination in public of the Hertfordshire plan. Later, at Bedfordshire's examination in public, Hertfordshire retaliated with its objections to the Bedfordshire plan, notably the proposals for the expansion of Luton which were discussed in the previous chapter.

5. District councils

'Because so much of the structure plan will eventually fall to be implemented by the districts, owing to the split of functions between counties and districts, it is essential that there should be full consultation and co-operation between counties and districts whilst the structure plan is being prepared.'[79] The problem of achieving consensus was evident in the responses of the district councils to the proposals in the structure plan. There was some suspicion at what was construed as an attempt by the county council to involve itself in district council responsibilities. A theme of the consultations was that the policy 'could pre-empt decisions which properly fall to them (Districts) as Local Planning Authorities, or say, as Housing Authorities'.[80] Some district councillors were openly hostile. A Luton councillor, for instance, accused the county council of 'seeking to impose dictatorial doctrines on this town' with policies 'designed to have us all neatly shepherded into cattle pens'. Such polemic should not conceal considerable unanimity on many of the issues discussed in the plan. The plan could assist the district councils in resisting development proposals. Its advantage to the districts was that it would 'provide guidance (and in our view unequivocal guidance) to development agencies on matters which affect the key issues in the plan'.[81] But certain major conflicts between the county and district councils, and between certain districts had to be resolved through the structure plan.

Both North Bedfordshire and Luton welcomed the employment strategy and the proposed concentration on the major urban areas. North Bedfordshire, following their established policy, were anxious to maintain the diversified economy of their area and felt that some employment and housing growth should be allowed in the rural area, a point which remained to be resolved by the county council. Luton adopted a pessimistic attitude on employment growth and felt the plan should be prepared to encourage

[77]Hertfordshire County Council (1975) *Hertfordshire County Structure Plan, First Draft Written Statement*, 1/10.
[78]Letter from the chairman of Bedfordshire Environmental Services Committee to the Planning Officer of Hertfordshire.
[79]Department of the Environment, Welsh Office (1974) op. cit., Para. 19 (see footnote 32).
[80]Report on consultation to Environmental Services Committee, 1 December 1976, p. 3.
[81]Ibid., p. 4.

growth from outside the county to maintain the employment needed to cater for population growth in the area. They felt Luton would be unable to accommodate its land needs within the borough's area and that 'one or more of the physical constraints would have to be compromised'.[82] South Bedfordshire had long been wary of Luton's expansionist philosophy. It was an area where considerable growth had already occurred, especially of commuter housing in Leighton–Linslade, and where the pressure on limited land resources was felt to be 'of such magnitude that it will be impossible to accommodate the local demand within the District'.[83] The district council's assessment of the situation was that population growth might outpace employment levels, leading to unemployment or greater commuting. The best solution would be restrict the release of land for housing and to allow Milton Keynes to absorb some of the area's housing needs. Since Luton would not accept the loss of young population and employment opportunities that any arrangements with Milton Keynes might involve, the views of the two districts appeared irreconcilable. In such circumstances the county council would have to suggest whether and where the expansion of Luton should take place.

Each district council was sceptical about the possibilities of meeting local housing needs in conditions of low growth given that so much housing land was already in private hands. Mid-Bedfordshire, for instance, felt powerless to control existing commitments, and suggested that more housing land would have to be released. It was on this issue that a crucial weakness of the structure plan became exposed, for if housing needs were to be met then the district councils, as housing authorities, would have to take a much more interventionist stance in the housing market. The plan was here, as elsewhere, utterly dependent on the degree of political commitment to its principles by the bodies controlling implementation.

PUBLIC PARTICIPATION

Several county councils have spent much time and money on attempts at public participation using special newspapers, questionnaires, and meetings to try to gain public interest and reaction to proposals. Such attempts have usually drawn a low response because the issues are difficult for the public to grasp, do not have immediate relevance to individuals, and the public do not feel confident that their views will be heeded. Public participation is seen by the planners as a process whereby information is given and public support for proposals is sought. It is a process which helps to legitimise the actions of the decision-makers. It is also a process which seeks consensus and thereby helps to eliminate opposition to the conclusions reached. If it can be clearly demonstrated that a particular viewpoint finds little public support, that viewpoint is inevitably weakened. In this way the attitudes of some of the decision-makers may be shaped as the preparation of the plan develops. Thus participation does have ideological implications in the context of structure planning in that it serves to neutralise political debate. Bedfordshire explicitly acknowledged this in opting for a programme of participation based on local organisations and interest groups since 'other types of participation have disappointing results, and the interpretation of any views received

[82]Bedfordshire County Council (1976) *County Structure Plan, Public Participation*, Phase 2 Report, June, p. 18.
[83]Ibid., p. 28.

would be the control in respect of extreme views.[84]

Participation was undertaken in two stages. The first, covering the first three months of 1976, took the form of a series of presentations to organisations and public exhibitions inviting comments on the Report of Survey and the Report on Alternative Strategies, with a short summary given in a leaflet. This phase purported to offer choices and invited ideas on the future strategy. The second phase presented the proposed policies of the structure plan in the form of a draft statement. As well as presentations there were public meetings chaired by councillors, a specially made film, and a newspaper. In both phases, TV and the press were used to stimulate interest. The first phase brought 162 responses from organisations while the second drew 98.[84]

The government agencies, amenity groups, and other organisations largely reiterated already known views on their specific interests. The groups concerned with the countryside, agriculture, and conservation were in favour of low growth and generally restrictive policies. Housing interests showed concern for the homeless and the problems of the construction industry. Industrial and labour organisations favoured a permissive attitude towards industrial development. Political parties adopted ideological positions which found some echoes in the council chamber. For example, Bedford Labour Party called for the nationalisation of the brick industry, describing the London Brick Company as a monopoly — 'hoarders who despoil the countryside'. The response from the parish and town councils generally favoured low growth with 34 preferring one or other of the low growth strategies out of 40 who stated a preference. There was considerable support for the improvement of public transport and for attempts to meet local housing needs. Many respondents expressed belief in the usefulness of the structure plan. 'A County Policy of *laissez-faire* would be suicidal. It is imperative to have a structure plan and an agreed strategy' (Toddington Parish Council). Others were more doubting — 'It is a waste of time Parish Councils expressing our views — you will not take any notice of them, it will be a political decision' (Houghton Conquest Parish Council). The most antagonistic response came from ratepayers' associations who commented on the waste of money involved in preparing the plan, one suggesting that 'Local government workers should go and do productive work in fields and factories' (Sharnbrook Ratepayers' Association).

It proved impossible to draw any general conclusions from the response from the general public elicited at public meetings and exhibitions and via the comment forms in the newspaper. The first phase stimulated 194 individual written responses and numerous comments at the public exhibitions. For the second phase 36,000 newspapers were distributed and 152 people used the reply form for comment. The planners construed this apparent lack of response to be due to general agreement with the policies or to lack of interest in a broad strategy over a long period of time.[86] No attempt

[84]Notes of the SPAG meeting 11 June 1975.

[85]Replies to the first phase were received from 76 parish and town councils, 11 government commissions or agencies, 11 statutory undertakers or public corporations, 13 amenity societies, 5 church groups, 15 community groups representing educational interests, 2 housing, 4 recreational, and 1 transport, 19 employers' or labour organisations, and 6 political parties (3 Labour, 2 Liberal, and 1 Conservative) — total 162. From the second phase responses came from 98 organisations — 35 parish and town councils, 6 government agencies and commissions, 8 statutory undertakers and public corporations, 47 general organisations, and 2 political parties (both Labour).

[86]Memorandum from the Assistant County Planning Officer (Policy) to the chairman Environmental Services Committee, 13 December 1976.

was made to classify the responses, and only broad attempts at generalisation were made such as: 'There appeared to be a widespread feeling that priority should be given to dealing with the problems and needs of the County's existing population and that low growth would provide a more appropriate context for this.'[87] The comments included detailed proposals, complaints about excessive detail (e.g. 'Why no policy on the size of toilet cisterns?'), and matters of concern to individuals or to particular parts of the county. Participation encouraged a cathartic response from some people. Among many examples was an attack on planners' attitudes to environmental design — 'your planners have already jack-booted their way over us and architects are an issue in themselves. Their motto is "All for one design, one design for all".' The sense of Us and Them reached its most apocalyptic pronouncement in a quotation from Churchill's *The Gathering Storm:*

'Thou art weighed in the balance and found wanting. And do not suppose this is the end. This is only the first sip, the first foretaste of a bitter cup which will be proferred to us year by year unless, by a supreme recovery of moral health and martial vigour, we arise again and take our stand for freedom as in the olden times.'

CONSULTATION AND PARTICIPATION — ASSESSMENT

It is difficult to assess the impact of consultation and participation on the structure plan since the process influences decision-makers in various ways. Consultation has more direct and measurable impact since certain organisations like government departments, statutory undertakers, and other local authorities are decision-makers themselves and influence both the inputs of the plan and its implementation. Participation with interest groups and the general public does not have such direct impact but helps to shape attitudes to the plan. Participation is a selective process. Organisations represent specific interests, only a few of the public become involved — often the more articulate or those with a particular axe to grind. In the Bedfordshire experience, participation was heavily weighted towards middle-class and rural interests. There was an absence of comment or interest shown by working-class people living in urban areas, and the few public meetings held in such areas were thinly attended. Organised labour also displayed little interest despite the increasing impact of the unions on national economic policies. There seem to be two reasons for the low response from the social groups whom the Labour group particularly considered themselves to represent. One is that the less well-off do not have the time or inclination to react to a structure plan and have other more pressing concerns. The second is that such groups are represented by trade unions who seek to achieve their objectives through other means. Structure planning has little relevance for them in that it cannot confer the power and influence they cherish. Participation provided a sounding-board for public opinion on a wide variety of issues, it forced the planners to make their intentions public and intelligible, and it uncovered a whole series of local matters which required attention and which might otherwise have been ignored. It led to the establishment of forums through which various interests and

[87]Bedfordshire County Council (1976) *County Structure Plan, Public Participation,* Phase 1, Report, June, p. 149.

the local authority could maintain a dialogue.[88]

Public participation, on the positive side, may be seen as part of the process of breaking down the secrecy which surrounds government in Britain. It is also an educative process enabling people to appreciate the constraints and the possibilities of government. Although it has been regarded by some planners and politicians as a necessary but unrewarding chore, its consequences should not be judged purely on its immediate impact, but rather on the long-term implications it has for public involvement in government. It adds a new dimension to the political process in that public opinion is actively canvassed and not taken for granted or assumed necessarily to coincide with that of the decision-makers. It is unlikely that, despite its obvious weaknesses, public participation can now be abandoned. Instead it is likely to develop in other fields as well, and may result in further checks on the power of local politicians and officials.

The involvement of politicians and planners with the general public may be a refreshing and sometimes salutary experience. The dialogue that was achieved during the two phases of Bedfordshire's participation led the County Planning Officer to claim 'It will never be the same again.' At one level that may be true, but at another level it must be doubted whether participation has any noticeable influence on the balance of power or the direction of planning policy. Participation in structure planning is a selective and bureaucratic concept, remote from the main concerns of people. As presently conceived and conducted it is safe and supports the notion of representative democracy but does little to strengthen it. The danger is that, by restricting the scope and impact of participation and by confining it to relatively privileged groups, public confidence in the planning process will be further eroded.

THE FINAL PLAN

Once the period of participation had been concluded, the plan had to pass through two more hurdles — the county council and the examination in public — before being finally approved by the Minister. On the two occasions the plan was debated by the county council, two issues dominated the discussions. One was the long-running and irresolvable conflict over the future of Bedford's transportation strategy which was covered in Chapter 5, and the other was the question of the expansion of Luton, which had aroused such passionate opposition from Hertfordshire interests and which was discussed in Chapter 6. Both these issues demonstrated the vulnerability of attempts at long-term strategic planning in an environment subject to short-term changes in political, economic, and demographic circumstances. They also illustrated the problems for a policy-making authority like the county council faced with the dispersal of power to implement policies. Both issues gave rise to considerable uncertainty about the future, an uncertainty unlikely to be removed by the policies finally adopted in the plan, which, by their very nature, would be expressed in such a way as to leave the way open for varying interpretation. In any event the process of monitoring and revising the plan meant that policies could be varied in accordance with changing political or economic assumptions.

[88]External Advisory Panels for Housing, the Economy, Environment, and Transportation were established as part of the monitoring process, 'The monitoring and review of the County Structure Plan', February 1978.

Apart from these issues there were others which emerged as major subjects for debate at the examination in public. The debate by the county council was restricted and most of the policies were passed without comment. This perhaps indicates that members were generally satisfied or considered the issues had been sufficiently explored in committee. It may also demonstrate the broad consensus that had been achieved over many policies. But perhaps the main reason for the comparative lack of interest by the council members was their implicit recognition that the plan did not, after all, interfere with those issues they regarded as most significant and which could be debated and decided upon at other times and in other forums. There is a tendency for politicians to think in the short term, to concentrate on issues of party or constituency interest, and not to engage in long-term forward planning. What matters most to them is the next budget, the need to build more schools or to develop or cut back the social services, not the esoteric and unreal prognostications required by a corporate or structure plan. Most members were content to leave structure planning to the committee responsible (and the committee in its turn had left much to a small group of interested members) and to interfere only when their immediate interests were threatened or when the hostility aroused by parts of the plan demanded a response.

At the county council meetings the inherent tension between urban and rural interests emerged. The plan had emphasised the need to concentrate development around the major towns and concomitantly to resist any proposals for additional residential development in rural areas. It was argued that such a policy would lead to dying villages losing their young people, services, and employment opportunities. This view was countered by the claim that there were large committed but as yet undeveloped sites in the rural areas (25% of the total in the county), that growth would not of itself ensure a healthy local economy with adequate services, that growth in rural areas would invade precious agricultural land, and that increased dispersal would vitiate a strategy based on urban concentration. In the past, rural residential development had not met local housing needs but had encouraged further commuting. This question of local needs and the growth of the population in the county became a central issue at the examination in public.

The plan was submitted to the Minister in April 1977 just before the county council elections the following month. The new council, in the first flush of their enthusiasm to demonstrate a new approach to policy-making, regarded the structure plan as a document developed by a socialist administration and consequently one requiring fundamental reappraisal. For a time there was talk of the plan being recalled and resubmitted after revision. However, the planning department managed to resist such a drastic course of action by pointing out that the plan had been subjected to intensive participation and consultation, that much of its substance had been generally endorsed, that it would hold up planning activity for a long period, and that detailed evidence for changes would be necessary. In other words, withdrawal of the plan would not only be extremely costly but would need to be based on something more substantial than mere political prejudice. The alternative course was to examine the plan and the objections to it in detail and to present a 'rejoinder' indicating which policies the council would be prepared to vary, amend, or reconsider. Consequently a group was established to review the plan and to indicate any change in attitude before the examination in public began.

Despite the rhetoric, little was eventually changed. Predictably, some policies were softened and flexibility became the order of the day when interference with the role of the district councils seemed in prospect. The council were prepared to modify the policies on the most controversial issues — Bedford's transport and Luton's expansion — as we saw in the previous chapters, though even here there was not a complete reversal — rather a more pragmatic and less definitive line. Most of the plan remained .unaltered. This process suggests that the plan had in reality become a consensual document, not a party manifesto. Some of its overtly ideological overtones had been eroded during drafting, and the need to achieve broad agreement had eliminated issues likely to divide opinion or set its implementation at hazard. Party political attitudes had weakened as the plan developed, and the bulk of the plan commanded the support of both parties. The change of administration did not undermine the plan, but apart from certain issues it served to strengthen it and ensure the continuity of its central strategy.

THE EXAMINATION IN PUBLIC

The idea of the examination in public 'is to provide the Secretary of State for the Environment with further information and arguments which he feels he needs to enable a decision to be reached on the plan'.[89] It is therefore the point at which the roles of the local planning authority and of central government interact. Up to this point the development of the plan has been in the hands of the local authority, though within the constraints of advice from government and the need to engage in participation. At the examination in public it is the government which is seeking information on the plan which will be interpreted before a final decision is made by the minister. The structure plan is a statutory instrument of control and as such must be endorsed by the central government.

The selection of the panel, the issues to be examined, and the participants are all made by the Department of the Environment. No doubt the idea of a disinterested approach to the issues is assumed, but the whole procedure is heavily weighted in favour of the vested interests in planning. Although the chairman of the panel was a QC, he was, quite naturally, experienced in planning matters. His colleagues were a senior Department of the Environment official and a planning inspector. Inevitably the debate would be heavily conditioned by the conception of the planning process possessed by the panel members. The list of participants (Table 7.3) and their degree of participation further emphasises the bias towards the big battalions. Apart from the county council, which was always present to defend its policies, local government was heavily represented. There were the 4 Bedfordshire district councils present at each session, and 5 county councils, making a total of 17 contributions, 5 district councils from neighbouring areas (14 contributions), the Milton Keynes Development Corporation (3) and 5 parish councils. Among the other interests who participated were 7 broadly classified as conservation groups, 5 representing transport interests, 9 representing industry, commerce, and farming, and 1 MP. Only three individuals unattached to any special

[89]Departments of Environment and Transport (1977) Bedfordshire County Structure Plan, Examination in Public, Notes for Participants.

Table 7.3 *List of participants at the examination in public*

The list includes all those who attended the EIP

County councils	District councils	Parish councils
Bedfordshire	Mid-Bedfordshire	Eastcotts
Buckinghamshire	North Bedfordshire	Elstow Beds.
Cambridgeshire	South Bedfordshire	Stotfold
Hertfordshire	Luton	Wilshamstead
Northamptonshire	East Northamptonshire	Harpenden, Herts.
Greater London Council	St. Albans and District	Bedfordshire Rural Community
	Dacorum	Council
	North Hertfordshire	
	Huntingdon	
	Milton Keynes Development	
	Corporation	

Conservation and amenity interests	Transport interests	Industry, commerce, and farming
County Landowners' Association	British Rail	Eastern Region of National Federation of Building Trades Employers
National Caravan Council Ltd.	National Bus Company	
	Automobile Association	Council for Small Industries in Rural Areas
Ramblers' Association	Cyclists' Touring Club	
North Bedfordshire Preservation Society	Midland Motorways' Action Committee	Luton, Dunstable, and District Chamber of Commerce
Harlington Conservation Area Committee		Luton Trades Union Council
Clifton Improvement and Preservation Society		Federation of Business and Professional Women (Bedford Branch)
The Harpenden Society		
Bedfordshire Association of Architects		National Farmers Union
Friends of the Earth		Akwood Property Co. Ltd.
Bedfordshire Action Committee Against Pollution		London Brick Co.
		Vauxhall Motors Ltd.

Others	Individuals
Anglian Water Authority	R. W. Burgess Esq.
Trustees of the Bedford Charity —	V. Goodhew Esq.
The Harpur Trust	Miss Carole Kuhlmann
	D. Madel Esq., MP

There were additional industrial interests represented at the separate hearing on mineral extraction, not recorded above.

interest participated during the three weeks over which the examination took place.

Altogether, eight issues were selected for examination. The procedure gave further opportunity to the major participants. The county council introduced each issue, the districts were invariably invited to respond, and other local authorities were given a large share of the time available. Special local interest groups and individuals were usually called at the end of a session. Where there were numerous objectors to an aspect of the plan, the objection was made by one person representing several interests. The proceedings were formal, consisting of submissions followed by questions from the panel. Although the examination was 'in public', the public were restricted to a gallery behind a glass partition for those sessions held at County Hall. There was no opportunity for any member of the public to intervene in the proceedings unless formally invited beforehand. The examination thus symbolises the power structure of local government. It is representative but remote, accessible to privileged groups, and conducted on lines that promise but do not encourage participation. Samuels has commented on the problem:

'Under the present system it is asking too much of the private organisation or person to test the plan of the planners, planners who have worked on the plan for five years, used large sums of public money to obtain professional and expert advice, and who sit there in serried ranks in order resolutely to defend the plan against anybody who dares to challenge it, or any part of it. Quite a few people take the trouble to sit in the public gallery. It should be possible to hold the occasional session just for the public at large. . . .'[90]

While it is true that opportunity to challenge the plan at this stage is denied to the general public, the plan does not go uncontested, for the examination provides the theatre for a major performance of all the conflicts and debates that divide the local authorities. Indeed, if the Bedfordshire plan is anything to go by, the examination in public is really the stage for the display of internecine strife between all those local authorities that can claim to have an interest in the plan. Much of the time at the Bedfordshire examination was devoted to attack and counter-attack by professional planners seeking to persuade the panel by a mixture of empiricism, selection, speculation, and assertion.

Much of the deliberation had an esoteric quality. One of the major issues was the level of growth that was implied in the strategy, and this became a recurrent theme of the debate at several points. The county council contended that the policy was for low growth to be achieved by meeting local needs for housing and employment, a net balance of commuting to be achieved by using up existing commitments of land, and concentrating any further development needed around the major urban areas. This was generally supported by three of the Bedfordshire district councils, notably by Luton who were concerned about the loss of manufacturing industry and the high unemployment rates in the town. South Bedfordshire, which had opposed the strategy in the earlier discussions, now found support from Hertfordshire and the Greater London Council. Hertfordshire argued that there was more growth potential in the plan than was realised (30% above the regional average) and that any release of land could put

---

[90]A. Samuels (1975) Structure plan examination in public, *Journal of Planning and Environment Law*, March, 137.

pressure on neighbouring areas for jobs or housing by encouraging in-migration. This would be in conflict with the Hertfordshire plan to restrain growth. The GLC considered there was more growth in the plan than was consistent with a low growth strategy, and any attempt to attracts jobs to Bedfordshire and to reduce commuting would affect the demand for and supply of labour in London at a time when efforts were being made to stimulate the capital's economy. To achieve a balance of jobs and labour supply in the county would require, on the GLC's calculations, 4000 extra jobs per year, which would be at the expense of other areas. With South Bedfordshire these opponents suggested that a 'growth spiral' was inherent in the plan. The plan was in reality an incremental strategy of releasing land as needs arose without acknowledging that there was a point when needs had been met and no further land could be released. The prospect of using Milton Keynes as the area for future growth should be explored. In response to this pressure the county council 'agreed that there might come a point when they would have to say that further growth would have to be accommodated at Milton Keynes', but in reply to a suggestion from the panel that the plan ought to state clearly that the time might come when there could be no further releases, they replied that the present council had not adopted a policy of 'putting the shutters up'.[91] The county's population projections were challenged as being too low and land had been released at a faster rate than had been originally forecast. If these trends continued then either more land would need to be released or, if that were not possible, the county would have to look elsewhere sooner than had been expected.

The relationship between population, employment, housing, and land needs was another recurrent theme. Other more specific issues (apart from Bedford's transport and the expansion of Luton) dominated some of the sessions. Among the transportation issues the conflict between proponents of public transport — urging subsidies, bus priorities, and a strengthening of the service — and those who advocated viability and no priority for buses, received its customary airing. On roads policy there were the anticipated claims for greater resources to be devoted to trunk roads and to bypasses and a late flurry of objections (37) urged the construction of a north–south bypass of Ampthill in the centre of the county, a scheme which had been abandoned in favour of an east–west route.[92]

Waste disposal policies aroused considerable interest with sixteen representations on the concept of using the brick pits in the centre of the county for this purpose. The capacity of this area was vast, 80 million cubic yards increasing by 4 million (30 acres) per year, and the policy of reclamation by using waste from other authorities and industry, and the possibility of the dumping of toxic substances, gave rise to apprehensions about safety, pollution, and traffic. The London Brick Company claimed that 'all toxic substances came originally from the earth. The permissible ones disposed of were relatively mild and innocuous and would degrade through domestic waste. Thus a land-fill site was like a compost heap'.[93] The county council held firm to the policy of using the brickfields for waste disposal, feeling that adequate control and safeguards

[91]Bedfordshire County Structure Plan, Examination in Public, Daily Summary, 24 November 1977, para. 8.
[92]The north–south route was not included on the strategic network and would not therefore be improved, much to the dismay of villages along the route one of which had recently experienced a petrol-tanker crash resulting in the demolition of several houses.
[93]Bedfordshire County Structure Plan, Examination in Public, Daily Summary, 7 December 1977, para. 16.

could be achieved through agreement with the owners, the London Brick Company. Shortly after the examination they had to face up to the implications of this policy when proposals to use an exhausted pit for waste from outside the county and for toxic substances from the local area was considered.

The policy for waste disposal and those for agricultural priority and environmental conservation were examples of long-term strategies which were generally acceptable until specific local interests were threatened. Although in general terms they could be consistently pursued, each would be tested from time to time and there was no certainty that in every case they would be upheld. In the case of the Green Wedge and Bramingham Farm, and no doubt in other future cases, the agricultural policy would be breached; environmental considerations would have to give way in some instances to the demands for mineral extraction; and the use of the brickfields depended on demand from outside the county, local interests within it, and the commercial advantages to the London Brick Company. Long-term policies in these areas were susceptible of varying interpretation and could be vulnerable to changing circumstances. Although the policies had achieved considerable consensus and continuity, their implementation could, in local instances, give rise to conflict and uncertainty.

THE LIMITS OF STRUCTURE PLANNING

The power to shape a structure plan and to control its implementation by those responsible for producing it would appear to be very limited. From Bedfordshire's experience the potential influence of decision-makers is greatest in the early stages of the plan's formulation when the parameters of the plan — its aims, key issues, and alternative futures — are defined. Even here the choices are more apparent than real, and 'unrealistic' possibilities are quickly eliminated. In the early stages, influence over the plan was restricted to a few central decision-makers. Although the Structure Plan Advisory Group had no executive functions, its recommendations were usually carried by its parent committee and ultimately by the council. The prospect of members outside this body securing influence was limited, although in the late stages of the plan other members were drawn into the debate on specific issues but effected little change in the plan's strategy. As the plan evolved so the influence of the members and officers producing it was diminished, and their role became increasingly that of arbiters between competing interests or interpreters of existing constraints. Thus the ideological content evident in the early drafts of the plan was gradually diluted as a plan embracing interests that went far beyond the county council was drafted.

The reasons for such an outcome have been explored in this chapter. Existing constraints and processes limited the available options; the implementation of the plan was in the hands of a diversity of governmental, public, and private agencies; and wide-ranging consultations and public participation were integral features of the plan's preparation. Where conflicts arose there was always room for interpretation, delay, or modification of the policies at a later date, should conditions or the pattern of influence shift. The structure plan could be presented as a reasonable assessment of possibilities for Bedfordshire, given existing constraints and the plurality of interests involved in both the preparation and implementation of the plan. The final plan presumed a consensus had been found either by general agreement, or by flexible policies that avoided antagonising specific interests, or by ignoring or playing down certain issues altogether.

The necessity for consensus presented as the strength of the plan also illuminates some of its basic weaknesses. Recognition that much of the plan was long term, but subject to later amendment and alteration, led to a low level of interest by the politicians both on the county council and the district councils. The plan failed to register as a decision-making document and was disregarded as having little relevance to the immediate affairs of the various authorities. In attempting to avoid partisanship and to achieve long-term objectives, it became vulnerable to short-term incremental decisions over a variety of fields which would commit the long-term strategy. In any event, an indicative plan which lacks control over resource allocation and is heavily dependent on co-operation and upon market forces cannot provide any assurance of fulfilment. This is the perennial problem of planning in a mixed economy, and was well summed up in the Review of the Strategic Plan for the South East: 'Power also resides, within much wider limits than are sometimes recognised, with a variety of private developers, large and small, who can be effectively restrained from developing, expanding or investing in certain areas, but who cannot be positively directed to carry out any operations unless they so wish.'[94] Over much of the area covered by a structure plan the planning authorities can only exert negative control. Initiatives to develop, to provide jobs, homes, and other facilities are, to a greater or lesser extent, dependent on the private sector. Although the public sector accounts for a substantial proportion of the gross domestic product, this is controlled by various central and local government bodies, public corporations, and statutory undertakers. Again the structure planning authority has no ultimate control but must attempt to co-ordinate the investment strategies of various bodies.

Despite the attempts to inaugurate comprehensive planning based on social and economic objectives, structure plans remain fundamentally land-use plans. One of their main functions is described as to state and justify 'the authority's policies and general proposals for the development and other use of land in the area concerned'.[95] Although in Bedfordshire it was stressed that the structure plan 'cannot be confined to a simple preoccupation with land-use',[96] it was recognised that 'in the final stage its direct concern is with the development and use of land, public and private'.[97] Certainly the issues which aroused most interest were concerned with the location or restraint of development (the expansion of Luton, rural policy). Although in its early stages the planners and politicians seemed willing to explore wide-ranging distributional issues, suggesting that the plan could improve the position of the disadvantaged or encourage the affluent, as the plan developed, its more comprehensive ideological pronouncements became refined into a set of policies confined to problems of development and restraint, expressed in the traditional environmental and land-use presumptions of planners.

As the structure plan reverted more towards the traditional concerns of town planning, so the opportunity for any radical changes was lost. Certain issues which had been partly exposed in the early stages were ignored. For example, a major environmental

---

[94]South East Joint Planning Team (1976) op. cit., p. 51.
[95]Department of the Environment, Welsh Office (1974) op. cit., para. 3a (see footnote 32).
[96]'Structure plan and corporate plan', an explanatory note for the SPAG, 2.6.
[97]Ibid., 4.i.

concern of the county, the pollution and dereliction caused by the brickfields, was to be the subject of a future plan on minerals. An eleventh-hour resolution calling on the government to bring the Oxford clay resources, extraction, and manufacture into public ownership was no more than an empty political gesture by the Labour group.

Even in those areas where the local authorities had more control, like social services, little attempt was made to integrate the structure plan with other long-term objectives. One district council complained of the 'meagre reference . . . to social issues throughout the county'.[98] The concern for social issues had disappeared during the various stages of drafting. The possibility of melding the structure plan with other long-term strategies has been advocated as the direction future planning should take. In Bedfordshire that opportunity was sacrificed when the structure and corporate planning processes were separated and the corporate plan subsequently foundered.[99] The structure plan proved a massive exercise undertaken by relatively few members who gradually surrendered many of the early hopes and ideals as the constraints and the power of external influences gradually revealed the impossibility of effecting any radical shifts in policy. Its scope was so large and its authority so weak that it could do little more than reflect the prevailing ideology and power structure. This tendency was underlined by the reality of participation confined to privileged groups and vested interests. The involvement of disparate interests to achieve a consensus led inevitably to an averaging of divergent viewpoints and to an assertion of the status quo.

Throughout the development of the Bedfordshire Structure Plan considerable scepticism prevailed among members, some officials, and the general public. Its lack of political commitment, of teeth, and of public excitement were evident and echoed the doubts expressed by many other authorities and by the Royal Town Planning Institute. Their diagnosis is precise: 'we are told . . . that the system is too slow and unwieldy; that it is ineffectual in achieving concrete results; that it is imperfectly related to other areas of local government activity, such as housing or social services or health; and that it does not promote a rational allocation of limited resources.'[100] The prescription is less easily perceived, and attempts at fuller integration of all services, of greater public involvement, and of resource-based planning have been stillborn. Given the need for consent, the existing institutional framework, and the multiplicity of agencies — public and private — involved, it is unlikely that any form of comprehensive planning can be inaugurated which will succeed where structure planning is said to have failed. It has only failed in that too much has been expected of it, its limitations are now exposed. Its success in improving the level and distribution of information, in bringing together divergent interests, and in attempting to inform and involve a wider public must also be recognised. Structure planning is, perhaps, more important as a forum for the collection and transmission of ideas than as a formal decision-making process.

[98]Bedfordshire County Council (1976) *County Structure Plan, Public Participation*, Phase 1, Report, South Bedfordshire's comments, p. 45.
[99]A. T. Blowers (1977) Checks & balances, the politics of minority government, *Public Administration*, Autumn, 305–16.
[100]Royal Town Planning Institute (1976) *Planning and the Future*, a discussion paper, November, p. 5.

CHAPTER 8

The Limits of Reform

CONCLUSIONS

There are considerable and obvious difficulties which face any researcher intent upon investigating the inner workings of a governmental system. The secrecy which surrounds the operation of central government is well known and accounts for the relish with which any morsel dropped by participants in governmental decision-making is devoured. Local government excites much less popular interest and its operations remain secret partly because there are few with the temerity to penetrate its inner recesses. Information about the background to policy-making has often to be wrested from participants in clandestine ways, and relevation may prejudice further inquiry.[1] Attempts to open up local government in recent years have been superficially successful. Fears of corruption have led to occasional press exposures, and the demands for open committee meetings and greater public participation have been met. But this should not seduce us into the belief what is visible is necessarily crucial. The assumption that analysis of decisions is sufficient to reveal the exercise of power has been successfully challenged, and it is widely recognised that we need to know about the interaction of decision-makers, their values, and the pressures exerted upon them which cause them to accept or reject certain courses of action before they enter the decision-making arena.

In the field of town and country planning the freedom available to policy-makers is both extensive and limited. It is extensive in the sense that planning, unlike other areas of local government, is not primarily an agency of central government, implementing policies within a national allocation of resources which leaves little scope for local discretion. Planning departments in local authorities are not responsible for large budgets to be spent on specific programmes. Rather, planning is a mechanism or mode of decision-making for the allocation of land uses and the spatial distribution of goods and services generated within both the public and private sectors. Herein lies the limits of its freedom. Planning has tended to be a responsive function, reacting to pressures rather than initiating development. Despite the call for more 'positive planning', town planning remains — and will always remain so long as the present system of resource allocation is retained — a passive activity. It is for this reason that planning has, in the past, been treated as a dependent, technical service attempting to secure an optimum

---

[1]Muchnik has commented on this problem encountered during his study of urban renewal policy in Liverpool. 'Hence, my academic colleagues in England have expressed their concern over the response to this study by the Liverpool Corporation and other local authorities generally. The questions involve the possible adverse implications for the efforts of future students and research workers. Will access to information be cut off? Will officials speak more guardedly, if they speak at all? My own political sensitivity makes the conflict with the essentials of academic freedom and the public right to information about public decisions a very real personal problem' (D. Muchnik (1970) *Urban Renewal in Liverpool: A Study of the Politics of Redevelopment*, Occasional Papers on Social Administration No. 33, G. Bell, p. 10.)

and rational spatial allocation of space and services. This helps to explain the lack of interest shown in planning among politicians. Although planning is severely limited in its freedom of operation, it is not, as is now widely recognised, an apolitical activity. There are choices to be made and these choices have distributional implications. The exercise of choice is a political matter, and therefore the process of policy-making is worthy of examination and explanation.

This book has focused on planning as a state activity. The state defines the limits of planning and establishes the local organisation through which planning policies are developed. Various interests (especially private ones) may secure their ends by using the planning process, by securing the necessary information, influence, organisation, and expertise. Those interests, which appear as a challenge or even a threat to the values or institutions of the state system, may be co-opted, subverted, or rejected by the planning process. Within the limits prescribed by the organisation of town planning, power over policy-making is concentrated among a few leading politicians and officials. Certain constraints on their power are exercised directly by the internal organisation of the political parties and bureaucracies, and by external factors in the shape of other organisations with which they share power or which are responsible for the implementation of policy. In addition, planning policy is formulated against a background of existing policies and processes and resource constraints over which decision-makers may exercise little control. The values on which policy is founded have their mainsprings in the political and social environment which conditions attitudes and defines the limits of the possible and desirable. Given these limitations it might be thought that planning policy is predetermined. In large measure this is true, and planning policy has been subject to less ideological conflict than some areas in local government, notably housing and education. Over a wide area of planning policy a consensus of values has occurred, or at least been assumed. Continuity has been characteristic, even during periods of apparent political change. However, in certain aspects of planning policy there is evidence of developing conflict which has led to uncertainty.

A major methodological problem confronted by any set of case-studies in local government or planning is the validity of any general conclusions that may be inferred from the empirical evidence presented. A great deal depends on the individual researcher's ability to make intuitive leaps from his own detailed knowledge to the wider issues which his study provokes. His knowledge of the whole is heavily conditioned by specific experience. Each researcher will wish to apply his own perspective to the examples he uses. In this book I have been chiefly concerned with the distribution of the power to develop planning policy among leading politicians and officials. It is unlikely that another researcher will adopt a similar perspective, and less likely that he will choose a comparable territory or examples. The problem of replication makes the task of generalisation difficult: 'it is hard to see how the somewhat indeterminate variables that characterise administrative situations could ever be rigorously and scientifically controlled, or how hypotheses could ever be systematically tested without an enormous number of cases so much alike as to become insufferably boring.'[2] Although there are several studies of local authorities which bear upon this present work, not surprisingly each adopts a particular orientation of concern to the author. Thus, while Lee[3] is interested in the leading decision-makers on a county council, he adopts a historical

[2] R. Gregory (1971) *The Price of Amenity,* Macmillan.
[3] J. M. Lee (1963) *Social Leaders and Public Persons,* Oxford, Clarendon Press.

perspective covering the management of the authority as a whole. Elkin,[4] Hampton,[5] Bealey *et al.*,[6] Jones,[7] Dearlove,[8] and Newton[9] concentrate on the role of politicians in the boroughs they have studied, and though there are certain common elements enabling comparisons to be made, each work adopts a different focus. Friend and Jessop[10] and Muchnik[11] are more concerned with the organisation and management of specific local authorities. Other researchers have attempted more generalised studies providing overviews of theoretical and empirical work in such areas as the sociology of public administration (e.g. Michael Hill[12]), or the organisation and administration of local government (e.g. Harvey Cox,[13] Buxton,[14] and Stanyer[15]) or the role of politics in local government (Bulpitt[16] and Gyford[17]). Similarly, there are several studies of planning policy, some dealing with the role of city governments in urban renewal and their relationship with the public (Dennis[18] and Davies[19]), and other studies with the nature and role of town planning in society (Eversley[20] and Simmie[21]). Each of these has contributed to our knowledge of how government operates at the local level. No work has attempted — and it is unlikely that one ever could — to interpret the growing number of empirical and conceptual works in terms of any systematic theory. Approaches such as that adopted by Harvey[22] are grandiose in conception and sweeping in theoretical canvass but are not clearly related to the detailed experience of local and national government as presently organised. Each piece of research in a developing field uncovers another aspect of the whole. The problem for each researcher is somehow to achieve a relationship between his unique material and the wider context of which it is a part. 'There is no formula for avoiding the twin hazards of excessive generality and excessive specificity other than cultivating responsiveness to the conscience pangs around by excess in either direction.'[23] My task has been to try to illuminate relationships of power through a detailed analysis of specific issues from the perspective of one organisation.

[4]S. L. Elkin (1974) *Politics and Land Use Planning: The London Experience*, Cambridge, Cambridge University Press.

[5]W. Hampton (1970) *Democracy and Community: A Study of Politics in Sheffield*, London, Oxford University Press.

[6]F. Bealey, J. Blondel and W. P. McCann (1965) *Constituency Politics*, London, Faber.

[7]G. W. Jones (1969) *Borough Politics*, London, Macmillan.

[8]J. Dearlove (1973) *The Politics of Policy in Local Government*, Cambridge, Cambridge University Press.

[9]K. Newton (1976) *Second City Politics: Democratic Processes and Decision Making in Birmingham*, Oxford, Oxford University Press.

[10]J. K. Friend and W. N. Jessop (1969) *Local Government and Strategic Choice*, London, Tavistock Publications.

[11]D. M. Muchnik (1970) op. cit.

[12]M. J. Hill (1972) *The Sociology of Public Administration*, London, Weidenfeld & Nicholson.

[13]W. H. Cox (1976) *Cities: The Public Dimension*, Harmondsworth, Penguin.

[14]R. Buxton (1973) *Local Government*, Harmondsworth, Penguin.

[15]J. Stanyer (1976) *Understanding Local Government*, Fontana.

[16]J. G. Bulpitt (1967) *Party Politics in English Local Government*, London, Longmans.

[17]J. Gyford (1976) *Local Politics in Britain*, London, Croom Helm.

[18]N. Dennis (1970) *People and Planning: The Sociology of Housing in Sunderland*, London, Faber, and (1972) *Public Participation and Planners' Blight*, London, Faber.

[19]J. G. Davies (1972) *The Evangelistic Bureaucrat: A Study of a Planning Exercise in Newcastle upon Tyne*, London, Tavistock.

[20]D. Eversley (1973) *The Planner in Society: The Changing Role of a Profession*, London, Faber.

[21]J. M. Simmie (1974) *Citizens in Conflict: The Sociology of Town Planning*, London, Hutchinson.

[22]D. Harvey (1973) *Social Justice and the City*, London, Edward Arnold; a more empirical Marxist study is by C. Cockburn (1977) *The Local State: Management of Cities and People*, London, Pluto Press.

[23]M. R. Stein (1960) *The Eclipse of Community*, New York, Harper & Row.

In several respects this book represents a unique approach. It is concerned with a county council under minority government during the years immediately after local government reorganisation. It is based upon the observations of one of the participants in the development of planning policy with all the problems that such a perspective entails (see Preface and Chapter 2, p. 8). The case-studies cover a variety of issues – land-development, minerals, transportation planning, and long-term strategic planning. They embrace a number of themes within the overall concern for the limits of power experienced by leading policy-makers. Among these themes are: the nature of planning, the role of different planning organisations, public and private interests, and the influence of public opinion and participation. A number of important planning issues are not consiered, including urban renewal, city centre redevelopment, rural policy, conservation, and local planning. From the evidence that is presented, certain general-isations may be suggested, some of them common to other approaches, others raised for the first time. The empirical work is used as the basis both for an academic analysis of the development of local planning policy and, in so far as its raises questions about the nature and organisation of planning in Britain today, as a contribution to the debate on the future of planning.

A number of conclusions can be reached through the studies. It is now possible to refine the arguments raised in the opening chapter in terms of general statements. They are interrelated but each offers a different perspective on policy making in local government.

1. Planning is a short-term incremental process

It is important to remember what is meant by 'planning' here (see Chapter 2, pp. 10–16 We are concerned with environmental planning as a process, not with planning as a mode of decision-making. By definition the latter, with its implication of comprehen-siveness, rationality, and a clear relationship between choice of objectives and their attainment by prescribed means, is the antithesis of incrementalism. Incrementalism is not a method of decision-making so much as a description of what tends to occur. It provides a rationalisation — some would perhaps argue a justification — for the approach to decision-making that characterises organisations. Planning as practised by local government planning departments may attempt to provide a synoptic view, to co-ordinate the various theatres of policy, and to resolve contradictions, but this does not enable it to claim that it is a method distinctively different from other policy-making processes. It may aspire to prevent waste of effort and resources, but this amounts to more intelligent and informed decision-making, not to a distinctive mode of policy-making.

In practice, as my examples demonstrate, planning often falls far short of achieving even these more limited objectives. Many planning decisions are taken in response to applications for development or changes in land use. Each case is judged on its merits according to planning principles which are laid down, in general terms, in a develop-ment plan. Development plans consist of structure plans prepared by county councils which provide the policy framework, and local plans usually undertaken by district councils. Although it can be argued that the existence of broad long-term planning principles conditions short-run decisions, these principles are often capable of different interpretations (as was seen in the case of fuller's earth). Certain, long-run strategies are quite robust, for instance the protection of areas of high amenity or the conservation of high-quality agricultural land. But such policies cover areas where competing pressures are not great. Where pressures do exist then long-term strategies may be breached, as was the case with the Green Wedge in Luton and fuller's earth at Aspley Heath. Decisions tend to depend on the balance of forces at any one point in time. Long-term strategies are open to continuing adjustment, and where pressures are great cannot withstand short-term demands.

This is not to argue that attempts at long-term planning are irrelevant. The very existence of policies aimed at controlling development within a particular pattern of land use ensures that breaches of policy are subject to public debate and justification. This is a very long way from a *laissez-faire* approach. But attempts to allocate land and development according to predicted outcomes are unlikely to succeed in the circumstances in which town planning operates. Transportation strategies are vulnerable to short-term political changes and resource constraints; structure plans are in reality guidelines rather than definitive statements of a future land-use pattern; and the Community Land Act, as was shown in Chapter 6, is unlikely to provide planners with the necessary control and investment to ensure the achievement of their long-term development proposals.

2. Planning tends to reflect the existing pattern of power in society

It is, therefore, conservative. As an element in the state system, planning clearly must help to support that system. Planning principles which openly challenge the balance of power are unlikely to be accepted. Thus nineteenth-century Utopian planning and its twentieth-century counterparts, which suggest alternative mechanisms for the allocation of resources, remain outside the institutionalised planning process. Planning is subservient to the need to maintain a balance between competing interests.

Experience of post-war planning has tended to emphasise the contradictions of a planning system superimposed on the market. There is growing evidence, developed at both theoretical and empirical levels, that planning has reinforced the existing pattern of distribution and, in some instances, has actually contributed to increasing disparities of income and wealth in society. For instance, rural settlement policies, by restricting development, have helped to force up house prices and have reduced the level of services available to those without the use of a car. In the cities dispersal and renewal policies tend to have favoured a relatively affluent and skilled population and contributed to the segregation of classes in the inner city, although this conclusion has not gone uncontested.[24] Other policies, in such areas as transportation and conservation,

[24]Fears have been expressed by the Greater London Council and other bodies that part of the reason for the decline of London's industrial base is attributable to regional, industrial, and new town policies which have encouraged industry and skilled workers to move from London to the development areas and the new towns. Industry has been prevented from developing in London by the operation of controls. There may be something in this argument but the processes are complex and cannot be explained by a single factor. Industrial decline has been a secular trend and there is little evidence to suggest that industry has actually been prevented from developing in London by planning controls. What has undoubtedly happened is that the death of firms has outweighed the birth of new ones. Any explanation of changes in the inner city would have to investigate housing, migration, and productivity trends among other factors. (See especially, Department of the Environment, *Inner Area Studies, Liverpool, Birmingham and Lambeth*, summaries of consultant's final reports, London, HMSO, 1977). It is difficult to get evidence on this and what evidence exists is equivocal.

are said to have favoured those who already command a disportionate share of resources. Radical opponents of planning point to such apparent contradictions as empty
office blocks, derelict land, blighted areas, uncompleted developments, failing public
transport, and lack of facilities as testimony to the inability of the planning process to
manage the market and public investment in any coherent manner. Such an analysis is
superficial. It is clearly convenient to attribute such evident deficiencies to planning but
planning is not answerable for the problems of society. Planners could rebut the charges
made against them with the argument that they lack the organisational framework and
control necessary to achieve environmental objectives.

At best, planning may succeed in achieving marginal changes in one direction or
another. For instance, there has been, in Bedfordshire, a small shift in transportation
policy towards the needs of those who lack mobility. But in terms of overall resources
and in terms of implementation the outcome has been to mitigate rather than counteract the effects of increasing car ownership. Any change in national or local policies or in
available resources could quickly reverse such a marginal change, and there was already
evidence in 1977 that interest in public transport was waning under a new administration. Plans may advocate meeting specific needs, e.g. housing and amenities. The
Bedfordshire Structure Plan laid some stress on this aspect, but it was powerless to
achieve its objectives without the co-operation of various agencies and the allocation of
resources for the purpose.

One reason for the inherent conservatism of planning is that it tends to advantage
those interests which are able to achieve access to the decision-makers. Despite the
opening up of planning to public scrutiny through open committees and public participation, certain interests retain decisive advantages in their ability to bring influence to
bear on politicians and planners. The less-advantaged section of the community are less
able or willing to respond (Chapter 6), and formal public participation is peopled by
highly organised and professional interest groups who have been able to resist certain
planning proposals. In the cases examined here we have seen the ability of a well-off
community to stall a proposed expansion scheme (Chapter 7) and of developers (in
land development policy in Bedford) and of industry (fuller's earth) to secure the access
necessary to achieve their objectives. The fuller's earth case is interesting in that it pitched
one private interest against a relatively well-off part of the community both of whom
were able to influence decision-makers, whether the officials (in the case of the
industry) or the politicians (in the case of the local interests). Special interests are often
able to describe their proposals in terms of the public or national interest, but they may
be ranged against other public interests which lack the same privileged access to
information.

3. Power over policy-making in planning is concentrated

4. Power over the implementation of planning policy is dispersed

The tendency towards concentration of power has been evident in the examples analysed. Power over policy-making is vested in chief officials who derive their power from a
hierarchically organised department. Politicians owe their power to influence in their

political party and the support they receive in terms of voting strength. This position enables them to possess considerable influence over leading officials. Informal interaction between chairmen and chief officers can be the mechanism through which the nature and timing of policy proposals is determined. The convention that the officer advises and the politician decides oversimplifies the reality where initiatives may come from either side, or a mutual agreement over certain policies may be secured through discussion. Thus, in Bedfordshire, Labour's initiatives in transport policy proved agreeable to the officials in the planning and surveyor's departments and accorded closely with government attitudes at the time. There was general agreement, too, over the main emphasis to be set in the structure plan. On some other matters the leading politicians and officials disagreed. In the case of fuller's earth the chief officer had the power to make the recommendation to his committee, which he did in the face of overwhelming opposition. Conversely, the chairman's attitude on car-parking policy, though firmly supported by his group, was opposed by his officials. Thus the power of leading decision-makers is limited by the effect they have on each other.

Although power is concentrated, it is not exercised independently of the political environment which surrounds the policy-makers. Chief officials may be able to decide on behalf of their department but they are dependent on politicians to ensure the success of their decisions. Leading politicians may be able to ensure policies through a vote but they must first gain the support at least of their group, and, in a case like Bedfordshire with minority government, often of some of their opponents as well. Decisions have to be rationalised in terms of policies, though these are, as we have seen, interpreted in the light of circumstances at the time. Even where there is apparently considerable freedom to take initiatives (e.g. in transportation and structure planning) freedom will, in practice, be limited by various constraints, among them resources, government policy, and the influence of public opinion.

Other organisations with policy-making powers, especially where some of these powers are shared, can be very effective in thwarting the implementation of proposals. The successful procrastination of Bedford Borough against the parking and transport proposals of the county council is a good illustration of this. The resistance of Luton Borough to the county council's attitude on the Green Wedge is a further illustration. The various illustrations where consensus over policy has secured results and disagreements have deferred or prevented action lead to my two final conclusions.

5. Continuity over planning policy requires consensus

In the past, planning issues tended not to arouse much political interest or conflict. It is still probably true that those councillors who wish to contribute to policy-making are most anxious to serve, if they can, on education or social services committees on county authorities, and on housing committees on district authorities.[25] Finance and estates

[25]Blondel and Hall, from their analysis of committee preferences in Colchester and Maldon, did not discover a very clear perception of the hierarchy of committees in terms of power. Although preferences were scattered, in Colchester, finance and general purposes, housing, and education came top followed by planning and development. There was little difference between the leading preferences, and over a third of the councillors had no preference. The authors concluded that councillors either 'do not see the committees clearly ordered in terms of power or they deny themselves the joys of even wanting to belong to powerful bodies'. (J. Blondel and R. Hall (1967) Conflict, decision-making and the perceptions of local councillors, *Political Studies,* **15** (3) (OctoberO 322—50, p. 329.)

committees are popular with councillors having an aptitude or special interest in those areas. Jefferson noted that 'council members often view town planning committees as the protectors of private interests and therefore not of great importance to action and change'.[26] The complexity of town planning legislation, the deference among members to the technical prowess of officials, and perhaps, too, the recognition of the feebleness of planning as an instrument for achieving political goals, may have accounted for the lack of popularity of town planning among members in the past. It was an area where consensus generally prevailed. The approach to transport planning in Bedford before 1973 illustrates this. Planning policy was largely in the hands of officials, and members merely gave it the stamp of legitimacy.

Although some aspects of planning are now controversial, considerable agreement can be achieved to ensure the continuity of planning policies. There are several reasons for this. Bureaucrats can persuade members to avoid divisive strategies by warning them of the consequences. Politicians may be prepared to trim policies to avert conflict. The Labour group compromised in several instances to maintain their transportation strategy. A compromise was arranged over the future expansion of Luton. A typical method is to increase the ambiguity of policies so that they can appear to satisfy different viewpoints. Occasionally a policy may be overplayed to ensure that its essential features are maintained. Labour's continued insistence on primacy for public transport quite possibly forestalled any attempt to remove subsidies altogether when the Conservatives achieved power. Continuity is also achieved where political differences over ends can be resolved by agreement over means. An example of this would be the reduction of the road-building programme, which attracted Conservatives because of its economy and Labour because it enabled a different emphasis to be introduced. Where general agreement over objectives can be secured, leaving open the possibility of different interpretations over means, then continuity of policy may be achieved though the question of implementation is left open. Such agreement over objectives enabled a structure plan to be produced which largely survived the political changes of 1977. But implementation of those objectives led to quite different interpretations over means, as the proposals for meeting local housing needs at Bramingham Farm demonstrated. Thus consensus at the level of objective setting need not involve consensus over implementation (and vice versa), and consensus among decision-makers may not be reflected among the public at large.

6. Conflict over planning policy leads to uncertainty

Political controversy over planning policy, or at least over elements of planning policy, has tended to increase. A number of factors have contributed to this. First has been the rapid growth of planning activity and the creation of large and powerful planning departments. This has attracted a political response, and the status of planning chairmen has correspondingly increased. Second, local government reorganisation has divided planning between the two tiers of local authority. This has encouraged conflict, often with an organisational impetus, but has required political involvement to support the embattled bureaucracies. At the same time reorganisation has raised the status of

[26]R. Jefferson (1973) *Planning and the Innovation Process*, Vol. 1, Part 3, of *Progress in Planning*, Oxford, Pergamon Press, p. 249.

planning relative to other functions. District councils have been left with few powers and, after housing, planning is their most important function. In the county authorities the demands of structure and transportation planning have enhanced the role of planning departments, and where planning has been organised in co-operation with transportation[27] the significance of this function in resource terms puts it on a par with social services, significantly less important than education but more important than the other functions of county authorities.[28] Third, widespread public concern about the outcomes of planning policies has led to pressure for more public participation and has emphasised the political issues inherent in planning. Finally, areas once immune from overt conflict are becoming increasingly controversial. An area where future conflict is likely to materialise would be the countryside, where the clash of agricultural and leisure interests is creating anxiety, and where the decline of village amenities is giving rise to concern. As a result of all of these developments, planning has become a source of increasing ideological and organisational conflict.

It is important to distinguish between these two forms of conflict. Ideological conflict exists between political parties each representing different interests and positions. Land development in Bedford is a good example. Transportation policy is another where Conservatives wished to maintain policies that would improve accessibility for car owners, while Socialists emphasised the mobility needs of those without a car. But this issue also involved organisational conflict between two bureaucracies each anxious to assert their authority. Conflict within organisations, between parties, or between politicians and officials (as in the example of fuller's earth) also occurred. More complex still were the conflicts within and between parties and organisations such as were witnessed in the case of the Green Wedge. Although politicians do not always adopt a party political posture in planning matters, bureaucrats — whatever their internal differences — present a united front within their organisation through their chief officer. This does not prevent bureaucratic differences between organisations. Of course there are many conflicts within party caucuses, departments, or between leading officials and politicians which are never made public.

Conflicts reduce the scope for innovation and change in policy. In the case of transportation in Bedford the conflict effectively prevented a new direction being fully achieved in practice although the parameters of policy shifted. Inability to resolve conflicts between organisations may lead to decisions being taken elsewhere, as in the examples of the Green Wedge and fuller's earth. In other cases conflicts prevented decisions being taken, as in the instance of the expansion of Luton. The existence of conflict also weakens the power to implement policy. Where control is lacking this can lead to other organisations acting contrary to the wishes of the body responsible for defining policy (e.g. Bramingham Farm).

[27] On reorganisation most of the non-metropolitan county councils retained separate departments of planning and transportation (surveyor's). Nottinghamshire was the one county where the two functions were amalgamated to form one department. Oxfordshire and Bedfordshire placed transportation planning (as distinct from implementation) under the planning department.

[28] Of the 1977–8 budget, gross revenue provision for Bedfordshire County Council social services accounted for £11.9 million and environmental services for £10.8 million. The value of capital projects in progress during 1977 were £3.9 million for environmental services and £1.1 million for social services, which would add £150,000 and £180,000 to the respective annual revenue costs. Thus there was very little difference in the resources required by these services, and it is worth noting that the cost of concessionary fares on public transport (approximately £1 million) was borne by social services. By contrast the comparable education budget was £81.8 million on revenue and £8.1 million capital.

It may seem paradoxical that an activity as weak as planning should be the focus of so much conflict. Much of the conflict is organisational rather than ideological, and this organisational conflict has concealed the real political conflicts within planning. These, as I have argued, are necessarily limited by the operation of planning within the framework defined by the activities of the state. But they are real and important. It is important to perceive and articulate the political conflicts, concealed and overt, for it is here that the significance of planning as a means of influencing the lives of individuals lies.

The ineffectiveness of planning leads to frustration among officials, politicians, and the public. Catanese sums up the situation like this: 'The basic problems with the planning process are that it promises to do too much, takes too long, covers too many problems, is too complicated, and produces results that are largely vague and esoteric.'[29] Part of the reason for the failure of planning is intrinsic in the process. It is the inevitable outcome of a system that is reactive, incremental, and limited by its bureaucratic and political structure as well as by various external constraints. These limitations have been the subject of this book. But even within these limits planning may be achieving less than its potential. As we have seen, much of its energy is directed not towards the achievement of planning goals but towards the negotiation of compromise or the resolution of conflict between organisations ostensibly serving a similar public. The effectiveness of town planning might be improved if some of the organisational problems were relieved. But the prospects for any fundamental change are weak, as the final part of this book seeks to demonstrate.

PROSPECTS

I have been concerned with town planning as an aspect of state power and have examined it in its local context. Alternative roles for planning outside the organisation of central and local government have been outside the scope of this book. My purpose has been to try to explain the role of local government policy-makers and the limits of power which they experience. In presenting possible changes in the development of planning policy I shall confine myself to what might be achieved within the present framework without threatening to overthrow it. I am not stating what I think is desirable, merely what I take to be possible. Each reform is limited by the conditions which have been analysed earlier and which have led to the conclusions stated in the first part of this chapter.

No system of government is static, but is constantly adapting itself to new circumstances or demands or attempting to improve its structures. Local government went through a major upheaval in 1973–4, though many would argue that the result was hardly an improvement. Since then efforts have been made in many authorities to improve the co-ordination of activities, consultation processes, and decision-making. All this may help to reduce conflict within an organisation. In Bedfordshire, planning and transportation functions were regarded as complementary and were placed under one committee. But the division of functions within the county council at departmental level allowed duplication of effort and rivalry, especially in the field of transportation

[29]A. J. Catanese (1974) *Planners and Local Politics: Impossible Dreams*, Beverly Hills, Sage Publications, p. 45.

where the planning department was supposedly responsible for policy and the surveyor's department for implementation. This uneasy partnership remained, although a proposal to merge the two departments altogether was made. This either could have had the effect of increasing the power of one department relative to others in the council, or could be represented as a stage in the development of corporate planning leading to the integration of policy-making and the reduction of internal conflicts.

The history so far of corporate planning in local government does not make one sanguine about its ability to subdue traditional departmentalism. It implies greater control by the centre over the activities of the various departments, a willingness of officials to surrender some of their independence, and a consistent political will to ensure the application of the corporate plan (from which presumably the scope for political disagreement will have been removed). It requires an ability to wrest power from chief officials and chairmen which few among them would be willing to surrender. It tends to focus on internal structure and ignores political realities.

While it might prove difficult to reduce internal problems of conflict and co-ordination, there does seem some prospect of minimising the scope for conflict between organisations. This would require the abolition of the two-tier system and certainly, as a first step if necessary, the concentration of planning powers in one authority. If less attention is paid to strategic planning and more effort goes into local planning, then the lower tier would be the most appropriate planning authority. A move to unitary authorities combining all the present functions of the two tiers, covering larger areas and populations than is normally the case with the present districts,[30] would be the most appropriate way out of some of the present problems. It is scarcely credible that a system of local government with so many detractors should be maintained purely because changes would cause too much upheaval. There is no justification for perpetuating a system universally condemned as costly, bureaucratic, and inflexible. In planning, the effect of separating functions has been little short of disastrous. The evidence of the case-studies in this book demonstrates the delays which can result from disputes or negotiations between two authorities essentially trying to do the same job. Where agreement is reached it takes longer than is necessary given the desirability for consultation and participation. Where conflict persists then decisions are deferred or, as was the case in Bedford, authorities spend their time undermining each other's strategies. This bureaucratic nonsense is raised to the highest plane of farce when, at the structure plan examination in public, presided over by ministry officials, the issues in the plan are disputed by two authorities representing the same electorate and presenting opposing policies. This ensures that the choice will be made, not by local representatives, but by means of a remote and centralised form of arbitration.

Another area where reform has been tried in the past is in the planning system. The 1968 Act replaced the land-use style of development plan with the indicative approach of the structure and local planning system. It solved some problems, created others, and

[30]Under the Redcliffe–Maud proposals there would have been sixty-one unitary authorities covering England outside the metropolitan areas. These would have been responsible for all local services. Bedfordshire would have been divided, with the northern part of the county joining north Buckinghamshire, the southern part joining central Hertfordshire, and the Biggleswade area becoming part of the east Hertfordshire area *(Royal Commission on Local Government in England 1966–9,* HMSO). The idea has been revived by the Labour Party who suggest that the country could be split into 12 regions and about 200 most-purpose authorities with an average population of 250,000 (The Labour Party (1977) *Regional Authorities and Local Government Reform,* A Consultation Document, July).

is subject to many of the same criticisms of the former system. An enormous amount of political and bureaucratic input has been devoted to structure planning. The attempt to create a framework for long-term planning flies in the face of one of the conclusions reached in this book — that environmental planning is essentially a short-term incremental process. Instead of providing a long-term strategy, a structure plan in reality is subject to continuous revision and has few powers of implementation. Despite its evident limitations, structure planning is one area where the full panoply of public participation has been unleashed and the public response has been derisory. In sum, there has been heavy intellectual investment into flexible and vague plans which have little meaning for the public and carry little conviction as blueprints for action.

Even more disturbing is the time taken to prepare such plans, delaying the preparation of local plans which are dependent on the county strategy. The new system of development plans was first introduced in 1968. By 1978 in the South-east region, covering a third of the country's population, only two structure plans had been approved, four had been through all the stages prior to approval, six had been published in draft form, and one had not even reached that stage.[31] The process of structure planning is cumbersome and complex, involving the preparation of surveys, alternatives, and draft plans, and going through various stages of consultation, participation, revision, and examination in public before eventual approval. Each structure plan has adopted a different approach in level of detail, nature of policies, and basic ideology, making compatibility between areas in terms of an indicative regional plan extremely tenuous.

Criticisms of the system have been voiced both within the planning profession and by the public at large. 'Among a wider lay public, planning — an activity associated not merely with statutory planning but with all the bureaucratic forces that shape one's life — is seen as too complex, extensive and costly.'[32] The House of Commons Expenditure Committee recommended a review of the planning system,[33] and the Royal Town Planning Institute argued for the evolution of a more integrated and intelligible approach to planning in its discussion paper, *Planning and the Future*.[34]

Any changes that are made should be seen in the context of organisational reform also. Thus, if the county councils are to be succeeded by unitary authorities, their strategic planning functions (notably the preparation of structure plans and transportation strategies) will either become redundant or handled by another level of government. I suggested earlier that long-term planning in the sense of achieving certain stated objectives is not possible in a society where the market is the predominant mode of decision-making. In reality, guidelines which are flexible and subject to revision must substitute for long-term plans. There would appear to be a case for the setting of strategic guidelines for the allocation of development land, and the conservation of resources such as agricultural land, minerals (see Chapter 5), and landscape. But these

[31]By the end of 1977, structure plans for East Sussex and south Hampshire had been approved. Those for Oxfordshire, Buckinghamshire, Hertfordshire, and Bedfordshire were awaiting approval; the plans for Kent, Surrey, Berkshire (3 parts), mid- and north-east Hampshire, and West Sussex were at various stages of consultation; the Essex plan appeared in mid 1978. London's plan had been something of a *cause célèbre* in terms of delays, scale, and political controversy during the late 1960s and early 1970s

[32]Royal Town Planning Institute (1976) *Planning and the Future,* discussion paper, para. 10.

[33]Eighth Report from the Expenditure Committee, Session 1976–7, Planning Procedures, Vol. 1, Report. para. 86.

[34]Royal Town Planning Institute (1976) op. cit.

hardly require to be supported by the excessive effort that presently goes into the preparation of structure plans at county level. These are matters which could be handled at regional level, giving a statutory framework where at present regional strategies are purely advisory. In the event of regional government being introduced, then strategic development plans could be integrated with other plans at a regional level, for transportation, health services, and so on. This might well provide a more satisfactory framework for development than the present system, which combines conflict and duplication at the local level with a totally ineffective system of resource allocation and co-ordination of services at the regional level. Some regional machinery would also remove the incentive for the proliferation of authorities (e.g. health, water) which carry considerable power with little accountability. It would achieve greater concentration of the power to implement the strategies developed at a regional level.

Whatever the arguments in favour of some regional planning machinery, it is at the local level that the present system demonstrates its most significant weakness. Local planning can affect the immediate environment and lives of people. Local plans should arouse public interest since the issues they deal with can be related to the individual's daily experience. But detailed local planning can raise false expectations if it fails to effect its proposals. There is a credibility gap between the plan and its performance. Effective local planning requires the commitment of manpower and resources. It probably requires also a reorientation of the approach of planners. At present most planning officers demonstrate more commitment to plan-making than implementation, more loyalty to their organisation and department than to the politicians and the public. It is the job of other workers — social workers, teachers, housing officers — to become involved in the day-to-day problems of ensuring that the needs of the community are met through the services supplied by local government. Planners are still regarded (and, perhaps, regard themselves) as remote from the public. In Bedford the County Planning Department occupies the sixth floor of a modern County Hall which overlooks an area with all the symptoms of the inner city problem — derelict land (much of it owned by local authorities and other public bodies), housing stress, and lack of open space. The contradiction of geographical proximity and intellectual distance is here symbolically realised.

Any devolution of planning towards a more community-based public service has wide-ranging professional, political and social implications. The germ of such an idea is to be found in *Planning and the Future*. Part of the integrated approach to planning advocated is described as 'community-based planning'. There are two aspects of this — involvement of the community in planning and involvement of the planners in the community. The document's ideas on participation go little beyond what has been tried in many areas already. In suggesting that participation should concentrate on 'important sections of the community'[35] there is the implicit recognition that planning serves the prevailing pattern of power — one of the conclusions established earlier in this chapter. As if to reinforce this conclusion, the paper goes on to suggest that for each participating group there should be 'a minimum guarantee of its representative and responsible character'.[36]

The fundamental contradiction of planning as a system which supports the interests

[35]Royal Town Planning Institute (1976), para. 65.
[36]Ibid., para. 66.

of the powerful and which, at the same time, asserts the needs of the underprivileged, is underlined in the following passage in the discussion paper. 'The elitist and authoritarian aspects of professionalism must give way to a new approach based on the ability of the professional to aid groups of citizens to come to a genuine expression of their own needs and the means of implementing them.'[37] This approach has intimations of an institutionalised form of 'planning aid' or advocacy planning.[38] Advocacy planning undertaken outside the organisational framework of bureaucratic planning is likely to be denied access to resources and decision-makers. Attempts to articulate needs within planning organisations suppose a system that is receptive and sympathetic.

The idea of decentralising planning departments and establishing community worker planners has, superficially, much to commend it. It could serve to strengthen the relationship between politicians, planners, and the community at large. But such a reform will succeed only in so far as it does not contradict the conclusions about the nature of planning in our society which were stated earlier. In the first place, decentralisation would appear to threaten the power located in the departments and vested in leading politicians. It would imply a new relationship between politicians and planners which neither would welcome. Community worker planners might be seen to subvert the representative role of local authorities. The planners, in their turn, will be anxious to avoid close identification with local political interests lest the need to mobilise support for specific policies loses them credibility with other parties or with part of the local electorate. This danger will be particularly great in politically marginal areas. Community worker planners will also not wish to risk their careers by supporting the local community against the department which employs them. In reality, decentralisation might betray the interests of local communities with planners acting as fifth columnists anticipating and heading off any confrontation which threatens the authority. Any form of decentralisation which merely places more stress on community involvement while doing nothing to alter the power relationships will inevitably continue to serve the interests of the powerful.

I have concluded that the power to implement planning proposals is dispersed. Decentralisation of planning activities would not of itself improve the prospects of implementation, though it might arouse expectations in the community. Already local authorities are hard-pressed to cope quickly and adequately with the demands made upon them — a situation that would become worse if the expression of local needs were to be deliberately encouraged. It would be difficult to discriminate between competing demands and to uncover genuine needs in order to make judgements on priorities and to act on them. In times of retrenchment in local authority expenditure, services are likely to be curtailed or reduced. Any exposure of the inability of planning to meet demands made upon it would not only diminish the prestige of planning but could nurture doubts about the effectiveness of the authority as a whole.

Decentralisation would not necessarily encourage any change in the distribution of resources. Relatively affluent groups and districts know how to take care of themselves. Opposition to schemes that are regarded as undesirable can be easily and successfully

[37]Ibid., para. 147.

[38]'Planning aid' is a means whereby professional expertise is placed at the disposal of groups in the community who wish to challenge a planning proposal affecting them or to help individuals negotiate the planning machinery. Advocacy planning implies that the planner supports specific ideologies or interest groups usually in contention with the planning authority. It was briefly discussed in Chapter 2.

mobilised. The idea that planning can be a positive activity able to promote specific interests has not been widely embraced, least of all by the most disadvantaged sections of the community. Relationships between planners and public, in so far as they exist at all, tend to be antagonistic. If a decentralised planning service were to be made available to all areas, then it is likely that the better-off would lay claim to resources which would then be denied to those in greater need. Decentralisation would need to be combined with positive discrimination in favour of certain social groups and areas if any redistribution was to be achieved. This is the essence of much recent legislation, culminating in the inner cities proposals.[39]

Quite aside from the problems of challenging the status quo in terms of power and patterns of distribution, there is the doubt about the function and relevance of planning to the problems it seeks to solve. Any councillor knows that the constituency problems he meets most frequently concern individuals and families, predominantly housing but also social services, education, and transport. Only in the broadest sense can these be described as environmental issues, and they are certainly not issues with which the planner has had to deal except in the most abstract sense in the preparation of plans. Even those issues more directly related to the environment which arouse local interest — such as street lighting, car and lorry parking, road and path maintenance — are hardly issues on which the planner can claim special competence. Planning expertise (as conventionally defined) may occasionally be required on matters of development control (building regulations, land uses) and, on a larger scale, the apprehension about comprehensive development proposals may require planning aid. But it is on these very issues that the resources of the professional planner seem to be mobilised in defence of the authority or in the promotion of private interests rather than in support of the community whenever a conflict is evident.

That planning, as defined and organised at present, is a bureaucratic activity basically reflecting and serving the prevailing system of values and the most powerful interests is in little doubt however much idealists may protest. Whether a reformed and rejuvenated planning system, moving away from plan-making more towards grass-roots activity, would in essence be much different must also be doubted. It is hardly surprising, at a time when public criticism of planning, recurrent self-doubt among planners, and strident calls for cutbacks in public expenditure are combined, that an attempt should be made by the vested interests in planning to redefine its role and assert its indispensability.

The changes being canvassed at present might bring certain improvements. Less emphasis could be placed on abstract, intellectually titillating, but largely irrelevant and remote structure planning. Correspondingly more attention could be devoted to the more useful work of local planning and implementation. Changes could be introduced to reduce the energy dissipated in organisational conflict and to encourage conflicts to be explicitly ideological. Decentralisation of large departments might help to provide more accessibility to decision-makers, greater participation by local politicians and public, and greater awareness of the needs of local communities. The education of those engaged in planning activities could be broadened, and the narrow-minded protectionism fostered by professionalism in planning reduced. But these reforms will be

[39] *Policy for the Inner Cities*, Cmnd. 6845, London, HMSO, 1977, Inner Urban Areas Act 1978.

strictly limited to what is permitted without directly challenging the power of established interests. They will come about, if they succeed at all, slowly and possibly in piecemeal fashion. Certain experiments now being undertaken in neighbourhood management schemes and comprehensive community programmes foreshadow changes that may be introduced to redirect planning and increase its effectiveness. Any shift to a position where planning would be the main if not the only means of allocation of resources and distribution of services implies a fundamental change that would not be seriously entertained. In any event there are few grounds for optimism that a change in the organisational structure will necessarily result in a shift in the balance of power. Merely to transfer more initiative and control from the market to the state could increase the delays, inflexibility, and cumbersome procedures which seem to plague large bureaucracies. To place control in the hands of planners equipped with vague social theories and blissful ignorance of economic and social processes will do nothing to inspire confidence in the ability of the state to succeed where the market has failed.

This conclusion may seem depressing but it is realistic. It does provoke the obvious question: Why, if conditions are such as to render planning impotent, should we bother to plan at all? The answer to this is, I suspect, because planning cannot be avoided. If the state is to survive then it must attempt to regulate economic and social life to prevent conflicts which threaten its existence. Town planning is part of the state's defence. It helps to relieve pressures, it protects resources, and it reconciles competing interests. It is when attempts are made to impose values that attack particular interests that planning begins to fail. There is clearly no likelihood of any rapprochement between an activity enshrined in the institutions of the state and defending its interests and any attempt to use that activity to challenge the status quo. Change can only come when planners return to the vision held by the early thinkers and state boldly what they want. This they are unlikely to do as long as planning remains institutionalised.

No doubt there is scope for improving the planning system. No doubt some of the structures and institutions of planning will change as they have done in the past. But we should not be beguiled into thinking that planning can ever become a positive and dynamic agent of social change. Social change requires political commitment. Town planning is not a highly politicised activity. Perhaps this is because the politicians recognise it for what it is — a passive, reactive, and dependent service. It is this function that both defines and limits the power of planning.

Epilogue

Anyone writing a book about the contemporary political scene is dealing with processes that continue after the book is finished. The studies in this book are set in one area and relate to a short time span, 1973–7. They focus on issues which were prominent at the time and which were likely to remain so. The period was an unusual one in local politics since it came immediately after local government reorganisation and during a period when Labour had a rare period of dominance both locally and nationally. An obvious question is whether the circumstances were so exceptional that the conclusions reached are largely atypical. To suggest this is to misunderstand the role of the studies. They are not presented as issues in themselves, interesting as each case may be, but as a contribution towards a greater understanding of the processes of planning, politics and power. For this reason they were set in a wider intellectual framework so that the work of other academics and the evidence of other studies in different places and at different times could be assessed. The relationship of these studies to this wider framework enabled certain conclusions to be drawn that are compatible with the evidence of the studies and that can be confirmed by experience elsewhere.

The political changes since 1977 have been dramatic and it is therefore worth establishing what impact they have had on the processes analysed in this book and whether they suggest any new issues or a need to modify conclusions. There is the obvious difficulty that the implications of some of the changes can only be guessed, but to await the results would render publication at any point impossible. Some of the changes of emphasis in planning policy coming in the wake of the Conservative victory at the county council election in 1977 have already been referred to at different points in the book. A philosophy of less intervention and greater pragmatism was evident in dealings with district councils and the conflicts between councils was, in consequence, less overt. Conservative control of county and district councils contributed to sympathetic relationships. A shift towards road building and away from public transport was also apparent though the balanced transportation strategy put forward in successive transport policies and programmes and in the structure plan was not put seriously at risk. The changes were significant and reflected quite different attitudes but did not disturb the underlying continuity of much of the planning and transportation policy. The election of a Conservative national government in May 1979 promised more sweeping changes brought about by a shift in priorities and attitudes towards planning.

The new government initiated another round of public expenditure cuts in line with its view that resources must be shifted from the public to the private sector. The cuts under Labour and those undertaken by the Conservative county council and their implications for transportation policy, have already been discussed in the book. It was argued that these cuts would not fundamentally alter services and that continuity would remain 'the typical pattern of local government' (ch. 2 p. 36). The cuts announced in 1979 in response to the government's requirement for reductions in current spending included further reductions in road maintenance, a fall in bus subsidies and a change in the concessionary fares scheme providing a half fare concession for a £1 charge. Thus, Labour's free scheme had been considerably diluted. But still the philosophy of a balanced transportation programme remained even though expenditure was at a reduced level.

Planning suffered as a result of the cuts and proposed legislation; hostile attitudes were expressed at national and local level. The county council proposed a restructuring of the planning department with an establishment reduced by about a third from that provided in the early years of Labour administration. This partly reflected the loss of planning functions to the county surveyor, and it partly accorded with the view that with the completion of the structure plan some of the workload had gone; it also satisfied the conservatives' antipathetic feelings towards the whole concept of planning. This cutback supports the view expressed in ch. 2, 'At a time of public expenditure cuts, planning is particularly vulnerable as the necessity for large, apparently non-productive planning departments is questioned' (p. 18).

Changes in legislation foreshadowed by the new government together with various ministerial pronouncements likewise suggested a lower profile for planning and for county planning departments in particular. The government announced its intention to repeal the Community Land Act. All my speculation about the implications of the Act presented in ch. 6 is, for the moment, largely academic. I am comforted by the thought that most of the comments on the Act were devoted to demonstrating its lack of impact (in the short term at least) and its disappearance hardly vitiates my conclusions. It now takes its place as the third in a series of attempts by Labour governments to address the problems of the land market and to encourage 'positive planning'. Meanwhile it will be interesting to see if speculative forces are once again unleashed in the land and property markets forcing the government to intervene as has happened before. In Bedfordshire little immediate change is likely since, as was shown in ch. 7, so much land is already committed for development.

Changes in the allocation of planning functions between the two tiers of local government could further weaken planning as a county council activity. Throughout the book criticisms have been made of the two-tier system of local government, particularly in connexion with planning. Neither Labour nor Conservative governments now appear willing to contemplate major changes such as the sweeping away of one tier (almost certainly the county councils) and the introduction of regional government. The upheaval would be considerable, could be costly in the short term and reform would be met with opposition from vested political and bureaucratic interests in local government. In 1979 the Labour government had promised to restore to the large cities (where it gained its greatest support) the powers they had held as county boroughs prior to local government reform. This idea of piecemeal but far reaching changes in the distribution of local authority powers has been described as 'organic change', and it met with a predictably hostile response from the county councils. Under the scheme counties would have been administering different services in different districts within their boundaries and would have possessed few powers at all in the largest cities. The government fell before the scheme could be implemented. The new Conservative government naturally sympathised with its supporters in the shire counties and put forward a more limited reform. The plan to transfer major services such as education and social services from the counties to some of the districts was dropped. Instead, reforms were to be limited almost entirely to planning functions. All development control powers (except minerals) would go to district councils. The county councils, as structure planning authorities, would have no powers of 'call-in' or direction on 'county matters', that is to say those proposals which had county wide or strategic implications. Districts would merely have to consult counties and have regard to the structure plan. The counties claimed that this would leave them 'without any power of decision in relation to critical planning decisions'.[1] At the time of writing the outcome of the debate is unknown. Exasperating as the proposals seem to the counties they do little to tackle the problems of the two-tier system and the much wider issues of local government reform.

The dropping of the Community Land Act and the proposed dilution of the powers of the structure planning authorities indicate a weakening of the role and functions of planning. Planning, for reasons set out earlier in this book, is weak both conceptually and practically, and this weakness becomes fully exposed when a government hostile to the idea of planning takes office. For a Labour government or council the impotence of planning is perceived to be a problem and efforts are therefore made to increase its powers and significance. The introduction of the Community Land Act was an attempt to strengthen planning. Locally, in Bedfordshire, Labour gave the planners responsibility for transportation planning and tried to use the structure plan as an instrument for achieving social objectives. By contrast, Conservatives see the weakness of planning as an opportunity to reduce interference in the market and to make savings on public expenditure. They have little time for esoteric conceptions of regional or structure planning. Apart from reducing the role of structure planning authorities, the new Conservative government quickly abolished the regional economic planning councils. The retreat from strategic planning was coupled with the well publicised view that structure planning was a wasteful and time-consuming process. The local response to this attitude was to reduce the size of the planning department. It is difficult to escape the conclusion that the attack on planning was widely welcomed and the protests so far have been muted. In the current political atmosphere the problems of planning outlined in ch. 7 not be solved by attempts to strengthen the system but rather by efforts to reduce the role of strategic planning.

Planning policy making at the local level is likely to reflect these broader changes in political attitudes. I have already traced some of the policy shifts that occurred after the change of political control in Bedfordshire in 1977. These changes were, in part, endorsed in the proposed modifications to the structure plan. The plan had been submitted in April 1977, a month before the county council elections. The new county administration had made certain 'rejoinders' indicating areas where attitudes might

[1]Association of County Councils, Local Government Act 1972, Planning and Development Control and Highways, Memorandum of the Association's Views.

alter, and the examination in public was held in November 1977. More than a year later (December 1978) the examination panel reported their findings to the minister who confirmed their recommendations in September 1979. Even then the procedure had not finished since time was allowed for representations to be made about the proposed changes in the plan before the minister made a final decision. More than six years had elapsed between the initial formulation of the plan and its final confirmation, a period of considerable political change in the county.

The minister largely supported the new council's transportation policy (ch. 5). He preferred the Bedford Western Relief Road to the Batts Ford Bridge. The relief road would, he considered, remove heavy traffic flows from the town. It would not ease congestion in the town centre but he was not satisfied a bridge at Batts Ford would do so either. His decision was entirely consistent with the changed political situation. The road still had two hurdles to overcome, resources and priorities. By 1979 the accelerated road programme (pp. 105–6) had fallen victim to expenditure cuts and the whole road programme had been revised. The first phase of the Western Relief Road had slipped two years to 1984/5 and phase 2 had been delayed by two years to 1986/7. But this was on the most optimistic assumption that there would be no further cuts and that the government would pay for a by-pass at Dunstable, a scheme given higher priority. If the county had to find the money for that scheme then the Western Relief Road was likely to drop out of the five year programme altogether. The council had maintained its priority for the south of the county and this had been backed by the minister in the structure plan. So, despite a favourable local political climate, construction of the Western Relief Road seemed as far away as ever. The uncertainty over the scheme resulting from political conflict in the 1970s had diminished its prospects and they were all but extinguished by the conflicts over priorities in a period of reduced resources foreshadowed for the 1980s.

Over other issues it was clear that the structure plan would reflect the prevailing pattern of power. In ch. 7 it was suggested that the process of consultation and participation provided privileged groups with the greatest access to decision makers and consequently enabled them to exert influence on the plan (ch. 7, p. 175). The remarks of the panel on the selection of participants at the examination in public underline this. 'The participants were selected on the basis of the effectiveness of the contribution they could be expected to make to the discussion of the matters to be examined'.[2]

It was clear, too, that the structure plan would only have limited value when it came to decisions over implementation. The debate about housing needs, employment policy, land availability and future growth had an air of unreality about it. The panel recognised they were dealing with imponderables. The concept of 'local needs' they felt, 'eludes both precise definition and positive means of implementation'.[3] They stressed the 'impracticability, if not the futility, of trying to achieve a balance between job opportunities and employment seeking population across the county'.[4] Nevertheless the panel were prepared to rewrite some of the assumptions of the plan and were prepared to arrive at different predictions of future housing needs by adopting different

[2]Bedfordshire Structure Plan, Report of the Panel, 1.2
[3]Ibid, 3.3.
[4]Ibid, 5.4.

forecasts based on their own assessment of housing vacancy rates and densities. They acknowledged that housing demand would, by the end of the plan, outstrip land availability, especially in the south of the county. Impressed with the opposition from Hertfordshire and South Bedfordshire District Council they considered that future expansion (apart from East Luton) should be accommodated at the new city of Milton Keynes. Thus had Hyde (pp. 132–4) escaped any prospect of future development.

This resistance to long term expansion in the south of the county was also a response to fears of a 'growth spiral' inspired by Hertfordshire and the GLC at the examination in public (ch. 7, pp. 175–6). In their comments the panel appeared obsessed by the prospect of growth which would put pressure on neighbouring areas and siphon off job opportunities from London. They feared the plan might run the risk of 'being inter-preted in an expansionist manner which could trigger off a growth spiral'.[5] Such a view seems remote from current apprehensions about a depressed economy when prospects of expansion in vehicle manufacturing on which the Luton area depends look bleak.

Problems of uncertainty were also inherent in conflicts of interest that could not be easily reconciled. For instance, the conflict between agriculture and conservation raised problems which the plan could not solve. The discussion confirmed, however, 'that there was indeed a conflict of policies in these areas and no criteria for reconciliation were indicated'.[6] These and other environmental conflicts, for example, between minerals and landscape protection, or between waste disposal and increased traffic were left to be resolved by 'negotiation, discussion, and persuasion'. Although much of the plan was endorsed demonstrating the continuity that results from consensus, there were areas — where conflict arose or where implementation was problematic — that were left to be determined. In such cases the plan, although of some value, offered no solutions.

The major changes that have occurred since the main part of this book was written have reinforced the conclusions reached in chapter 8. Changing economic and political circumstances have resulted in attitudes to planning which further undermine its pretensions to be a long term or comprehensive decision making process. It will remain an incremental process arbitrating conflicts between powerful interests at specific points where decisions are taken. Strategic planning has been further weakened by expenditure cuts, the abolition of regional councils and the proposed transfer of powers to district councils. The consensus that is assumed in such plans can be quickly trans-formed into conflict when policies need to be implemented. The need to take decisions can expose conflicts which have long lain dormant.

This point is being demonstrated as I write. Bedfordshire has become the scene of a debate of national, even of international dimensions. The application by the London Brick Company to replace their existing brickworks in the Marston Vale by two large new works has aroused passions that have smouldered for years but have, until now, lacked the opportunity for direct confrontation. The despoliation of the Marston Vale by the brick industry has long been an issue, but the scale of the problem and the vagueness of the original planning conditions have failed to secure any effective restoration. Over the years a much more significant issue, the danger of air pollution

[5]Ibid, 5.8.
[6]Ibid, 8.4.

from brickmaking, has been largely suppressed by reassuring comments from the company and the public authorities. Efforts to monitor pollution and to undertake research into its risks have been sporadic and inconclusive. Now the company's need to re-negotiate their planning permissions has unleashed a debate about the suspected danger to vegetation, cattle and human health from the emission of fluorides. It has become linked to widespread international concern about the dangers of toxic substances in the air. The power of experts, of companies, and of the research and information industries is a matter of concern to social scientists, and it raises issues that go far beyond the horizons of Bedfordshire and the relationships of politicians and planners that have been the subject of this book. In this book I have tried to appreciate the limits of power in planning by a detailed analysis of local case studies. The fascination of a wider canvass must await another volume.

Bedford, October 1979

Sources

The literature on planning, politics and local government referred to is listed in the bibliography. In addition a range of other sources produced by government bodies and local government, and other authorities were consulted. These are all referred to in the footnotes to the main text. The major sources used were the following:

Chapter 4. Bedfordshire County Council (1972) *County Review,* Minerals Aspect Report; 1976 *County Structure Plan: Report of Survey:* (1978) *Minerals: Appraisals and Issues; Minerals: Appraisals and Issues, Public Consultation,* (1977) Extraction of fuller's earth at Baulking, Oxfordshire, Inspector's Report; (1977) Extraction of fuller's earth, land at Old Wavendon, Inspector's Report: Proofs of evidence and statements prepared for the public inquiry, held at Aspley Guise in 1976.

Chapter 5. HMSO (1976) *Transport Policy: A consultation document;* (1977) *Transport Policy,* Cmnd. 6836. The Max Lock Group (1952) *Bedford by the River,* London, John Murray. Borough of Bedford (1970) *Bedford: Urban Transport Plan, 1968–77.* A. M. Voorhees and Associates (1974) *Luton, Dunstable and Houghton Regis Transportation Study Phase Two;* (1974) *Public Transport in Bedfordshire.* Bedfordshire County Council and A. M. Voorhees, *Bedford Urban Transportation Study* (1974) *Project Report;* (1975) *Survey and Immediate Action Report; Community Involvement Programme,* various reports; (1975) *Development of Transportation Alternatives;* (1976) *Evaluation of Alternatives* and *Transport Recommendations;* (1976) *A Transportation Plan for 1991.* Also various statements made by North Bedfordshire Borough Council for the examination in public of the Structure Plan.

Chapter 6. School for Advanced Urban Studies (1976) Community Land Training Programme, Background Papers. HMSO (1974) *Land,* Cmnd. 5730. Bedfordshire County Council (1974) *Luton/Dunstable Green Wedge,* Joint Appraisal. Borough of Luton (1976), Little Bramingham Farm, Outline Development Plan.

Chapter 7. South East Joint Planning Team (1970) *Strategic Plan for the South East;* (1976) *Strategy for the South East: 1976 Review.* Department of the Environment (1978) *Strategic Plan for the South East, Review: Government Statement.* Bedfordshire County Council, *County Structure Plan* (1976) *Report of Survey* January; (1975) *Draft Report on Alternatives:* (1976) *Alternative Strategies, Consultation Report,* January; (1976) *Public Participation Phase 1 Report,* June; (1976) *Written Statement Consultation Report,* September; (1976) *Public Participation Phase 2 Report,* December; (1977) *County*

Structure Plan. Also rejoinders to objections to the Structure Plan, statements by district councils on the matters to be examined in public, summaries of examination in public, and (see Epilogue) Report of the Panel at the Examination in Public (December 1978), List of proposed modifications, and Statement relating to the Secretary of State's proposed modifications (1979).

Other sources

Throughout the book references are made to various documents relating to the decisions and policies discussed. In particular the agendas, minutes and reports of the Environmental Services Committee were a vital resource in the compilation of the evidence on which the studies rest. In addition these were a variety of internal memoranda, reports and working papers, letters and comments which came my way and which have helped me to provide a more comprehensive perspective of the processes of planning and politics.

Bibliography

Abercrombie, P. (1945). *Greater London Plan*. HMSO, London.

Agriculture, Fisheries and Food, Ministry of (1975). *Food from our own Resources*. Cmnd. 6020. HMSO, London.

Allison, L. (1975). *Environmental Planning*. Allen & Unwin, London.

Almond, G. A. and Verba, S. (1965). *The Civic Culture*. Little, Brown, Boston.

Altshuler, A. (1965). The Goals of Comprehensive Planning. *Journal of the American Institute of Planners*, Vol. 31 (August).

Ambrose, P. (1976). *Who Plans Brighton's Housing Crisis?* Shelter Local Report, 1 March.

Bachrach, P. and Baratz, M. S. (1962). Two Faces of Power. *American Political Science Review*, Vol. 56, pp. 947–952.

Bains (1972). *The New Local Authorities: Management and Structure* (The Bains Report). HMSO, London.

Banfield, E. C. (1959). Ends and Means in Planning. *International Social Sciences Journal*, Vol. 11, No. 3.

Barratt, J. (1976). *Land and Inequality (Patterns of Inequality)*, Unit 10). Open University, Milton Keynes.

Bealey, F., Blondel, J. and McCann, W. P. (1965). *Constituency Politics*. Faber, London.

Benevolo, L. (1967). *The Origins of Modern Town Planning* (translated by J. Landry). Routledge & Kegan Paul, London.

Blondel, J. and Hall, R. (1967). Conflict, Decision-Making and the Perception of Local Councillors. *Political Studies*, Vol. 15, No. 3 (October), pp. 322–350.

Blowers, A. T. (1970). Council Housing: The Social Implications of Layout and Design in an Urban Fringe Estate. *Town Planning Review*, Vol. 41, No. 1 (January), pp. 80–92.

Blowers, A. T. (1973). Planning Residential Areas. *Urban Development*, Unit 29, pp. 91–139. Open University, Milton Keynes.

Blowers, A. T. (1974). Land Ownership and the Public Interest: The Case of Operation Leapfrog. *Town and Country Planning*, November, pp. 499–503.

Blowers, A. T. (1976). Consensus or Conflict: A Case Study in Planning. *Patterns of Inequality*, Unit 30, pp. 55–104. Open University, Milton Keynes.

Blowers, A. T. (1976). Transport Planning: A New Direction? *Town and Country Planning Summer School*, Report of Proceedings, Nottingham, pp. 16–20.

Blowers, A. T. (1977). Checks and Balances: The Politics of Minority Government in Bedfordshire. *Public Administration*, Autumn, pp. 305–316.

Blowers, A. T. (1978). Future Rural Transport and Development Policy. *Rural Transport and Country Planning*, Cresswell, R. (ed.), Blackies. Glasgow.

Bottomore, T. B. (1966). *Elites and Society*, Penguin, London.

Brocklebank, J. *et al.* (n.d.). *The Cases for Nationalising Land*. Campaign for Nationalising Land, 139 Old Church Street, London.

Bruton, M. J. (1974). Transport Planning. *The Spirit and Purpose of Planning*, Bruton, M. J. (ed.), Hutchinson, London.

Bruton, M. J. (1975). *Introduction to Transportation Planning* (2nd ed.). Hutchinson, London.

Buchanan, C. D. (1963). *Traffic in Towns*. HMSO, London.

Bulpitt, J. G. (1967). *Party Politics in English Local Government*. Longmans, London.

Burridge, M. (1973). Education for Urban Governance: Education for Whom? Centre for Environmental Studies, CES CP10, London.

Buxton, R. (1970). *Local Government*. Penguin (1973), Harmondsworth.

Castles, F. *et al.* (eds.) (1971) *Decisions, Organisations and Society*. Penguin, London.

Catanese, A. J. (1974). *Planners and Local Politics: Impossible Dreams*. Sage Publications, Beverly Hills.

Centre for Environmental Studies (1973). *Education for Urban Governance*. Conference Paper 10, London.

Cherry, G. E. (ed.) (1974). *Urban Planning Problems*. Leonard Hill, London.

Cockburn, C. (1974). Urban Government. *Urban Planning Problems,* Cherry, G. E. (ed.), Leonard Hill, Aylesbury, pp. 213–242.

Cockburn, C. (1977). *The Local State: Management of Cities and People.* Pluto, London.

Countryide Commission (1974). *New Agricultural Landscapes,* HMSO, London.

Cox, W. H. (1976). *Cities: The Public Dimension.* Penguin, Harmondsworth.

Cresswell, R. (ed.) (1978). *Rural Transport and Country planning.* Blackies, Glasgow.

Cullingworth, J. B. (1976). *Town and Country Planning in Britain* (6th ed.) (The New Local Government Series, No. 8). Allen & Unwin, London.

Dahl, R. A. (1961). *Who Governs? Democracy and Power in an American City,* Yale University Press, New Haven.

Dahl, R. A. and Lindblom, C. E. (1953). *Politics, Economics and Welfare.* Harper & Row, New York.

Davidoff, P. and Reiner, A. (1962). A Choice Theory of Planning. *Journal of the American Institute of Planners,* Vol. 28 (May).

Davies, J. G. (1972). *The Evangelistic Bureaucrat: A Study of a Planning Exercise in Newcastle upon Tyne.* Tavistock, London.

Dearlove, J. (1973). *The Politics of Policy in Local Government.* Cambridge University Press, Cambridge.

Denman, D. and Prodano, S. (1972). *Land Use.* Allen & Unwin, London.

Dennis, N. (1970). *People and Planning: The Sociology of Housing in Sunderland.* Faber, London.

Dennis, N. (1972). *People Participation and Planners' Blight.* Faber, London.

Diamond, D. and McLoughlin, J. B. (1973). *Education for Planning* (Progress in Planning, No. 1). Pergamon, Oxford.

Dror, Y. (1972). *Ventures in Policy Studies,* American Elsevier, New York.

Elkin, S. L. (1974). *Politics and Land Use Planning: The London Experience.* Cambridge University Press, Cambridge.

Environment, Department of (1973). *Planning and Noise.* Circular 10/73. HMSO, London.

Environment, Department of (1974). *Land.* Cmnd. 5730. HMSO, London.

Environment, Department of (1974). *Structure Plans.* Joint Circular, 98/74, 168/74. HMSO, London.

Environment, Department of (1975). *Housing Land Availability in the South East, Consultants' Study.* HMSO, London.

Environment, Department of (1977). *Inner Area Studies, Liverpool, Birmingham and Lambeth.* HMSO, London.

Environment, Department of (1977). *Local Government Finance,* HMSO, London.

Etzioni, A. (1967). Mixed-Scanning: A 'Third' Approach to Decision-Making. *Public Administration Review,* December.

Eversley, D. (1973). *The Planner in Society: The Changing Role of a Profession.* Faber, London.

Eversley, D. (1976). The Education of Planners. *Growth and Change in the Future City Region,* Hancock, T. (ed.), Leonard Hill, London, pp. 221–255.

Fagence, M. (1977). *Citizen Participation in Planning,* (Urban & Regional Planning Series, No. 19). Pergamon, Oxford.

Faludi, A. (ed.) (1973). *A Reader in Planning Theory* (Urban and Regional Planning Series, No. 5). Pergamon, Oxford.

Fay, B. (1975). *Social Theory and Political Practice.* Allen & Unwin, London.

Foley, D. (1960). British Town Planning: One Ideology or Three? *British Journal of Sociology,* Vol. 11.

Friedmann, J. (1966). Planning as a Vocation. *Plan,* Vol. 6, No. 3, pp. 99–124.

Friend, J. K. and Jessop, W. N. (1969). *Local Government and Strategic Choice.* Tavistock, London.

Glass, R. (1957). The Evaluation of Planning: Some Sociological Considerations. *International Social Sciences Journal,* Vol. 11, No. 3, pp. 393–409.

Grauhan, R. R. (1969). Notes on the Structure of Planning Administration. *A Reader of Planning Theory* (Urban and Regional Planning Series, No. 5), Faludi, A. (ed.), Pergamon (1973), Oxford.

Gregory, R. (1969). Local Elections and the 'Rule of Anticipated Reactions'. *Political Studies,* Vol. 17, pp. 31–47.

Gregory, R. (1971). *The Price of Amenity.* Macmillan, London.

Gyford, J. (1976). *Local Politics in Britain.* Croom Helm, London.

Hague, C. and McCourt, A. (1974). Comprehensive Planning, Public Participation and the Public Interest. *Urban Studies,* Vol. 11, pp. 143–155.

Hampton, W. (1970). *Democracy and Community: A Study of Politics in Sheffield.* Oxford University Press, London.

Hancock, T. (ed.) (1976). *Growth and Change in the Future City Region.* Leonard Hill, London.

Harvey, D. (1973). *Social Justice and the City.* Edward Arnold, London.

Helco, H. H. (1969). The Councillor's Job. *Public Administration,* Vol. 47, pp. 185–202.

HMSO (1976). *Devolution: The English Dimension.* HMSO, London.

Hill, D. M. (1974). *Democratic Theory and Local Government* (The New Local Government Series, No. 12). Allen & Unwin, London.

Hill, M. J. (1972). *The Sociology of Public Administration*. Weidenfeld & Nicholson, London.

Hills, P. J. (1974). Transport and Communications. *Urban Planning Problems,* Cherry, G. E. (ed.), Leonard Hill, London.

Hindess, B. (1971). *The Decline of Working-Class Politics*. MacGibbon & Kee, London.

Housing and Local Government, Ministry of (1970). *Development Plans: A Manual of Form and Content.* HMSO, London.

Howard, E. (1902). *Garden Cities of Tomorrow*. Faber (1965), London.

James, J. R. (1965). The Future of Development Plans. *Town and Country Planning Summer School, Report of Proceedings,* University of St. Andrews, pp. 16–30.

Jefferson, R. (1973). *Planning and the Innovation Process.* (Progress in Planning Series, Vol. 1, Part 3). Pergamon, Oxford.

Jones, G. W. (1969). *Borough Politics*. Macmillan, London.

Kilbrandon Commission (1973). *Report of the Royal Commission on the Constitution, 1969–73.* Cmnd. 5460 and 4560–1. HMSO, London.

Labour Party (1977). *Regional Authorities and Local Government Reform.* A Consultation Document, July.

Lee, J. M. (1963). *Social Leaders and Public Persons*. Clarendon, Oxford.

Lee, T. P., Wood, B. Soloman, B. W. and Walters, P. (1974). *The Scope of Local Initiative: A Study of Cheshire County Council, 1961–74.* Martin Robertson, London.

Lindblom, C. E. (1959). The Science of 'Muddling Through'. *Public Administration Review,* Spring.

Lock, D. (1965). Structure Plans: A Review of Public Participation Methods and Current Ideas. Paper at Town and Country Planning Association Conference, Shepperton, 25–27 April.

Lock, D. (1976). New Towns in the Future City Region. *Growth and Change in the Future City Region,* Hancock, T. (ed.), Leonard Hill, London.

Lucking, R. C., Howard, K. and Greenwood, M. J. (1974). Corporate Planning and Management: A Review of their Application in English Local Government. *Town Planning Review,* Vol. 45, No. 2 (April), pp. 131–145.

Lukes, S. (1974). *Power: A Radical View*. Macmillan, London.

Marx, K. and Engels, F. (1848). The Communist Manifesto. *Selected Works,* Marx, K. and Engels, F., Lawrence & Wishart (1968), London.

Maud Committee (1967). *Management of Local Government*. Vol. 2, *The Local Government Councillor,* Moss, L. and Parker, S. R. HMSO, London.

Max Lock Group (1952). *Bedford by the River*. John Murray, London.

Maynard, A. (1975). An Economic Analysis of the Land Act 1975. Paper presented at Seminar of Chartered Institute of Public Finance and Accountancy. Also in *Local Government Studies*, July, 1976.

Meyerson, M. and Banfield, C. (1955). *Politics, Planning and the Public Interest.* Free Press, New York.

Michels, R. (1915). *Political Parties*. Free Press (1959), New York and Dover.

Milibrand, R. (1973). *The State in Capitalist Society*. Quartet Books.

Ministry of Agriculture, Fisheries and Food (1975), *Food From Our Own Resources,* HMSO, London.

Muchnik, D. M. (1970). *Urban Renewal in Liverpool: A Study of the Politics of Redevelopment.* Occasional Papers on Social Administration, No. 33, G. Bell.

Newton, K. (1976). *Second City Politics: Democratic Processes and Decision Making in Birmingham.* Oxford University Press, Oxford.

Planning Advisory Group (1965). *The Future of Development Plans*. HMSO, London.

Polsby, N. W. (1963). *Community Power and Political Theory.* Yale University Press, New Haven and London.

Price, M. (1976). *Houghton Regis Town Development Scheme: A Study.* Cranfield Institute of Technology, March, Cranfield, Bedfordshire.

Rabinovitz, F. F. (1967). Politics, Personality and Planning. *Public Administration Review,* March.

Ratcliffe, J. (1976). *Land Policy*. Hutchinson Educational, London.

Reade, E. J. (1976). An Attempt to Distinguish Planning from Other Modes of Decision Making. Seminar Paper, Department of Town and Country Planning, Manchester University, 24 November.

Reade, E. J. (1977). Some Educational Consequences of the Incorporation of the Planning Profession into the State Bureaucracy. Paper presented to the Annual Conference of the Sociologists in Polytechnics Section of the British Sociological Association, Oxford, April.

Redcliffe-Maud Commission (1969). *Royal Commission on Local Government* in England, Report. Cmnd. 4040. HMSO, London.

Rein, M. (1969). Social Planning: The Search for Legitimacy. *The City: Problems of Planning,* Stewart, M. (ed.), Penguin (1972), Harmondsworth.

Ridley, T. M. and Tressider, J. O. (1970). Replies to Comments on 'The London Study and Beyond'. *Regional*

Studies, Vol. 4, No. 1, pp. 81–83.

Roberts, M. (1974). *An Introduction to Town Planning Techniques.* Hutchinson, London.

Robinson Committee (1977). *Report of the Committee of Enquiry into the System of Remuneration of Members of Local Authorities.* Cmnd. 7010. HMSO, London.

Rossi, H. (1975). Community Land — The Conservative Viewpoint. *Estates Gazette,* 21 June, pp. 889–895.

Royal Town Planning Institute (1976). *Planning and the Future.* Discussion Paper, November.

Russell, B. (1938). *Power, A New Social Analysis.* Unwin, london.

Samuels, A. (1975). Structure Plan Examination in Public. *Journal of Planning and Environment Law,* March.

Schattschneider, E. E. (1960). *The Semi-Sovereign People: A Realist's View of Democracy in America.* Holt, Rinehart & Winston, New York.

Self, P. (1972). *Administrative Theories and Politics.* Allen & Unwin, London.

Self, P. (1975). Strategic Planning for Quality of Life. *Growth and Change in the Future City Region,* Hancock, T. (ed.), Leonard Hill, London, pp. 32–52.

Sharpe, L. J. (1960). The Politics of Local Government in Greater London. *Public Administration,* Vol. 38, pp. 157–172.

Sharpe, L. J. (1962). Elected Representatives in Local Government. *British Journal of Sociology,* Vol. 13, No. 3, pp. 189–209.

Simmie, J. M. (1971). Public Participation: A Case Study from Oxfordshire. *Journal of the Royal Town Planning Institute,* Vol. 57, No. 4, pp. 161–162.

Simmie, J. M. (1974). *Citizens in Conflict: The Sociology of Town Planning.* Hutchinson Educational, London.

Skeffington, A. (1969). *People and Planning* (The Skeffington Report). HMSO, London.

Smart, G. (1977). Structure Plans. *County Councils Gazette,* Vol. 69, No. 11 (February), pp. 286–288.

Stanyer, J. (1976). *Understanding Local Government.* Fontana/Collins, Glasgow.

Starkie, D. N. M. (1973). *Transportation Planning and Public Policy* (Progress in Planning Series, Vol. 1, Part 4). Pergamon, Oxford.

Stein, M. R. (1960). *The Eclipse of Community.* Harper & Row, New York.

Stewart, M. (1972) ed: *The City: Problems of Planning,* Penguin, Canada.

Thomas, R. (n.d.) *Planning, Housing and Land Values.* Land and Liberty, London.

Thorburn, A. (1975). Structure Plans and Local Government. Paper at Town and Country Planning Association Conference, Shepperton, 25–27 April.

Trade, Department of (1974) *Maplin, Review of Airport Project,* HMSO, London.

Trade, Department of (1975). *Airport Strategy for Great Britain,* Part 1: *The London Area.* A Consultation Document. HMSO, London.

Trade, Department of (1976). Airport Strategy for Great Britain, Part 2: *The Regional Airports.* A Consultation Document. HMSO, London.

Transport, Department of (1976). *Transport Policy: A Consultation Document* (2 vols.). HMSO, London, April.

Transport, Department of (1977). *Transport Policy,* Cmnd 6836, HMSO, London.

Uthwatt Committee (1942). *Expert Committee on Compensation and Betterment.* Cmnd. 6386. HMSO, London.

Weber, M. (1947). *The Theory of Social and Economic Organizations* (edited with an Introduction by Talcott Parsons). Free Press (1964), New York.

Wibberley, G. (1974). The Proper Use of Britain's Rural Land — A Critical View. Royal Town Planning Institute, Diamond Jubilee Conference, 13–15 June.

Wildavsky, A. (1973). If Planning is Everthing, Maybe It's Nothing. *Journal of Policy Sciences,* Vol. 4, No. 2, pp. 127–153.

Wilson Committee (1963). Final Report of the Committee on the Problem of Noise. Cmnd. 2056. HMSO, London.

Wiseman, H. V. (1967). *Local Government at Work.* Routledge & Kegan Paul, London.

Index

URBAN AND REGIONAL PLANNING SERIES

Other Titles in the Series

CHADWICK, G. F.
A Systems View of Planning. 2nd Edition (Volume 1)

BLUNDEN, W. R.
The Land Use/Transport System (Volume2)

GOODALL, B.
The Economics of Urban Areas (Volume 3)

LEE, C.
Models in Planning: An Introduction to the Use of Quantitative Models in Planning (Volume 4)

FALUDI, A. K. F.
A Reader in Planning Theory (Volume 5)

COWLING, T. M. & STEELEY, G. C.
Sub-Regional Planning Studies: An Evaluation (Volume 6)

FALUDI, A. K. F.
Planning Theory (Volume 7)

SOLESBURY, W.
Policy in Urban Planning: Structure Plans. Programmes and Local Plans (Volume 8)

MOSELEY, M. J.
Growth Centres in Spatial Planning (Volume 9)

LICHFIELD, N. *et al.*
Evaluation in the Planning Process (Volume 10)

SANT, M. E. C.
Industrial Movement and Regional Development: The British Case (Volume 11)

HART, D. A.
Strategic Planning in London: The Rise and Fall of the Primary Road Network (Volume 12)

STARKIE, D. N. M.
Transportation Planning, Policy and Analysis (Volume 13)

FRIEND, J. K. & JESSOP, W. N.
Local Government and Strategic Choice, 2nd Edition (Volume 14)

RAPOPORT, A.
Human Aspects of Urban Form (Volume 15)

DARIN-DRABKIN, H.
Land Policy and Urban Growth (Volume 16)

NEEDHAM, D. B.
How Cities Work: An Introduction (Volume 17)

DAVIDSON, J. & WIBBERLEY, G.
Planning and the Rural Environment (Volume 18)

FAGENCE, M.
Citizen Participation in Planning (Volume 19)

FALUDI, A. K. F.
Essays on Planning Theory and Education (Volume 20)